AF506064

THYSSEN-BORNEMISZA
ART CONTEMPORARY

A QUESTION OF EVIDENCE

AMAR KANWAR / RAQS MEDIA COLLECTIVE /
RITU SARIN & TENZING SONAM / NIKOLAUS
HIRSCH & MICHEL MÜLLER IN COLLABORATION
WITH CYBERMOHALLA ENSEMBLE /
MARINE HUGONNIER / PAK SHEUNG CHUEN /
HEMAN CHONG / KHIN KHIN SU / GONKAR
GYATSO / QIU ZHIJIE / AMNYE MACHEN
INSTITUTE

WITH CONTRIBUTIONS BY
FRANCESCA VON HABSBURG / DIANA BALDON
/ AMAR KANWAR / GABRIELLE CRAM / AUNG
MYINT HTET / T. J. DEMOS / RAQS MEDIA
COLLECTIVE / MARINE HUGONNIER / SYBILLE
KRÄMER / MONIQUE BEHR / JEEBESH BAGCHI
/ CYBERMOHALLA ENSEMBLE / CHARLES
MEREWETHER / TENZING SONAM / ARADHANA
SETH / DANIELA ZYMAN

EDITED BY
DANIELA ZYMAN & DIANA BALDON

VERLAG DER BUCHHANDLUNG
WALTHER KÖNIG

EVIDENCE OF DOUBT

In 2001, as part of a field trip to Laos, where I was involved in a UXO de-mining project, I traveled to Burma (Myanmar). Both Laos and Burma are struggling under ruthless dictatorships. A shift to democracy in these nations is impossible without the will and support of the international community. When I look at an issue of the Condé Nast Traveler magazine that carries the cover line "The Ethics of Travel to Myanmar after the Saffron Revolution", I see the tourism industry trying to dissolve the recent protests into something colorful and nostalgic, even tempting to tourists, while gliding gracefully over the tragic loss of life in the low-lying Irrawaddy Delta that could have been avoided by a timely evacuation of the population. The junta subsequently tried to cover up its failures by blocking foreign aid to the region for more than a month, whilst making tourist package deals on the other side.

But we, on the other hand, are overwhelmingly concerned with our own survival, all the more so in the wake of the recent economic meltdown. Even if we put more effort into it, we would have little impact on dictators like Robert Mugabe in Zimbabwe, Kim Jong-il in North Korea, Omar Hassan Ahmad al-Bashir in Sudan, Bashar al-Assad in Syria, and Muammar Abu Minyar al-Gaddafi in Libya who invest enormous efforts and resources in retaining their grip on control, exclusively at the expense - economically, physically, and emotionally - of their own people. Systems based on the denial of the human being are not merely upheld but presented as a god-given eternal state by the ideologies designed to support them. A strong enough impulse to change is unlikely to come on its own, without coercion through massive outside pressure. Building up that pressure seems to me to be the task of activist groups and human rights advocats.

CAN CONTEMPORARY ART MAKE A DIFFERENCE, BE THE SEED FOR POLITICAL INNOVATION? NOTHING IS IMPOSSIBLE. WE MUST EXPLORE WAYS TO SHIFT THE POLITICAL PARADIGMS THROUGH INCENTIVE RATHER THAN PRESSURE. INSTEAD OF POWER CENTERS, FORUMS AND INSTITUTIONS, ART ADDRESSES PEOPLE'S MINDS—AND THAT IS ITS GREATEST STRENGTH.

We can out a face to peace and tolerance. We are intimately familiar with the portraits of His Holiness Dalai Lama Tenzing Gyatso and Daw Aung San Suu Kyi. The Dalai Lama received the Nobel Peace Prize in 1989, shortly after the 1988 Tibetan uprising, in an unexpected show of support for his peaceful protest. Two years later, Václav Havel nominated Daw Aung San Suu Kyi, who won 82% of the popular vote in 1990 for the National League for Democracy Party (NLD) in Burma, but she has never been allowed to hold office. In 1991, she won the Nobel Peace Prize "for her non-violent struggle for democracy and human rights."

HOW EASILY DOES EVIDENCE BECOME QUESTIONABLE AS THE AUTHORITIES, THE MEDIA, OR THE TRAVEL INDUSTRY MANIPULATE IT? WHAT IS EVIDENCE, AND WHAT BECOMES OF IT?

These are difficult questions to ask ourselves, let alone to answer. Facts can become evasive, and with them, our notions of right and wrong. Some of mankind's greatest minds have interwoven the philosophy of knowledge with the philosophy of morals. In a way, this tells us that we cannot value Good without the True. To me, the two merge into our personal wisdom which is much more a perpetual goal than a static quality and I believe that the key is to give everyone a chance to explore his or her own ethics parameters through awareness.

Amar Kanwar's brilliant work was made in collaboration with video makers from the underground movement within Burma. Incorporating his own footage as well, it is the beginning of this exploration of ourselves and our own curiosity and consciousness as we experience his interpretation of violence and cruelty. We need to read the stories through our own eyes and not be blinded by what others want us to see. We are numbed by television, bored by news, and we are becoming immune to forced consciousness, as indeed are the people who live under those autocratic regimes. So where do we go from here?

A Question of Evidence was conceived during a trip that T-B A21's chief curator, Daniela Zyman, and I made to India in 2006 to visit the Dalai Lama in Dharamsala. We passed through Delhi upon our return, and met up with Raqs Media Collective, Amar Kanwar, Tenzing Sonam, and Ritu Sarin. Together we have approached this exhibition as a work in progress, an exploration of data and images and their interpretation or lack of it. It asks all of us to take the time to reflect on these issues just enough to be able to ask a few vital questions. Those are the questions that sometimes lead to the right answers and, hopefully, to more of the right questions. The project is highly interactive, with an Internet café, a library, blogs, and a notice board where everyone can post a comment. We are networking and reaching out to millions of people though the

Internet, Facebook, and MySpace, as well as our own website, and hope that we may trigger a clear, comprehensible, doable strategy for the future. I know this sounds ambitious, but art can and does move people intellectually as well as emotionally through its poignant and provocative language.

I particularly want to thank Daniela Zyman and her associate curator, Diana Baldon, for their instrumental work in finding the right balance for this message, and for curating such a refined exhibition. I also want to thank Aradhana Seth for her invaluable contribution to this project. I truly appreciate above all the incredible team spirit that evolved though this project and how much fell into place as a result of that effort. I would also like to thank Barbara Horvath and Philipp Krummel for the installation of the exhibition, which is imaginative and sensitive to the material and the timeliness of the exhibition. Kristina Pia Hofer worked on all the networking, blogging, and websites, and I really appreciate the new dynamic she brings to our communication strategy at T-B A21. I am extremely grateful to all the artists who have responded so enthusiastically to our call for special commissions. We have never had a show with so many new works that have materialized in such a short time-frame; it's quite a miracle! I would like to make a special mention of Tashi Tsering, one of the founders of the Amnye Machen Institute in Dharamsala, who donated a number of books and maps to the exhibition, but more importantly generously shared his knowledge and extensive expertise with us, which was extremely inspiring. I am deeply indebted to everyone who has helped to make this happen, especially the authors of this catalogue and all the researchers, and particularly to Tsewang Gyatso for his dedication to Tibet21 and the tireless work that he has devoted to the cause.

I am grateful to Dr. Karl Fink, the vice-chairman of the Vienna Insurance Group, for his unflagging support of T-B A21. The sponsorship we receive on an ongoing basis from the Vienna Insurance Group is a sign of genuine support of the program that we put forward. This is rare and much appreciated by all of us here at T-B A21. Last but not least, I am grateful to His Holiness the Dalai Lama for his words of encouragement two years ago, when we visited him in Dharamsala, and again at the Reichstag in Berlin in May 2008. He has made sure that we all participate in this project with an unbiased heart and that we share the pain not only of the victims but also of the perpetrators of these crimes, and that we work hard to forgive them for the past and help them find a peaceful solution for the future. I do humbly confess to His Holiness, however, that I still find it hard not to point the finger at those who continue to commit crimes and to violate the understanding the world has about human rights.

— FRANCESCA VON HABSBURG

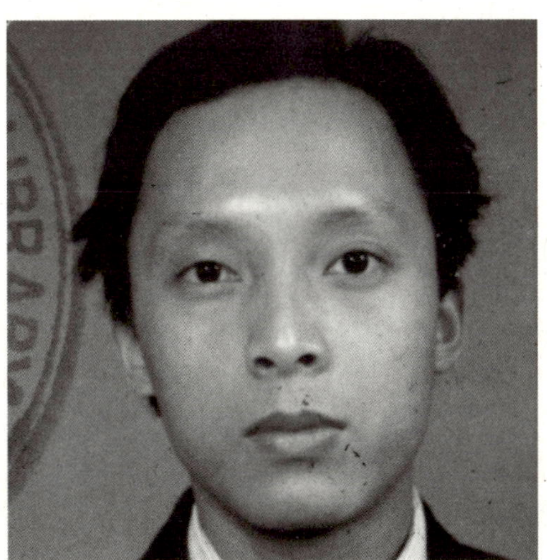

And how to remember you, Thet? A lifetime and fifty-nine years in a single moment.
Thet Win Aung who was killed in prison in Burma on 16th October 2006.

A QUESTION OF EVIDENCE

A Question of Evidence presents works by artists and cultural practitioners who engage with, or comment upon, the difficulty of creating, collecting, and disseminating evidence-based material around issues such as identity politics, the suppression of human rights, democratic reform, and restrictions on free expression and representation. As "narrations of urgency," the projects in the exhibition often present multiple perspectives on conflicted and rapidly changing realities. While restricted in its geographical scope—most participants were born in and/or work in South and Central Asia—the exhibition does not overlook, but rather intends to illuminate, the essential differences in the role and presence of artists and practitioners within the public realm in their respective contexts. Therefore it incorporates a variety of artistic and cultural approaches—including moving image, still photography, sculpture, books, maps, archives, and live-feed blogs—that encompass diverse viewpoints on the nature and function of representation in the face of "real" events and sociopolitical circumstances. Some participants present a different side of their artistic work, which emphasizes a more discursive, collaborative, or hybrid aspect of their practice, as in the case of Heman Chong, Nikolaus Hirsch & Michel Müller, Marine Hugonnier, and Raqs Media Collective. Some in fact regularly collaborate with grassroots collectives that, often faced with restricted channels of communication, manage to conduct research and disseminate information through Internet-based networks, video and film databases, open-source initiatives, and other means. In this regard, these works exemplify the imparting of knowledge production in the transformation of the concept of visual arts to that of visual-intellectual culture, in line with the elucidations of art theorist Sarat Maharaj, who has commented on the fervor of such practices:

"THERE IS MUCH ACTIVITY IN INDIA, CHINA, AFRICA THAT IS RADICALLY INTERDISCIPLINARY. IT DETERRITORIALIZES RECEIVED CONCEPTS OF ART. GROUPS WORKING ON THE INTERNET OR WITH FILM, VIDEO, PERFORMANCE, AND OTHER PRACTICES ARE INVOLVED IN MODES OF KNOWLEDGE PRODUCTION THAT OFTEN HAVE OBLIQUE RELATIONS TO THE VISUAL.

Are such practices more like research machines through which social, political, visual, statistical, epidemiological data are telescoped?

[...] For me, it's a marker for ways we might be able to engage with works, events, spasms, ructions that don't look like art and don't count as art, but are somehow electric, energy nodes, attractors, transmitters, conductors of new thinking, new subjectivity and action that visual artwork in the traditional sense is not able to articulate."[1]

Central to these works is the concept of evidence, which can be defined as the act of testifying or bearing witness in a broad cultural sense. Evidence is, in its fullest definition, a paradoxical and contested notion, as it may refer to a highly privatized object (image, symbol, artifact) that serves as a trace or indication of a past event or experience. It can also indicate a sign acting as an "orientation" device, an anchoring object for (often) anxious and subjective testimonies. In the legal context it can be either object-based (an exhibit) or written or oral testimony, referring to an objectivist order or to the status of a witness. Because it is derived from and overlaps with other disciplines—anthropology, ethnography, history, philosophy, law, literature, politics, religion, and sociology—evidence serves as a useful guiding principle in the analysis of the assembled works and practices, which cross genre lines—encompassing art, film, music, narrative, poetry, and performance—thus involving an eclectic use of competing discourses.

Clearly the sociopolitical contexts in which these productions originate radically differ in the degree of possibilities of artistic creation and relative freedom of expression. They also vary in regard to the issues of contest, hardship, and protest expressed by the works on display.

Since 1962 Burma has been ruled by one of the world's harshest military dictatorships, currently under the leadership of General Than Shwe. The popular protest movements of 1988—generally referred as "8/8/88"—and, most recently, of September 2007, mediatized under the label of the "Saffron Revolution," have created a fragile opposition movement both within the country and in exile. With thousands of protesters and human rights activists in prison, the "virtual prisoners of the conscious," as Aung Myint Htet calls them in her interview in this catalogue with Miss K., a disclosed practitioner from Rangoon, are artists, journalists, and writers who have developed precarious or clandestine identities as bloggers, citizen journalists, chroniclers of the everyday.

The surprising parallelism of events between this uprising in Burma and the riots in March 2008 in the Tibetan regions within China (Tibetan Autonomous Region, Amdo, and Kham) deserves much deeper analysis than this preamble allows. Symbolically, the open brutality against the monks—the "sons of the Lord Buddha," endowed with absolute religious and high social authority—were possibly the most provocative afflictions against the moral values of both societies, still dominated by the Theravada and the various traditions of Tibetan Buddhism. These protests, however, not only demonstrated the failure to create a benign and compassionate autonomous region made up of a dwindling Tibetan population within the People's Republic after sixty years of Communist rule, but also reignited the debate about the political status of Tibet within the community of nations altogether. The official "Middle Way" approach, advocated by the Dalai Lama since the 1970s and uncontested until recently, fails to meet the political vision of today's exile community, which has become more sophisticated and independent in its political articulations.

The religious, ethnic, and economic conflicts within the People's Republic of

China remain among the many unresolved issues surrounding the Chinese government's policies and its autocratic rule, heightened by the politically restrictive climate following the Tiananmen Square protests in 1989. Yet it is the overall lack of freedom, equality, and justice that seems to concern creative communities within China. The recently reawakened "Middle Kingdom," as China has also historically been called, has demonstrated an unparalleled rise to economic power accompanied by a deeply felt moral and intellectual vacuum that became most manifest during the recent Olympics. This has been outspokenly described by Ai Weiwei in the British daily newspaper *The Guardian:* "Real public contentment can't be pirated or copied. No matter how long our politicians order people to sing songs of praise, no matter how many fireworks they launch into the heavens, and no matter how many foreign leaders they embrace, they cannot arouse a genuine mood of joy and celebration among the people. Neither fairness nor justice, neither reality nor humanity can be simulated or manipulated by wires or remote control. Those who staged the opening ceremony stopped at nothing to create a fantasy. They faked the footprints of fire with computer graphics. They exploited an innocent child by making her lip-synch to a patriotic song. These people are shameless."[2]

Ai has been posting his writing on a blog that, since its inception in 2005, has become one of the most visited web-logs published in Mandarin. The blog is devoted to political commentary and art world documentation, a daily activity that has revealed a thought-provoking intellectual whose sharp observations, critical attitude, and sense of social engagement voice outspoken views on contemporary China's cultural, social, and political conditions. In the context of *A Question of Evidence*, we had commissioned him to realize an artist book which included a selection of texts and photographs taken from his blog—http://blog.sina.com.cn/aiweiwei—to underline how the discursivity of such a critical project can be a paradigm for people who, like him, have remained integral and faithful to their opinions and (political) positions. However, just before going to print with the catalogue, he withdrew his participation from the exhibition, an occurrence we deeply regret.

Similarly, India's reckless exploitation of resources (human, spatial as well as natural), its ethnic tensions and marginalization of populations endowed with very limited rights, infringements on free speech, the unpredictability of its juridical system, the corruption of its political elite, and the striving to gain economic and geopolitical power within and beyond the South Asian subcontinent are among the sources of a discontent that has prompted energetic activist engagement by a vast number of grassroots and media organizations. Specifically in New Delhi, Mumbai, and other urban centers, the gentrification process has been steadily erasing long-standing squatter settlements which, although invested with various rights, were undeniably "unauthorized". Their vast network of street markets and neighborhood manufacturers—or the "bypass," to use a term coined by scholar Ravi Sundaram to describe the "pragmatic appropriation of the city, perhaps more *in medias res* than 'marginal'"[3]—has created a fast-changing and proliferating assembly of practices of resistance that are dedicated to systematically recording and opposing the social and economic transformations on daily existence. According to Sundaram, "The bypass was equally the site of vast everyday violent encounters between urban population and speeding road machines, exposing public display of technological death."[4] These cursory descriptions of various backgrounds are just one layer of the extremely complex issues under scrutiny: in fact, the production that we have selected, combined, and cross-referenced in the exhibition translates visually into an open, unfinished and amorphous field of critical thinking. It underlines the effort and desire on our behalf to, on the one hand, contextualize the works on the basis of recent historical events that, in our view, need to be reinstated into a debate and, on the other, to spatialize them within specific geographies that seem immensely vast and, in many respects, also haunting. In this sense, we have been less interested in the homogenizing powers of consolidation and aggregation that such topographic analysis might offer and, instead, have aligned ourselves with the notion of geography as defined by scholar Irit Rogoff: "An epistemic category [which] is in turn grounded in issues of positionality, in questions of who has the power and authority to name, of who has the power and authority to subsume others into its hegemonic identity."[5] Consequently, we are interested in a plurality of critical and visual approaches that allow for the access, rehearsal, and negotiation of contemporary conditions. Locality is in fact construed by the different experiences in participating in sociopolitical and cultural processes.

In more than one respect, haunting has been a feeling that has accompanied the preparation and thinking behind this project. The Burmese "Saffron Revolution," the riots in the Tibetan regions, and Beijing's 2008 Olympic Games unfolded during the course of its planning, and the personal sufferings, confusions, and restlessness that were the direct effects of such events, are woven into the exhibition display as well as the pages of this catalogue. Thus, the following comments by our collaborator Kristina Pia Hofer in regard to this exhibition and the work of sociologist Avery F. Gordon seem to well capture these concerns and personal enmeshments. According to Hofer, "haunting seems a fitting strategy for two reasons. First, the exhibition itself speaks of problems that have a 'ghostly' quality to Western audiences: we know totalitarian regimes exist, and we shudder when we feel their presence, but we might not always acknowledge that they are 'real,' or that they concern us and our reality in any way. More often than not, we try to exorcise our knowledge of them. Second, evidence—especially evidence of something ghostly, like a blurry photograph always carries an element of not-quite, of non-presence, of stories untold left to discover, of mystery. Ghosts make us want to make sense of things that scare us, that threaten to harm us, that we cannot explain. If we, like Gordon, understand ghosts as social phenomena with a highly political meaning, ghosts can help us make sense of the ways we deal with political conflict."[6]

The notion of the haunting presence is not dissimilar to the ideas of the Lebanese writer Jalal Toufic. No better description can be given about the impossible task of the recorder, narrator, or redactor: "With regard to the surpassing disaster, art acts like the mirror in vampire films: it reveals the withdrawal of what we think is still there. [...] Does this entail that one should not record? No. One

should record this 'nothing,' which only after the resurrection can be available. We have to take photographs even though because of their referents' withdrawal, and until their referents are resurrected, they are not going to be available as referential, documentary pieces—with the concomitant risk that facets relating to the subject matter might be mistaken for purely formal ones. A vicious circle: what has to be recorded has been withdrawn, so that, unless it is resurrected, it is going to be overlooked; but in order to accomplish that prerequisite work of resurrection to avert its overlooking, one has initially to have, however minimally, perceived it, that is countered its withdrawal, i.e., resurrected it."[7]
Occupying a central position in the exhibition, Amar Kanwar's extensive video installation *The Torn First Pages* (2004–08) manifests such concerns in terms that are poetic yet political. An ode to the thousands engaged in the struggle for democracy in Burma, *The Torn First Pages* is presented in honor of the bookshop owner Ko Than Htay, who was imprisoned for tearing out the first pages of all books and journals that contained ideological slogans from the military regime. The video installation directly, elliptically, and metaphorically engages themes of the struggle for a democratic society, contemporary forms of nonviolent resistance, political exile, memory, and dislocation. For Kanwar, the poetical and its nature as evidence are reconcilable by nature, as he suggests: "Imagine the formal presentation of poetry as evidence in a future war crimes tribunal. Imagine nineteen sheets of paper floating forever in the wind." His work is counterbalanced by a second large multichannel video installation by Ritu Sarin and Tenzing Sonam. *Middle Way or Independence?* (2008), which unfolds around a comprehensive and multifaceted discussion on the Tibetan question, setting the "Middle Way" approach of partial autonomy within China against the demands for independence by the activist community. The video-fragments interweave scenes from recent Free Tibet activities with interviews with members of the Tibetan community in exile in India, and Chinese intellectuals engaged with the Tibetan question who confront their own spiritual and political engagements. Qiu Zhijie has been traveling to Tibet over the past few years in an ongoing art project that can be understood as a journey, a pilgrimage of ideas, a collection of factual evidences. In *Lhasa Is Far Away, America Is Far Away* (2007) and *A Railway from Lhasa to Kathmandu* (2006–07), the artist retraces the steps of the first historic Tibet explorer of the 19th century, of the pundit Nain Singh. Furthermore, he references the Qinghai-Tibet Railway, which opened on July 1st 2006, and now connects Lhasa to the Chinese railway system, a symbolic and infrastructural exploit with lasting impact: "It struck me that nothing the British could have done back then, nor even the imposition of Chinese sovereignty (in 1959), will have as much impact upon Tibet and the traditional way of life as the opening of a railroad connection between Golmud and Lhasa. The railway will be the instrument that will destroy the myths about Tibet, as it will allow everyone to discover its mysteries."
Other works in the exhibition explore the contradictions embedded in the notion of the document, revealing its susceptibility to secrecy or deliberate acts of self-censorship. This is metaphorically shown by Pak Sheung Chuen, whose "miracle cash register receipts" reveal hidden, encrypted messages behind the formal

transaction of an exchange of goods. Similarly, Heman Chong's collages *Deleted Scenes* (2008) resemble portraits whose subjects, having been removed, seem to have been permanently imprisoned, a thorny issue in many Southeast Asian countries. Khin Khin Su, in contrast, looks at the human condition under different sociopolitical realities in Burma through confrontational performances, large banners, and installations that indirectly question the role of the artist in Burmese society.

Marine Hugonnier's book takes a more art historical turn. It contains a constantly growing collection of loose pages recording thoughts derived from Buddhist concepts, such as that of "prajna," which is a kind of intelligence attained when one lets go of certain ideas, compiled by the artist and drawn from interviews based on concepts defined by the Chilean neuroscientist Francisco Varela, in particular those of "autopoesis" and embodied knowledge. The artist, together with art theorist Sarat Maharaj and curator Hans Ulrich Obrist, among others, has attempted to bridge these ideas with issues encapsulated by the title of her work: *An Artwork Which Is Not An Artwork* (2008).

Many of these works present an ongoing character, evolving over time through reediting or the addition of further research, thus remaining by default always incomplete. In fact, the exhibition prominently features selections from diverse archives and collections, including the Tibetan Amnye Machen Institute. Based in Dharamsala, India, since 1992, the AMI has undertaken a systematic scientific examination of Tibetan history, culture, society, and politics, studying the past to help independent creative thinkers to understand their present. A second archive is hosted within a structure designed by architects Nikolaus Hirsch & Michel Müller in collaboration with the Cybermohalla Ensemble, a community of young practitioners aged fifteen to twenty-three who have been gathering in media labs in squatter settlements of New Delhi. "Mohalla," which in Hindi and Urdu means "neighborhood," are places for sharing thoughts, ideas, and creative energies in the form of songs, blogs, photographs, videos, magazines, and so forth. Hirsch and Müller's *Cybermohalla Hub* (2008) is a temporary construction that, during the exhibition and thanks to the support of T-B A21, will be newly erected in Ghevra, an area at the borders of New Delhi. Considering itself a space giving form to such productive forces, this "hub" is dedicated to collecting Cybermohalla's vast database, which connects the Foundation to the hard reality of the destruction, relocation, and rebuilding of these young practitioners' work spaces in the context of the wild urbanism of the Indian capital.

In the role of social commentators, the Cybermohalla Ensemble produce documents that are not residual traces, marks of the occurrence of events that are changing these young practitioners' lives forever, but evidential agents for contesting injustice and economic interests of political lobbies that are behind the spread of the government's measures. Most importantly, these records exist digitally, and hence they possess a fundamentally different nature from that of printed or physical archives, being virtual files that are readily retrievable online, hence more ephemeral to trace or embody. Placing texts, songs, images, videos, and other materials on the Internet prevents data from disappearing into an eternal void. Equally, the easy access to readily available information at all times

THE CONCEPT OF THE DOCUMENT, AS THE ARTIST ALLAN SEKULA SUGGESTS IN HIS WRITINGS ON THE PHOTOGRAPHIC ARCHIVE, ENTAILS A NOTION OF LEGAL OR OFFICIAL TRUTH AS WELL AS AN IDEA OF PROXIMITY TO AND VERIFICATION OF AN ORIGINAL EVENT.[9]

The proliferation of scattered archives in the exhibition does not, however, function as evidence of events claiming to be based on a true narrative, on documents constituting ultimate means of proof. What gives then an archive, a blog, or a book the authority to validate the facts recorded and deposited within them? Inscriptions serve as supplements to memory, and yet they cannot provide testimony because they are incapable of attesting to anything but their own survival, distanced from that which has happened, offering material for phantasmagorical fictions or mythical tales: in other words, they sometimes are simply effects of the real underpinning orders of knowledge. This idea is exemplified by Raqs Media Collective's *Unfamiliar Tales* (2008), a piece confronting the nature and power of inscriptions beyond local definitions. This photographic and text work elaborates on and reinvents the lightly humorous and moral subtext of the Jataka fables incorporated by both Burmese and Tibetan Buddhism. It illustrates the philosophical significance of the Buddha's incarnations into a state of "notself"-ness—a manner of sentience that locates its origin and existence within a web of dependence and reciprocity that encompasses the ever-changing nature of the material universe. For these artists, it is the willful or involuntary setting aside of the recognition of this web of dependence and reciprocity that lies at the root of all tyranny.

This work, together with the infinite and transient nature of digital archives, negates temporality and impermanence. In this respect, the Sri Lankan art historian and philosopher Ananda K. Coomaraswamy has indicated how antiretinal images can be forms of "embodied viewing" conceived by a word, or the intellect, that needs to be distinguished by those imitating a physical object or the memory of it. Similarly, bringing into the equation Coomaraswamy's understandings of the "retinal" with the proto-conceptualism of an artist like Marcel Duchamp, as Hugonnier's work does thus creating a theoretical framework for touching upon this kind of interpretative apparatus, it is possible to notice how both views emphasize the notion of open-endedness, whereby the issue of evidence remains at the mercy of changes in context, control, and conditions. Even though polarized in different representational models, their approaches show how facts are, in the end, constructs decided on the basis of what survives the test of the most coherent and prevailing evidence. As Sarat Maharaj illustrates it, in the constant stream of revising facts, artists, activists, and cultural theorists alike are not that constrained, even though they are aware of treading on water.[10]

In the game of claiming credibility or describing images as undeniable or fabricated evidence, different philosophical doctrines about the nature of truth, meaning, and knowledge are questioned. The evidence supplied by a photograph, video, blog, or object can correspond to the physical imprint of the real. We are familiar with the belief that facts are "hard" like a stone, in particular scientific data that is pieced together in the course of theoretical and argumentative evaluations of the pros and cons of what is being observed. Even so, facts remain open-ended in their final reception because, within the accepted premise that there are multiple perspectives, their evidence is "retinalized" to conform to how, within such convoluted and manipulative exchange, we believe it should perform, far from being neutral to external conditions. Yet in the context presented by this exhibition, what is striking is how the works by artists and media practitioners intersect critique, rigor, and play with shifts in the modalities of real and fabricated evidence that, rather than making claims of definitive truth or clear-cut paradigms, open up avenues of inquiry above, beyond, and around what can be called evidence.

— DANIELA ZYMAN & DIANA BALDON

1. Birnbaum, Daniel (2002), "In Other's Words: Sarat Maharaj Talks with Daniel Birnbaum", in *Artforum International*, February Issue, p. 109.
2. Weiwei, Ai (2008), "Happiness Can't Be Faked," *The Guardian* website, August 18, http://www.guardian.co.uk/commentisfree/2008/aug/18/china.chinathemedia
3. Sundaram, Ravi (2008), in "Manifesta 7: Companion", Rana Dasgupta, with Raqs Media Collective (eds.), Cinisello Balsamo [Milan]: Silvana, p. 35.
4. Ibid.
5. Rogoff, Irit (2002), "Parallel Lives," in "Kutlug Ataman: A Rose Blooms in the Garden of Sorrows", Vienna: BAWAG Foundation, p. 11.
6. Hofer, Kristina Pia (2008) on "A Question of Evidence", and Gordon, Avery F. (1997), "Ghostly Matters", unpublished material.
7. Walid Raad quoting Jalal Toufic, http://www.unitednationsplaza.org/seminar_raad.html
8. Kirsch, Gesa E., Rohan, Liz (eds., 2008), "Beyond the Archives: Research as a Lived Process", Carbondale: Southern Illinois University Press.
9. Sekula, Allan (1986), "The Body and the Archive", in Charles Merewether (ed., 2006), "The Archive", London: Whitechapel Art Gallery; Cambridge, Mass.: MIT Press, p. 14.
10. Maharaj, Sarat (2004), "Unfinishable Sketch of 'An Unknown Object in 4D': Scenes of Artistic Research", in Balkema, Annette W., Slager, Henk (eds., 2004), "Artistic Research", Amsterdam: Rodopi, pp. 39–58.

The State Peace and Development
Council, Government of Myanmar has
also informed the people of Burma of
what the four main People's Desires are.

FOUR PEOPLE'S DESIRES

*   Oppose those relying on external
    elements, acting as stooges,
    holding negative views

*   Oppose those trying to jeopardize
    stability of the State and progress
    of the nation

*   Oppose foreign nations interfering
    in internal affairs of the State

*   Crush all internal and external
    destructive elements as the
    common enemy

FOUR POLITICAL OBJECTIVES

* Stability of the State, community peace and tranquility, prevalence of law and order;

* National reconsolidation;

* Emergence of a new enduring State Constitution;

* Building a new modern developed nation in accord with the new State Constitution.

FOUR ECONOMIC OBJECTIVES

* Development of agriculture as the base and all-round development of other sectors of the economy as well;

* Proper evolution of the market-oriented economic system;

* Development of the economy inviting participation in terms of technical know-how and investments from sources inside the country and abroad;

* The initiative to shape the national economy must be kept in the hands of the State and the national peoples.

FOUR SOCIAL OBJECTIVES

* Uplift of the morale and morality of the entire nation;

* Uplift of national prestige and integrity and preservation and safeguarding of cultural heritage and national character;

* Uplift of dynamism of patriotic spirit;

* Uplift of health, fitness and education standards of the entire nation.

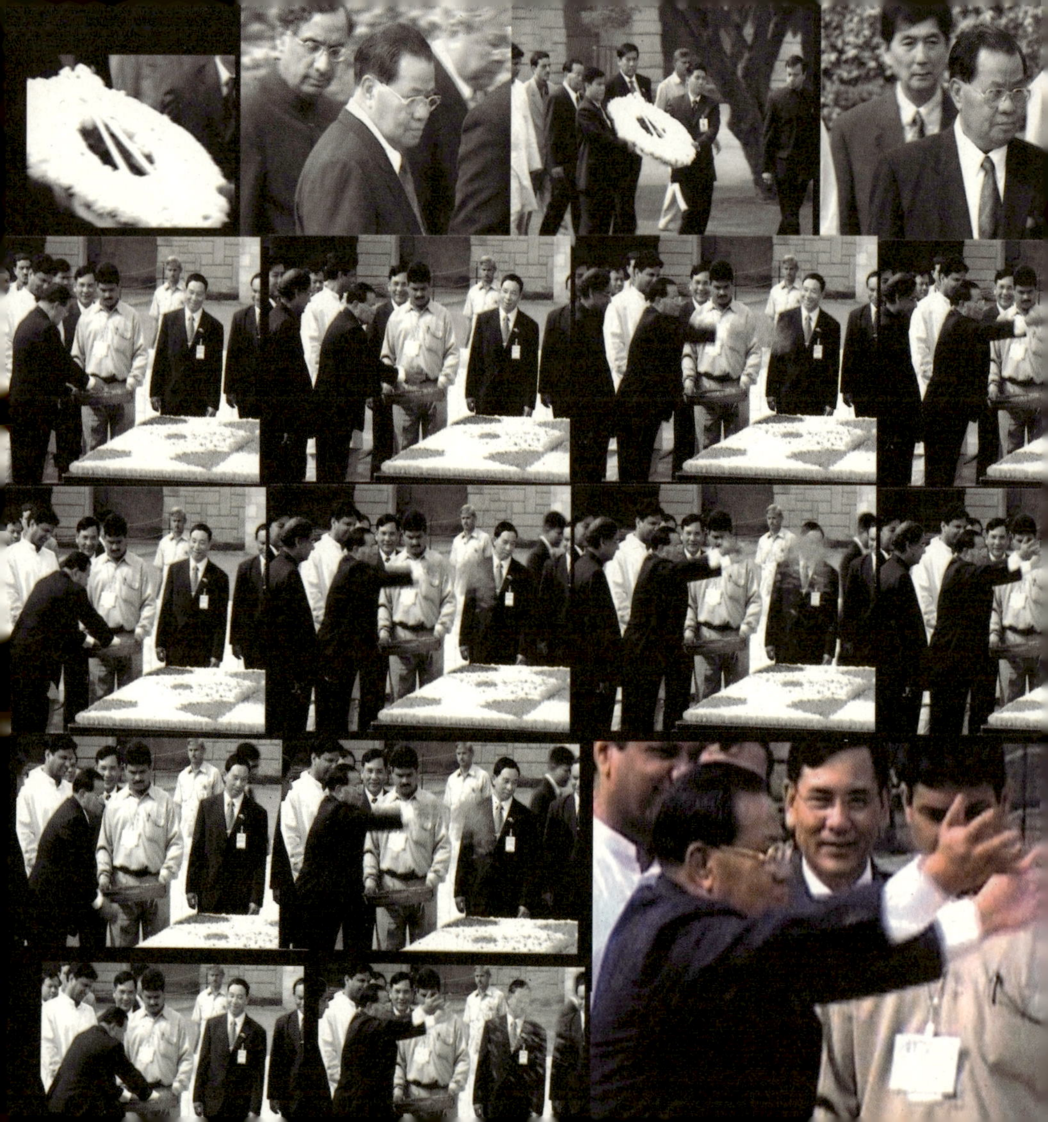

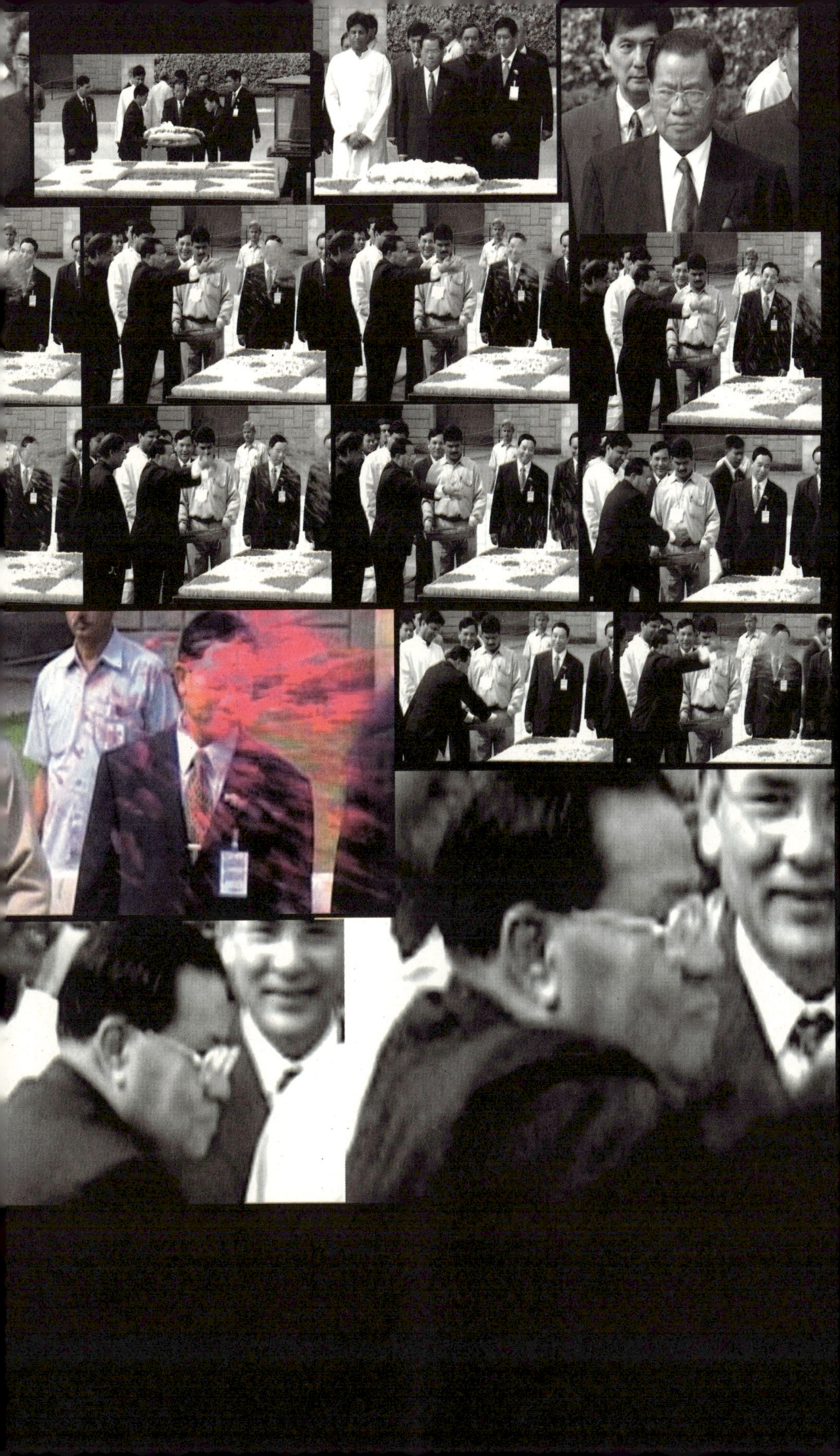

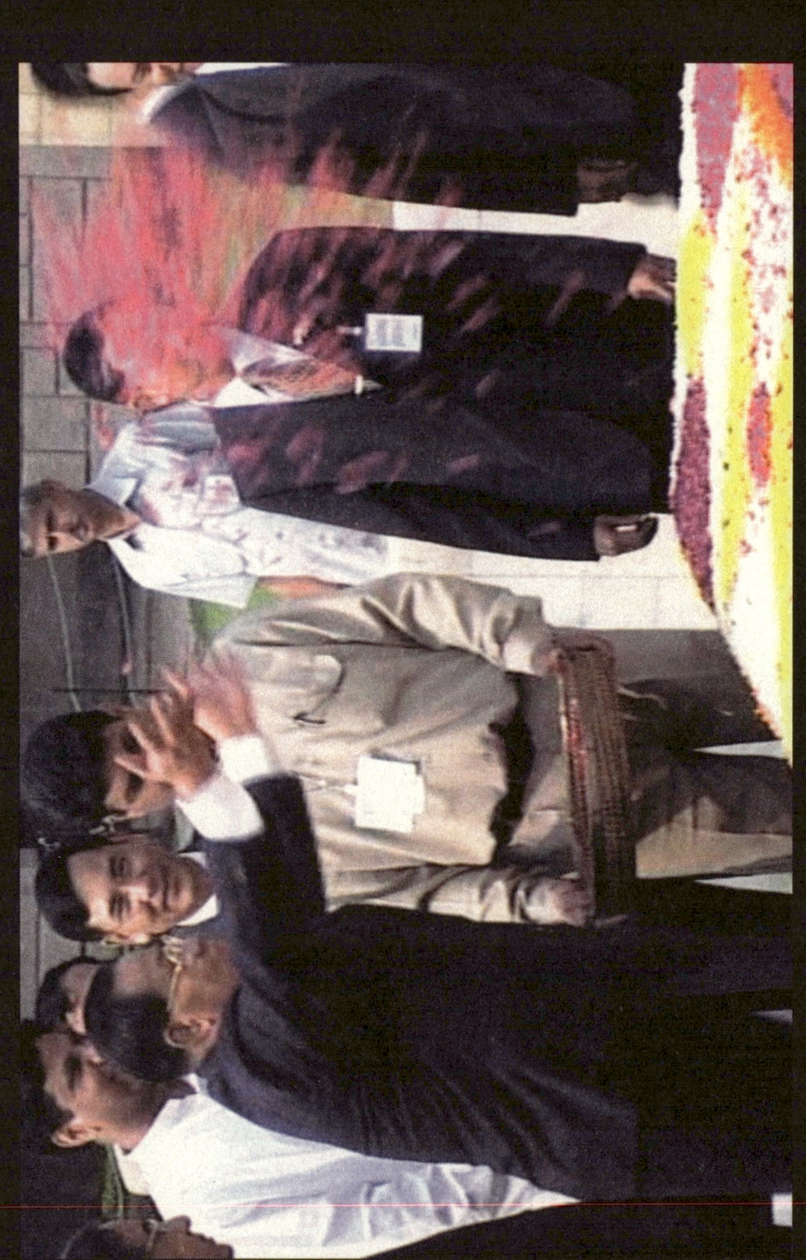

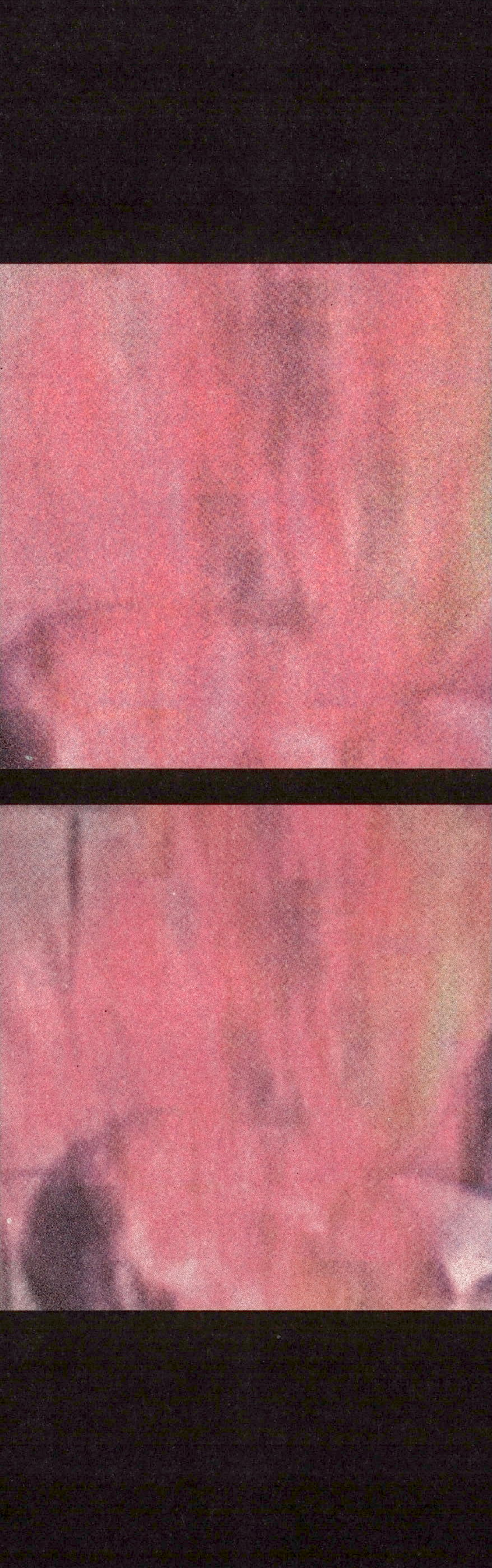

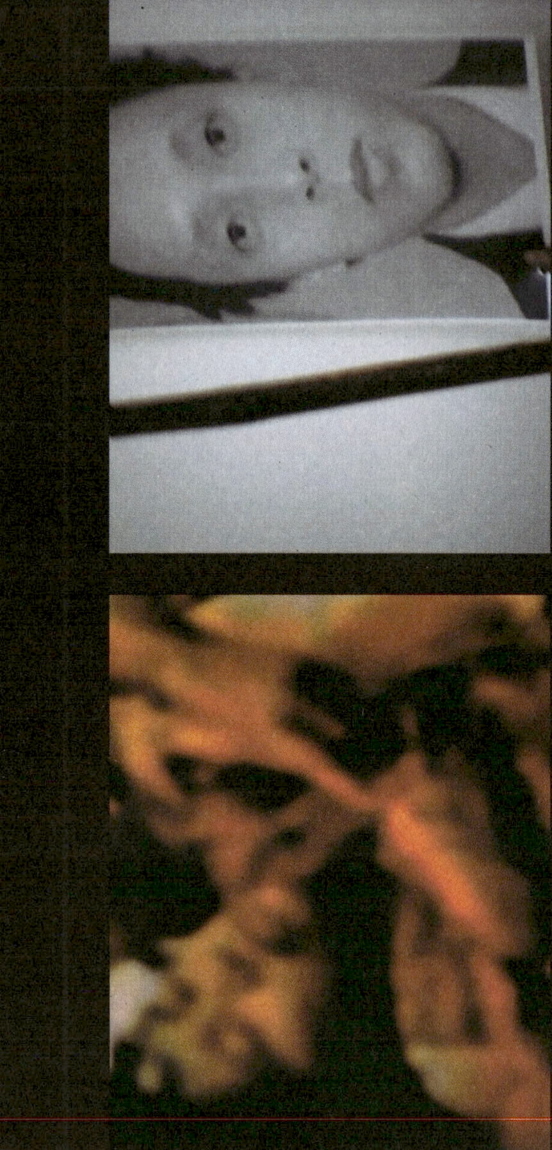

THE NOBEL
PEACE PRIZE
ONE HUNDRED YEARS FOR PEACE

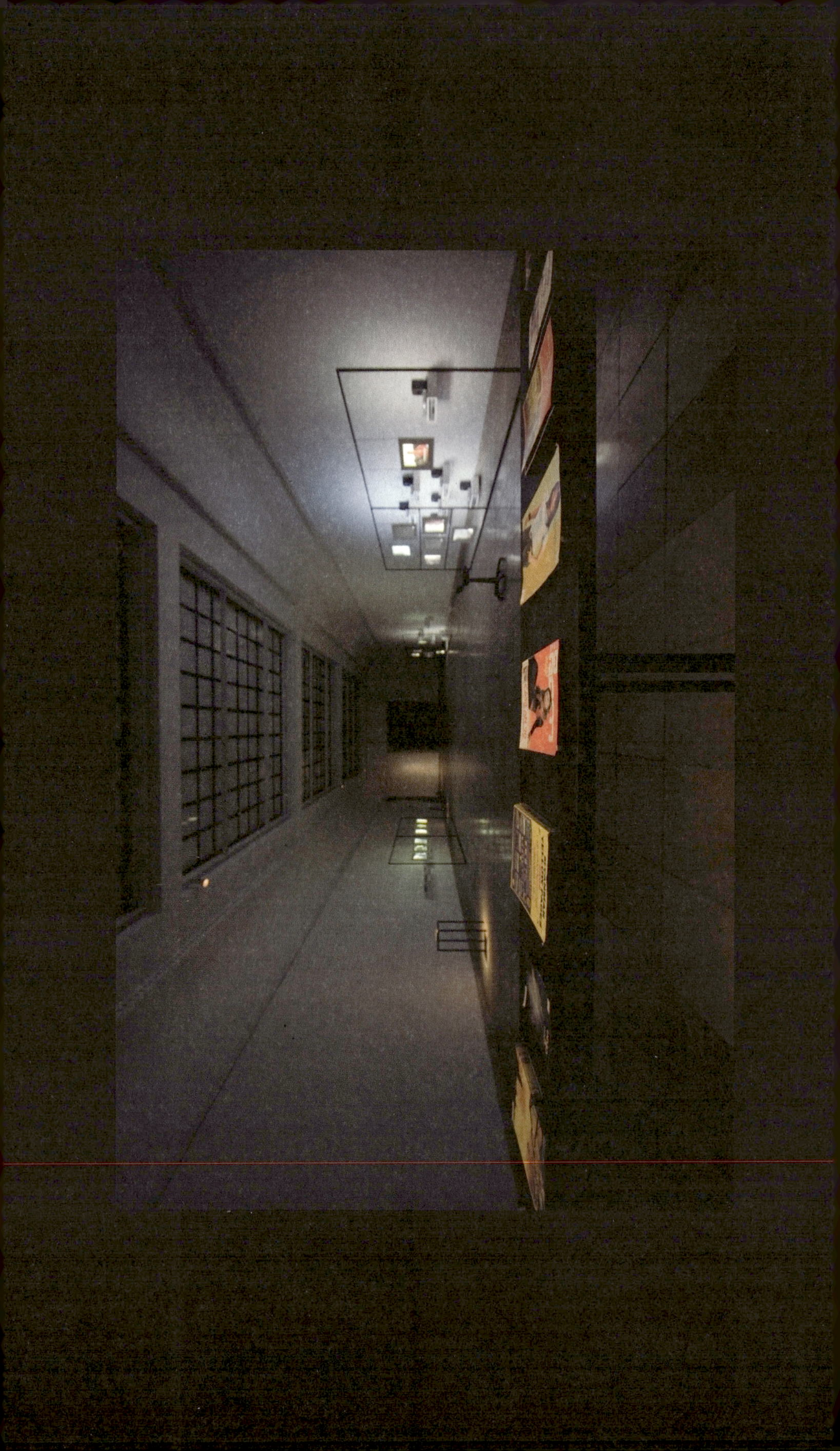

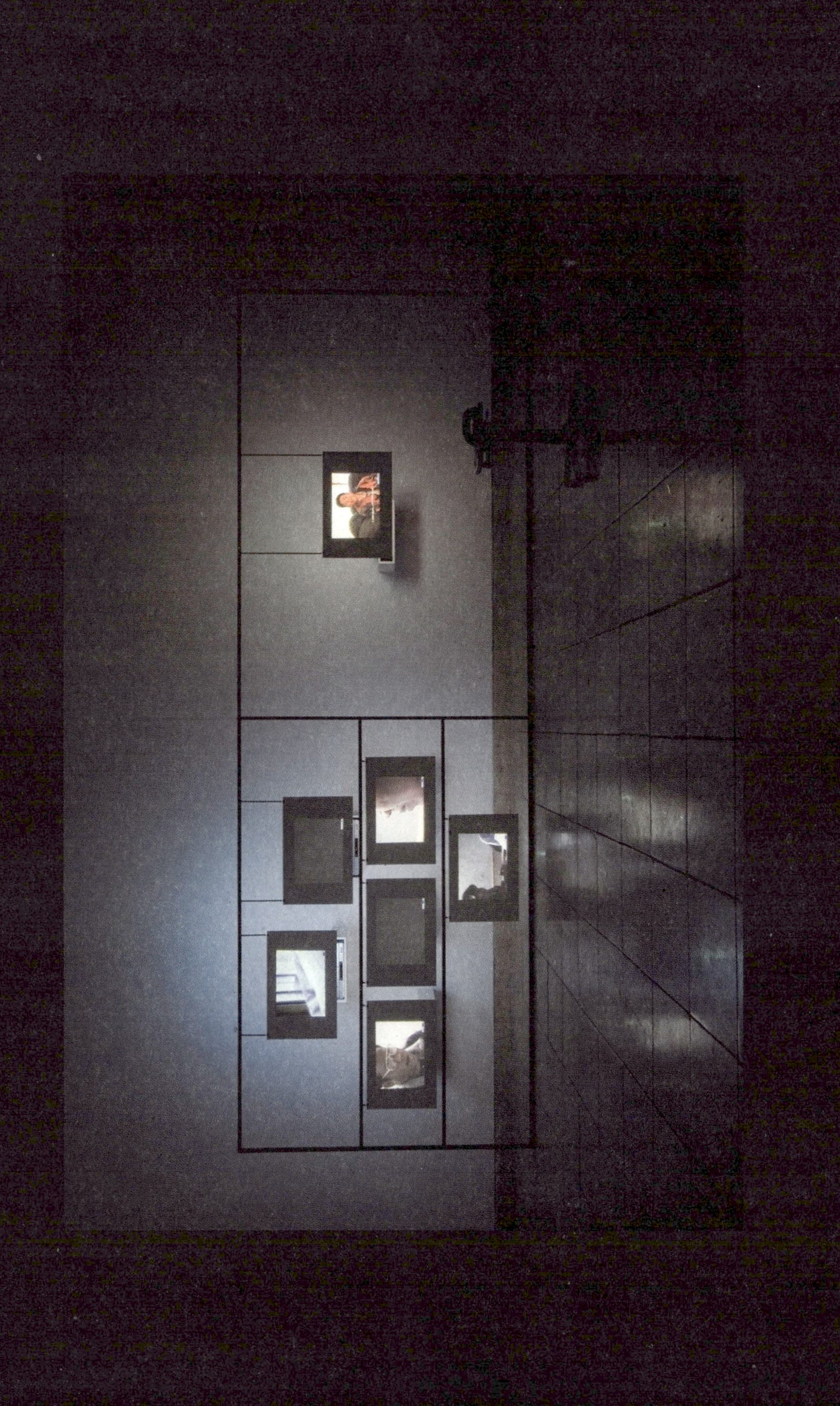

EMBEDDED SCRIPTS /

WITNESSING THE WORK OF AMAR KANWAR

"The kind of reading I have in mind would not assume a direct correspondence between words and things, nor confine itself to single meanings, nor aim for the resolution of contradiction. It would not render process as linear, nor rest explanation on simple correlations or single variables. Rather it would grant to 'the literary' an integral, even irreducible, status of its own. To grant such status is not to make 'the literary' foundational, but to open new possibilities for analyzing discursive productions of social and political reality as complex, contradictory processes." (Joan W. Scott, "Experience", 1992)[1]

The Torn First Pages by New Delhi–based filmmaker Amar Kanwar, conceived as a continuous investigation and taking the form of a nineteen-channel video installation, treats the conflicts in Burma (Myanmar) from 2004 onto the present day. The work is dedicated to the Burmese bookshop owner Ko Than Htay in Mandalay, who was imprisoned for tearing out the first page of all books and journals before selling them. By law the first page of every book and any published printed matter—such as magazines or newspapers—is reserved for the ideological slogans of the military junta and a denunciation of democratic forces, which renders their removal a direct act of resistance against the regime punishable by prosecution. For his defiant gesture, Htay was arrested in December 1994 and sentenced to three years imprisonment and torture in the infamous Mandalay prison. He carried out his resistance against the military dictatorship as an individual act of civil courage. Kanwar's three-part installation consists of nineteen video projections onto papers hung as *floating scripts* on three separate metal constructions. The piece is also accompanied by a little book consisting of imagery, some of which is included in the installation, and additional texts and materials. The first page had not been torn out and contains the military doctrine as described above. In part one we see six distinct films, of which five are a series of portraits. In one of the moving images I recognize a man in a suit tossing something pink, perhaps flowers, onto a bigger field of color. He is accompanied by other men in suits who stand in line, many with static and serious expression, while others look at the ground. The gesture of the general is repeated. At first the rhythmic repetitions, accompanied by the sounds of camera clicks, causes me to feel a certain aggression, perhaps rage; in time, though, that feeling gives way to the impression of being witness to a nonsensical gesture, an empty meaningless ritual. Upon further investigation I discover that the footage for *The Face* was secretly shot at a ceremony in Rajghat on October 25, 2004, during an official visit by General Than Shwe, supreme head of the Burmese military dictatorship, who had been invited by the Indian government. It is the General who is tossing rose petals at the cremation memorial site of Mahatma Gandhi in Delhi, a gesture that had been restaged for the international press. What happened before, I cannot know from what I see, but then I read Amar Kanwar's text in the *Himal Magazine* published in Kathmandu, Nepal. The cover story is entitled "Gandhi and the

/ RELATIONAL GRAMMARS

Witnessing *The Torn First Pages* we find ourselves in a space in which each viewer discovers their own unique relationship to the narratives embedded in the imagery. It consists of a whole range of dissident voices, which again contain another range of dissident conscious and unconscious narratives, personal or collective memories, (hi-)stories and experiences, all of which speak to us, draw us into a *conflict zone*—to use a phrase Amar Kanwar deploys to describe and link his investigations across the South-Asian subcontinent. There will also be multiple distances or closenesses in relation to the many centres within the *The Torn First Pages,* as every viewer also carries their own multiple and multiply related stories into the exhibition.

"IF WE WERE TO JUST LOOK AT YOUR OWN SELF, YOU WOULD FIND THAT THERE ARE MANY EXPERIENCES, THOUGHTS, DEFINITIONS—FRAGMENTS THAT SPAN A VERY LARGE AMOUNT OF TIME IN HISTORY THAT ALL CONSTITUTE YOUR OWN SELF."[2]

If we look at the fabric of opinions, information, experiences, feelings, triggered memories ... I tried to construct this in the first part of the text in order to show the obvious contradictions and gaps that we encounter between described realities, the information inscribed in images, and their actual visual/visceral representations. We realize that everyone is likely to experience something different or many different things. I can see a man in uniform, whereas another might only see a man, a third a general, and yet another will see *the* General, recognizing his face easily from an international newspaper or from physical familiarity, one as a politician and another as a family member, one in hate and one in love. One will see something pink, another will see flowers, a third will be able to identify the memorial site, and a fourth will know the precise name of the flower used on such occasions—what it means symbolically and/or personally. In his essay "'Getting to Know You…': Knowledge, Power, and the Body," Bill Nichols writes, "How do we come to know others and the worlds they inhabit? If knowledge arises, in large part, from subjective, embodied experience, to what extent can it be represented by impersonal and disembodied language? What strategies are available to us for the representation of people, their experience, and the encounters we wish to have of them?" He continues: "To what extent can the particular serve as an illustration for the general? Not only *what* general but *whose* general principle does the particular illustrate? To what extent are generalizations misunderstandings of the nature of the particular, the concrete, the everyday and what does this mean for historically located individuals?"[3]

General" and the paragraph is titled "Blood-red petals." He writes, "The moment finally arrives. Than Shwe has come back to the place where Gandhi's feet laid at his final resting place. It is the twenty-first century. Aung San Suu Kyi is still imprisoned. Thousands of political activists, artists, poets, journalists across three generations have been killed, lie in prisons, or are scattered in exile across the globe. Blithely, the Supreme Dictator picks up a handful of soft rose petals and tosses them gently into the air. They fall silently on the cremation site of Gandhi. The Supreme Dictator reaches out again toward the basket. There is still no change in his expression."

According to Kanwar, the projected footage contains the repetition of the original action, as a photographer missed it and shouted in panic: "Excuse me, sir, excuse me! Once more! Once more, please!"

What is it that we actually see? Let's look again at the image of General Than Shwe at the memorial site of Mahatma Gandhi. What do we detect beneath the surface of the images? The rarely seen General, who according to rumor carefully avoids his public depiction, spreads flowers on the cremation site of the spiritual and political leader of one of the biggest non-violent civil right movements in history. A movement identified with a form of resistance that in essence opposes to the form of dictatorship that the General masterminds in Burma. In an interview with Martijn van Nieuwenhuyzen, Kanwar describes how through his artistic intervention of repetition The Face develops an energy that suddenly renders it a "homage to Gandhi, (it) critiques the Indian government's support of the Burmese military as well as (it) becomes evidence of a moral and spiritual crime," the depiction of a violation, the simulated and hypocritical act of pretended tribute—an act of appropriation in fact. Kanwar, in another text, asked: "We know what Pinochet and Idi Amin looked like but have you seen the face of the Supreme Burmese dictator Senior General Than Shwe?" Ida Kierulf remarks: "The Face presents us with the mask-like face of a public figure that is seldom seen in public—the Burmese General and Head of State."

In the same part of *The Torn First Pages* we find imagery of Thet Win Aung, student leader of the protests in 1998, who was sentenced to fifty-nine years in Mandalay prison for having helped to organize student protests since 1988, when he was a high-school student. At the age of thirty-four, on October 16, 2006, Aung was killed in prison. A text on the exhibition of Kanwar in the Whitechapel Gallery in 2007 describes the piece as follows: "Kanwar's silent elegy shows a black-and-white photograph of Thet Win's youthful face being delicately hoisted into place, positioned high on a white wall, a place traditionally reserved for icons and heroes. The tenderness with which an anonymous individual installs the piece is in stark contrast to Thet Win's barbaric treatment. The respectful silence that accompanies this ceremony not only highlights the solemnity of the occasion but references the gagging of the Burmese media by Than Shwe's government." Aung Din, of the US-based Campaign for Burma, has said: "We believe that physical and psychological torture inflicted on Thet Win Aung by his captors was the main reason for his untimely death." In another projection in part one of *The Torn*

In my relation to the *conflict zone* I can only understand and maybe try and decode some parts of what is thoroughly encoded, as Amar Kanwar cannot fulfil the task to encode and represent the conflict itself in its completeness since he has access to neither a singular inside nor an outside perspective and is part of it in a relational way always. Maybe we will share some experiences; maybe we will share none at all. Some images might contain a veracity that the artist himself could not know, and can only predict as an uncertain feeling of unease. Or, on the contrary, perhaps a feeling of freedom or even bliss touched him when seeing and deciding upon an image. Maybe he picked it for a different reason than someone else would and maybe he'll never hear about another person's strong relation to this same picture. Kanwar doesn't think in terms of singularities: "Once you see and accept that there is a heterogeneous audience, that each member of the audience has a complex history of life experience and memory, it is a bit pathetic if you are going to start making unilateral messages for such a rich, complex audience."[4]

"Ce n'est pas une image juste. C'est juste une image," stated French New Wave filmmaker Jean-Luc Godard in 1969, in the Dziga Vertov Group film *Le Vent de l'Est.* He was being confronted with telling a left-out true story based on historical realities, and thereby asking for the potential meaning and capability of the depiction and reconstruction of reality and the role an image could take within it. In fact discovering that the actual veracity and emergence might lie in what is not shown and in what is not said, or in what cannot be depicted—the *unrepresentable.* Let's close our eyes and think again about the second part of the exhibition: Seven blank paper screens are linked through the fragmented stories inscribed, simultaneously one and simultaneously together shattered in times and spaces, overlapping: a house, English lessons, a still life of food, machines, workers, paintings of Aung San Suu Kyi and Gandhi, children playing and drawing and writing in English and in their native language, supposedly traditional dancing classes, the recall of a resistant member, tears, unspeakable words, silences, "my father was also involved in the uprising." Images pass by, filmed from the inside of a moving car, a hand bearing a cigarette, smoke, a song from Santana on the radio interrupted by the radio announcer, the Statue of Liberty, a seagull, a man, a poem, "my cheroot's burnt down / the sun has set / take me home," Tin Moe, a cigarette, a baby brought to bed in slow motion. "How do we recall?" Kanwar seems to ask, and, "How could we recall?" The imagery and the sounds the artist proposes—closed-up parts of bodies, still lifes, wide-angle shots of objects, colored dissolves, gestures, details of spaces, breathing, sounds of sites, spoken words—seem to stand for or contain something more, they seem to work like windows into realities. Kanwar wrote to me: "If you try and recall you see that the nature of recall is often fragmented—and yet the images come together—in a way there is a larger narrative that comes together inside your head that is far greater, larger than a certain journey and the poem."

First Pages we rediscover the forgotten photograph of Ma Win Maw Oo, a high school student who was shot dead by Burmese soldiers during the 8888 Uprising in 1988. The film is based on one picture, which contains the moment in which Ma Win Maw Oo was carried away by two medical students immediately after she had been shot. "The killing gained worldwide publicity for a day as a news photograph before it disappeared from public memory," Kanwar has noted. *Thet Win Aung* and *Ma Win Maw Oo* (both 2005) center on and pay tribute to two Burmese citizens killed for their resistance to the Burmese military dictatorship. Both films are short and based on a single photographic depiction and emerge from a "single frame" in which Amar Kanwar "wanted to explore a universe." Another witness to the work, Devika Singh, in her article "The Compass that keeps Spinning," described her experience of this pair of works in the following manner: "In the first seconds of the four-minute visual essay, blurred and indistinct black-and-white forms appear. Gradually, the face of the young political activist […] appears on a large photograph suspended on a wooden pole and is slowly hung onto a wall. By contrast, in *Ma Win Maw Oo,* bright red and orange hues invade the screen and then recede to reveal two medical students trying to rescue the thirteen-year old girl […]" Further, she remarks: "Here, Kanwar does not attempt to reconstruct his subjects' stories; by putting still photographs in motion, he points to the irreversible gap between them and the living." What does Khin Htay Htay Win, the mother of Ma Win Maw Oo, see and remember and feel when looking at Kanwar's images? "I still miss my daughter every day," she says. "Today, I want to cry the way my daughter cried. They said that they opened fire in the sky. But they aimed at her straight. That's why she died straight away. In my heart, my daughter did it for her country; she gave up her life for the country." Kanwar asks: "And how to bring back your memory, Ma Win Maw Oo, and that day in 1988?"
As I watch the vibrant colors of the rhythmically pulsing blurry and distorted imagery—before it dissolves into its resolution—other images flicker into my consciousness: open wounds, a heart beating, a feeling of fragility but also warmth, sympathy, and security, which I experience as a space of memory, a space for the depicted victim to remain and rest, perhaps.

Another film, also within the first part and entitled *The Bodhi Tree,* contains the story of Sitt Nyein Aye, a well-known Burmese dissident painter who had to escape from Burma after the military crackdown on pro-democracy demonstrations in August 1988. Now living in exile in New Delhi, he continues his work as an artist in a small studio under a bodhi tree. The scene in which two men carry a painting of Mahatma Gandhi and Aung San Suu Kyi through the streets, Kanwar describes as follows: "the fleeting glimpses of a painted portrait of Aung San Suu Kyi and Gandhi being carried down the streets, and the faces in a crowd during a political rally demonstrate how portraits become representations of opposition." As the moving images depict a man preparing something we later identify as canvases in his outdoor studio, a strong wind starts and it seems about to rain. We hear the noises of worked wood, rain,

The images Kanwar proposes don't depict or illustrate reality as such. They rather contain or bear realities. They even have the capacity of activating memories as complex psychological processes that, on the one hand, offer a site or a space for their negotiation and/or reconciliation, but, on the other, could also affect and thus have the potential of effecting not only a change in reception but one's script or grammar as base or place of departure of (future) operations. As was Godard in his famous quotation, we are not just speaking of realities in general. The work of Kanwar is located in zones of conflict, treats war and its effects, and is mostly related to traumatic experiences. As Katy Rogers points out in her essay "Creating a Dialogue with Historical Traumas" on Kanwar's film *Ma Win Maw Oo:* The artist "fills a traumatic, indelible void in collective Burmese consciousness by granting life to the one who lost it," and he "forces memory back to his viewers," relating them to their/everybody's *own* past. She even takes it a step further in making the comparison to the psychoanalytic goal of "bringing the patient to terms with a past trauma so as to incorporate it into his or her psyche, thus allowing for its productive negotiation in the future."[5] Kanwar's work offers a way for oppressed memories and narratives of traumatic events to find a way (back) into the present consciousnesses while respecting the multiplicity of its audiences. This allows for each viewer to find a *personal way,* according to different times and spaces, for diverse rhythms to emerge that respect the different social, political, personal vantage points brought to bear upon them, as well as how fast, when, or where to approach the embedded scripts, or how close to get or how distant to remain at any one time. These multiple *personal ways,* of course, can cross at any time and/or (temporarily) overlap, but also reverse and move in many other ways.

Ravi Vasudevan wrote in the context of Amar Kanwar's film *A Season Outside* (1997): "In contrast to the campaign or activist documentary, with its own, very important field of pertinence, the reflective form opens the possibilities of inquiry rather than making the definitive truth claims and establishing clear-cut critical paradigms."[6] Elsewhere, Anne Rutherfords asked Kanwar this question: "If you're working in this way there's a lot of open-endedness about how the images get interpreted. How do you work with that politically, given that your project is to make political films?" Kanwar's response: "I don't think that dealing with multiplicity and putting forth your point of view are contradictory. Further, I think in the global political situation, any political activist would know that the audience he is trying to reach out to is of many kinds, with many rationales and many histories. Even if you want to make just a convincing kind of argument film, you will find that you don't end up convincing at all."[7] Kanwar's poetic approach to the political constantly oscillates along the boundaries of the touched-upon *conflict zones,* keeping them intact and breathing, making them visible instead of disguising them.

The notion of reality that Amar Kanwar proposes to us already incorporates the problematic field of its representability/representation, but tries nonetheless leaves in the wind, and other sounds from the immediate environment— in between we see imagery of the sky, leaves, the fragile roof, a fabric, white, dissolved blanks. Aye and some other men become agitated and begin to wrap up his paintings with black plastic sheets in order to protect them from the rain, since inside there is not enough space. As the film progresses, we see people sitting, possibly waiting, and clapping hands, as well as a Buddhist monk standing in a gallery in front of black-and-white images of other monks whose names are written below them. "Are they alive?" I ask myself.

Each of the metal frames of *The Torn First Pages,* within which hang the paper screens with the rear-projected videos, are like the centre-spread pages of a large book. On the right, hanging alone, is another film, titled *Somewhere in May.* The text describes it thusly: *"Somewhere in May* lies within the intersection of freedom and claustrophobia, democracy and its simulation, the holy mission of great national projects and the individual's relationship with the politics of today. In the torturous normalcy of exile two events occur on the same day in the city of Oslo. The May 17th celebrations of the Norwegian National Day in 2004 was also the day the Burmese military dictatorship began a sham National Convention for Democracy inside Burma. Through the Democratic Voice of Burma (DVB), a small radio station in Oslo, the Burmese resistance reported on this sham convention as it broadcasted news that was secretly heard by thousands within Burma."

In the second thematic section of *The Torn First Pages* we experience a story in pieces, fragmented and distributed across seven screens. The narratives tell of a community in exile, from within which—according to the words of the artist—"shoots out a tangent that heads to New York in search of a poet and a poem," a long journey with another Burmese activist. At the end of this adventure they finally find the famous poet Tin Moe, exiled from Burma, and recorded him reciting his famous poem that was also found scribbled on the walls of prisons inside Burma. The poem goes: "My cheeroot's burnt down. The sun has set. Take me home." Kanwar writes: "The haiku metaphorically represents the state of Burma under the military and the aspirations of the people." This section emerges, somewhat surprisingly, from the small town of Fort Wayne, Indiana, where a large Burmese community lives in exile with activists from Burmese and ethnic nationalities from several generations. While still politically active, they make their living as assembly-line workers in the ancillary industries of major automobile factories. The screens are simultaneously linked by blanks, which are sometimes lightened by the imagery of the projected stories. And as the blanks—which seem to take up more time than the projected images—I entertain the sneaking suspicion that these empty spaces could also contain many more stories than the visuals represents or could represent. Are the underlying stories that are too difficult to be told set free through this format? Do they find a way into our presence?

In the third part of the exhibition we encounter "old and new archival footage to redefine what we by habit are used or trained to acknowledge and define as reality. He opens up the notion in order to fill it with a whole range of new possible contents, containers, and activators. I remember a scene from the recent film *Stalags,* by Ari Libsker, on pornographic fiction in Israel. It uses archival footage from the infamous Eichmann Process in Jerusalem in 1961, during which the fiction writer Yehiel de-Nur / K. Tzetnik—a survivor of the Holocaust and the Auschwitz concentration camp—is called to the witness stand. He recalls the place and of Auschwitz as "another planet." He faints. He claims that everything described in his fiction is real. Where do we find evidence, when we redefine what is part of this reality, besides factual knowledge? Knowing that the traces traumatic events leave behind could even be untraceable, that a victim to crime could show even *invisible* symptoms such as partial or complete amnesia, denial and many others, where do we find evidence? Could the act of (re-)collecting evidence, the attempt to find an *image juste,* become the evidence itself? When Kanwar sends the words

"IMAGINE THE FORMAL PRESENTATION OF POETRY AS EVIDENCE IN A FUTURE WAR CRIMES TRIBUNAL. IMAGINE NINE-TEEN SHEETS OF PAPER FLOATING FOREVER IN THE WIND..."

ahead of his exhibition, I would read exactly along the attempt of (re-)negotiating the boundaries of the already defined in order to create a space of future potentialities in the reading and recalling of violence and crime by means of different, unseen, overlooked, or erased sources. Kanwar again: "To keep collecting evidence when confronted with continuous brutality is only possible when there is hope for a better future."[8]

— GABRIELLE CRAM

anonymously and secretly filmed inside Burma," which contains "black-and-white footage from the time of the independence of Burma, the generals, the 8888 Uprising, the recent rebellion by the monks" shot by both well-known and anonymous professionals as well as amateur filmmakers whose names remain protected by anonymity or by organizational cover. On three projections we watch people on the streets, dead bodies, bloodied bodies, fire, smoke, people in uniforms, monks in robes, the army attacking people and monks… On a second set of three paper screens I see the projection of a man in uniform again accompanied by other men in uniforms, and barely legible fragments of texts underly the images. Kanwar writes: "The three screens distort the archive in order to create the laughing triptych of General Ne Win, the first Burmese dictator, along with his coterie." The underlying texts, which are printed directly on the paper sheets, consist precisely of the texts as on the aforementioned torn-out first pages, and describe the restrictions invented by the military dictatorship.

In texts, the little book, Wikipedia ghost writings, weblogs, and other sources I discover more about the economic and historical background of the conflict zone depicted in the work. From an article on the website of Mizzima News on "Media in Burma" I understand that the image takes on a different meaning in the context of the much publicised September Uprisings of 2007. In the 1988 uprising, information (and especially visual documentation) of the events were not easily available and were censored by the military regime; the Internet was not accessible and news reports had been continuously blocked by the government. The detention of journalists also marks a certain continuity in the history of the repression in Burma. Since the "8888 Uprisings" in 1988 hardly any images, save for the aforementioned photograph of the assassinated student Ma Win Maw Oo, managed to escape into public realm. Reading another chapter of the same article entitled "Media as Counter Offensive: Junta Way of Looking at Media," I need to ask myself what uncomfortable truth could lie in the self-legitimisation of information detention of the military regime when Burmese Minister for Information Brig-Gen Kyaw Hsan states, while attending the inauguration of a journalists' training program in Rangoon in September 2005, that "the countries with the strong media arm" are trying to "bully and dominate small nations through the practice of neo-colonialism." Devika Singh describes that while watching Kanwar's work she listens to the recurrent voice-over of the artist and reads first-person commentaries as subtitles, which are experienced as an "omniscient presence addressing the victims he portrays. But it is not so much with them as with the viewer, who becomes part of the collective we often referred to in the voice-overs and subtitles, that Kanwar connects." *The Torn First Pages,* with films shot in India, Norway, and the United States, plus archival material secretly filmed in Burma, is conceived—according to the words of Kanwar in the interview with Martijn van Nieuwenhuyzen—"to exist as a moving image constellation that tangentially engages with the Burmese resistance and the question of democracy, exile and individual courage. It intends to draw us all into the Burmese resistance no matter where and how far away we are."

1. Scott, Joan Wallach (1992), "Experience", in "Feminists theorize the Political", Scott, Joan Wallach, Butler, Judith (eds.), New York: Routledge.
2. Rutherford, Anne (2005), "'Not Firing Arrows': Multiplicity, Heterogeneity and the Future of Documentary: Interview with Amar Kanwar", in *Asian Cinema,* Spring/Summer.
3. Nichols, Bill (1993), "'Getting to Know You…': Knowledge, Power, and the Body", in Renov, Michael (ed.), "Theorizing Documentary", New York: Routledge.
4. Rutherford, Anne (2005), ibid.
5. Rogers, Katy (2006), "Memory's Void", in "Image War", ISP Exhibition, Whitney Museum, New York.
6. Vasudevan, Ravi (2003), "Selves Made Strange. Violent and Peformative Bodies in the Cities of Indian Cinema, 1974–2003", in Chandrashekhar, Indira, Siehl, Peter C. (eds.), "body.city", Delhi: Tulika Books.
7. Rutherford, Anne (2005), ibid.
8. Van Nieuwenhuyzen, Martijn (2008), "Amar Kanwar. Collecting Evidence," in *Flash Art,* January/February.

THE ARTIST HAS CONSIDERED THIS WORK OF ART POLITICALLY SENSITIVE TO A CERTAIN EXTENT AND THEREFORE DECIDED NOT TO FULLY EXHIBIT IT DUE TO THE THREATS IMPOSED UPON HERSELF, HER FAMILY AND FRIENDS BY THE RULING MILITARY JUNTA OF BURMA.

KHIN KHIN SU
WE HAVE TO BE VERY CAREFUL
THESE DAYS BECAUSE...

The phrase "We have to be very careful these days…" is widely used in Burma among its 55 million inhabitants for several (if not infinite) reasons. Among locals, this phrase is used on a daily basis in response to the living conditions, in a state of constant fear, a state of vague but very real threats. For example, in Burma, simply saying the name of an opposition party leader in public can result in a minimum 7-year imprisonment. The simple act of wearing a white shirt and praying for the livelihood of the political prisoners can be interpreted as an action that disturbs the stability of the state with the consequence of spending the rest of one's life in prison. In such a country—where freedom of expression and speech is non-existent—everyone has to be very careful about what they say, how they say it, what they see, how they see it, what they do, and how they do it, because one reckless action or careless phrase can result in a chain of troubles and miseries—as state-sponsored thugs have been made the watchdogs of general public. Therefore the phrase "We have to be very careful these days…." has become a part of daily conversation and communication among Burmese. To stay alive and out of trouble (or in order to avoid torture, pain, suffering, harassments, rape, and other types of miseries in life), one has to be very careful these days in Burma.

However, the artist has questioned whether this issue could be taken not only locally but also universally. Providing that every single action of each individual on the surface of earth has its own consequences, it is important to for us to be aware of our actions and how we execute them. The fact about us being careful may concern any subject ranging from personal issues to social issues to political issues to environmental issues to cultural issues to ethical issues to other infinite issues concerning humanity and human conditions.

In this project, A0 size color paper with the phrase "We have to be very careful these days because…." will be pasted not only on the surface of the intended exhibiting space but also in other public places. The aim of this intervention is to engage the general public (not only gallery visitors) by presenting a warning, or rather enigmatic message, so as to force them take part intellectually. At the same time, this project can be taken as an interactive work between the artistic concept and the imagination of the public because no particular reason for which we have to be careful is given. However, what we (the entirety of humankind) have to be careful about is totally up to the public. In another sense, the project contracts time: the message tells us to be careful and, thus, the viewers are forced to contemplate themselves and their actions in the present, how they effect the future, and how their past actions and the consequences thereof effect both present conditions and future plans.

This project is an ongoing public intervention—by using color posters in the manner of post-it notes as reminders of what one is obliged to do.

WE
HAVE TO BE
VERY

CAREFUL THESE DAYS BECAUSE…

INTERVIEW WITH MISS K.

My name is Aung Myint Htet. I am a Burmese journalist and stringer for exile media. Today, Miss K., who has been organizing various educational projects in Burma, is interviewing me. For security reasons, neither her name nor those of other people, groups, and organizations can be revealed here. Thank you for your understanding.

AUNG MYINT HTET: Miss K., thank you for being with us today. First of all, tell us what you do in Burma.

MISS K.: I organize workshops, training, lectures, and seminars in Rangoon. This is an attempt to fill the educational void in Burma. The military junta has controlled the country for nearly half a century and their main focus is to suppress and restrict the enlightenment and empowerment of citizens; as a result, the education system has totally collapsed—the public education system is (unsound). Therefore, there have been efforts by independent organizations, NGOs, and citizens, in and out of the country, to provide education to people in Burma, covering different fields. My focus is on art, film, video, and media. Education in modern and contemporary art, film and video making, communication, and media, these are all non-existent in Burma, so these are the areas I have been trying to cover. One of these projects now has grown to an extensive center that deals with film and video, and I collaborate with foreign institutions for this project. We have provided regular film/video workshops and as a result, we now have a growing number of local film/video makers. So we needed to set up a database and archive of these Burmese film/video works and producers, as well as provide production and post-production services and distribution assistance so that Burmese people can create truly independent films and videos—documentary, drama, experimental, any genre.

I can confirm your description of the state of education in my country. Since I cannot find journalism or media communication in course lists of any of our universities, I had to look for training here and there, sometimes sneaking across the border to get training in a neighboring country. Foreign groups and NGOs provide the training and to take part in them I must take great risks—from being on the government's watch list to imprisonment. I am always afraid.

The risk is the same for our participants. Some have been imprisoned in the past and some not, I mean not yet, but all are equally afraid. This is the very basic environment of any of our workshops and seminars. Still, some cannot help shouting out loud because of the daily frustration and a great desire to express themselves more freely, while some others are more cautious.

And about crossing the border, even that is a high-risk operation. Most Burmese who are engaged in activities that seek greater freedom live illegally in neighboring countries. If found out, they can be arrested, deported, and imprisoned. Most exiled journalists have no ID, no documents or papers, nothing that can protect them. Even those who have had a document from UNHCR in Thailand, for example, had to tear it up and go completely underground because the holders of these documents were sent to camps where they are not allowed to go out, or use any means of communication to reach the world outside the camp. How can you work as a journalist in such conditions? In the West we now fashionably call this "bare life," but this is the very state you are in.

Sadly, yes. In the West they can call us whatever to suit their conceptual frame, but for us, we just have to survive under any circumstance. Our minds are concentrated on thinking about how to adapt to the condition, how to minimize risk and maximize what's offered. No space for theory here.

Sorry, we cannot help but theorize. About people like you, for example. I call it the "virtual prisoner of the conscious". You may, fortunately, be out of prison in the physical sense, but you are restricted anyway and that's because of your consciousness. I actually admire the sense of survival and vitality of your people, and this may be an Asian thing. I give workshops and training on the border area, too, and always admire how the Burmese living on the border can negotiate—with local people, administration, police, military, and with the economy. This negotiation practice has created a whole alternative world where few laws of the real world apply. In one town on the Thai border, where most of the Burmese exile groups and organizations operate, more than 200 of them, for example, none of them have legal status. The more they are politically and socially "conscious," the more they are illegal, as economic migrants and seasonal workers can get work permits, however limited they are. So the local police are in a way fed by these "illegal exiles"—whenever they want to "drink a cup of coffee" they wait for the Burmese and catch them. The exile organizations, therefore, include this "coffee-for-police-fee" (my term) in their annual budget. Thai military intelligence unofficially allows the exile organizations to operate with an expectation that they can obtain useful information from them. But of course, once the political wind changes direction, they can easily close down the organizations, deport individuals or send them to camps, and this happens from time to time.

BURMESE EXILES LIVE AND WALK ON THIS EXTREMELY THIN EDGE—THE EDGE OF THE BORDER, THE EDGE OF THE REALITY, AND THE EDGE OF THE MIND.

And they all survive this with negotiations.

What about how people inside are dealing with the situation?

Because I operate in the capital, Rangoon, and almost all the participants live in the capital, and many are engaged in cultural activities, I can only talk about that particular group of people, which I can even call the cultural elite. We are talking about a country where the gap in education and information levels between big cities and rural areas is huge, with hundreds of different ethnic minorities that depend on their community's level of education and information. So what I say here may not be relevant in talking about the whole country. As far as this cultural elite is concerned, they rely on a cultural code—this is their weapon. They are much more trained and informed about elaborate modes of expression that imply hidden subtexts than the military generals, who are totally

ignorant of any new and sophisticated cultural language. In the early period of
my involvement, I started by screening good films and videos, I mean literary-
"good", and organizing follow-up discussions at teashops.[1] And afterwards, we
would normally (if our screening is not disrupted by the authorities) go hunting
for DVDs downtown. The streets are full of DVDs and VCRs; contrary to outsid-
ers' imagination about heavily restricted Burma, there is an abundant supply
of videos, and they are mostly coming from China and some from Thailand and
India. The problem is not the amount that is available to the citizens but a lack
of education on how to find "good" ones among them. And this is an interesting
fact about censorship in Asian totalitarian countries, perhaps with the exception
of North Korea: it's more about depleting our sense of judgment than about re-
stricting physical materials. So our DVD hunting became part of the field training,
I called it "mushrooming," a training in how to pick edible and good ones and to
judge which ones are poisonous. And which ones are poisonous in a culture?
The hundreds and thousands of films and TV soaps that the authorities want
you to indulge in—passively and without thinking deeply. You decide to be out
of this tempting status quo and to enlighten yourself, to train yourself, and to
take the trouble to dig in the mound of trash and be able to see what is useful.
This is already a big, big step forward and a huge advantage over the ever-more
ignorant junta. Every time I visit the country, I ask local colleagues what they
have found while I was away. You will be surprised by their answers—"Kiaros-
tami," "Dogville," "Karel Zeman" …

Yet the arrests continue.
… and so do the routine submission of manuscripts by editors to the censorship
board, the visits of censorship officers to an exhibition before the opening, the
practice of sentencing innocents without a fair trial …
What I have observed in this situation is the battle between the cultural eloquence of the elite, I mean hidden eloquence, and the ignorance of the junta
that has opted for random censorship. When writers, editors and publishers
submit their manuscripts to the censorship board, usually 40 to 70% of the
text will be taken out after weeks of waiting. This is devastating for those who
wish to publish their original work. What's worse, they usually don't know why
these parts have to be withdrawn and they cannot argue with the officers. It's
the same for art pieces in exhibitions. Artists must take down their works, and
why? Because of the use of the color red, or because a member of the artist's
family works for a foreign news agency? They will never know for sure. This is
how the authorities show off their power while maintaining their ignorance, and
it creates more fear in peoples' psyche.
In a film workshop, there are always some participants who want to make a
strong political statement in their films. In one of the workshops, for example,
one team (we usually divide the participants into small teams) made a ten-
minute film entirely focusing on hands of various professionals and in various situations. Among them, we see some hands dealing with exchanging money under
the table, some nervously trying to hide sensitive documents, and some appar-
ently fed up with never-ending bureaucratic routines. This film was shown at an
official screening (where we cannot avoid a presence of officials and state intel-

ligence officials) without any problem. Another short film consists of a collection of shots of public notice boards that are all over Burma, telling people such and such is prohibited, is not allowed. This was also shown without any disturbance. This suggests that these expressions, while they are obvious to us, are not fully grasped by the authorities. But then even the most innocent boy-meets-girl drama can become a problem if the authorities decide to make trouble for us. We don't know when the time will come; it can happen at any time.

In your perception, which is stronger among the Burmese—a desire to express themselves or the fear of doing so?

Fear dominates in everybody's mind in Burma. Naturally, cultural practitioners have a strong desire to express themselves, but among common people, the desire to communicate is overwhelming. In the last year or so, hundreds of Internet cafés have popped up in every corner of Rangoon, and they are always full. Users are mainly talking to family and friends who live abroad, reflecting the mass exodus of Burmese out of the country.

DURING THE "SAFFRON REVOLUTION," BURMESE BLOGGERS BECAME A SENSATION IN THE WORLD MEDIA BECAUSE OF THEIR 'CITIZENS' JOURNALISM,' REPORTING THE SITUATION ON THE WEB MINUTE BY MINUTE UNTIL THE AUTHORITIES FINALLY SHUT DOWN THE NETWORK. THIS IS NOT NECESSARILY THEIR DESIRE TO BE ENGAGED IN POLITICAL ACTIVITIES; BLOGGERS GENUINELY WANTED TO COMMUNICATE TO THE WORLD, WANTED TO TELL WHAT WAS HAPPENING, WANTED TO DESCRIBE THE SITUATION THAT THEY WERE IN. THIS DESIRE TO COMMUNICATE OVERCAME FEAR.

When I watch people flocking to Internet cafés despite their intimidating atmosphere and the many regulations and restrictions, I cannot help but think that their desire to communicate will eventually push the junta out. Of course, the authorities are fighting back; after the "Saffron Revolution" blog fiasco[2] they sent their people to a foreign boot camp to work as blogger-infiltrators. So the informers are not only ubiquitous in teashops but on blogs, too; these agents recently even staged a DDoS attack on exile media. It's a war, a media war, but it's also a war on desire. The Burmese government has this "People's Desire" slogan that every licensed media outlet is required to publish[3]—and this is often made the butt of jokes by locals as well as foreigners—but the more they try to manufacture the people's desire, the more will people even consciously take hold of their genuine desire and eventually drive it forward.

In the field of art, this true desire of people to communicate is most evident in performance art. In fact, performance art in Burma is among the strongest now in comparison with anywhere else because of its earnestness and urgency. It is a manifestation of the body not as a servant but as an autonomous medium of expression. Poetry is everyone's favorite medium here, too (this is also a characteristic of Burmese blogs: many like to send poetry to others), and performance art is probably second to it. The brand value is high, and even a shopping center recently organized—somewhat innocently—a performance event as a promotional event. The Serbian curator Bojana Pejić once told me that in former Yugoslavia during the socialist era, censorship of art was primarily focused on figurative art. But in Burma and also in other Asian countries, the authorities are wary of performance artists, and they have been imprisoning them—probably because for Asian authorities, such thing as an independent body does not exist; their belief is that a body must belong to a higher authority. They will not tolerate a body manifesting as a representation of its owner's powerful mind. So I hope performance art can happen in more places all over Burma, disseminating its message for an individual body to liberate itself from the empire of autocracy.

— AUNG MYINT HTET

1. The Burmese have a teashop culture where lively discussions take place on any subject. Some teashops are favorites of writers; some are occupied by artists, musicians, and so on. This is a place where you can find anybody you want to meet. Naturally, because of this, teashops are the most watched places too.
2. At the beginning of the uprising, when monks started to march on the street in the capital from September 22, 2007 on, it took the authorities three days to realize that local bloggers were sending out pictures to the world at large until they finally shut them down.
3. Together with the "People's Desires", media must also publish the "Four Objectives" (see pp. 20/21)

POETIC JUSTICE: ON THE ART OF EVIDENCE

Exhibit A: A photograph by Raqs Media Collective depicting a squarish pond, surrounded by rocky banks and situated in the midst of grassy hills and fields. Inserted into an exhibition that questions the nature of evidence, the photograph begs the question—to what truth does it bear witness, beyond the truth of its own existence? The query illuminates something fundamental about the question of evidence—that is, evidence is never enough in and of itself.

The term "evidence" derives from the Latin *videre,* meaning "to see," the "evidentiary" being "what is distinctly visible," according to the *English Oxford Dictionary.* In this regard, the word most immediately calls to mind the legal context—blood on a knife connects investigators to the perpetrator of a crime, like a piece of a puzzle, so that a material object, "DNA evidence," provides verification of an event. Even in courtrooms, however, evidence must be placed within a narrative, so that its facticity, its indisputable presence as a material object or faithful reproduction, if accepted, leads to belief in something beyond itself—a set of circumstances, a probability, a guilty party. And this narrative necessity points to its paradoxical quality—while evidence should be "obvious to the sight" and "recognizable at a glance," it in fact requires elaborate contextualization to establish its meaning.

ALTHOUGH EVIDENCE IS MEANT TO BE INDUBITABLE AND INCONTROVERTIBLE, GROUNDING STORIES IN SCIENTIFIC TRUTH, IT REQUIRES ARGUMENTATION AND DELIBERATION, AND THIS IS WHERE THINGS GET TRICKY.

Returning to our Exhibit A, the photograph of the pond of water: the text that accompanies the image—entitled "How The Most Terrible Solitude Was Overcome," one of two diptychs that comprise *Unfamiliar Tales* (2008)—has it that the photograph documents the present liquid state of "a small piece of sky" that landed on earth, leaving its playmates, the clouds, behind. In an act of compassionate and unselfconscious enlightenment, the "skylet" transformed into a pool of water in order to nourish its surroundings. The artists, in other words, contextualize the photographic evidence of the pond by recourse to a story inspired by the "Jataka" fables popular in Burmese and Tibetan Buddhism. These tales relate the Buddha's incarnation as various selfless, peaceful, and environmentally interconnected modes of being, allegories frequently posed against the tyranny of dependency, egoism, and political domination. The photograph, then, serves to ground that Buddhist tale in proof, presenting, irreconcilably no doubt, a scientific exhibit, the documentary photograph of a pool of water, to verify a matter of subjective belief, a religious fable.

Photography, we know, has been traditionally viewed as possessing what the French literary critic Roland Barthes terms "an evidential force" and a "power of authentication," which offers a way of "evaluating 'truth' in discourse" by virtue of its "photomechanical reproduction" of reality, as historian John Tagg has written.[1] But in the case of the Raqs Media Collective's work, photography is diverted from the legal context in which agreed-upon interpretation becomes legally binding or actionable. Instead, by resituating the evidential power of photography within a religious framework in the context of an artistic exhibition, the group mixes sacred and secular paradigms, establishing the truth of a Buddhist fable by recourse to scientific methodology, thereby disrupting the latter's rationality and logic; just as, conversely, it directs scientific truth-claims to validate a theological parable. The result, in both cases, is an explosive combination of modernity's secular and scientific positivism with Asian religious tradition. Beyond the multiple interpretive possibilities of that provocative juxtaposition, what we end up with is the acknowledgement that

THE DEFINITIONS OF EVIDENCE AND TRUTH—AND PARTICULARLY WESTERN ONES COMMONLY ASSUMED TO BE UNIVERSAL AND HEGEMONIC—ARE NOWHERE CERTAIN OR CONSTANT—

in fact, they change meanings according to different cultural and historical contexts.

One particular model of evidence—or epistemological paradigm—that dominates current-day definitions of "evidence" emerged in Europe in the late nineteenth century, and is constitutive of our understanding of the modern social sciences. Consider the disciplines of art history, criminology, and psychoanalysis, which, as Italian historian Carlo Ginzburg has noted, display telling methodological parallels in terms of how each interprets material evidence—for instance, the art historian Giovanni Morelli's approach to the attribution of historic artworks (i.e., determining authorship on the basis of a painting's style) parallels the fictional character Sherlock Holmes's way of discerning the significance of clues in criminal investigations, which in turn corresponds to Sigmund Freud's psychoanalytic procedure of reading symptoms. All three, it turns out, revolve around the probing of small, seemingly insignificant physical details to reveal the key to a deeper reality, which, for Ginzburg, defines the "conjectural paradigm" that governs numerous scientific disciplines, including history, archaeology, geology, physical astronomy, and paleontology, in addition to art history, forensic science, and psychoanalysis. "Reality is opaque," Ginzburg writes, "but there are certain points—clues, symptoms—which allow us to decipher it."[2] At the same time, this process of "deciphering" points to the subjective, interpretive mode that belies the "scientific" pretence of the conjectural paradigm (e.g., its assumptions of objectivity, truth, and neutrality) as it had developed and was institutionalized in nineteenth- and twentieth-century modernity. Intriguingly, Ginzburg goes on to note the historical origins of "conjecture" in the practice of divination, reminding us that "the *coniector* was a priestly soothsayer or diviner."[3] In other words, it is the disciplinary authority of the social sciences that ultimately establishes the truth of its procedures, rather than the intrinsic value of its evidence. What the historian reveals about this method correlates with Tagg's point that "photographs are never 'evidence' of history; they are themselves the historical."[4] In this regard, it is not "the power of the camera" that guarantees the authenticity and meaning of images, but rather the authority of interpretive contexts, such as institutions and the state, that invests the camera with its evidential power, just as the ritualistic context guaranteed the diviners' conjuring of truth.

The nature of truth and of evidence has shifted considerably in recent decades in the postmodern era—in philosophical, scientific, and cultural discourses alike. And it has done so in ways that reverse the terms of the conjectural paradigm of the social sciences, privileging the subjective and imaginary aspects of truth and the uncertainty and contingency of evidence in the place of older beliefs in neutrality, facticity, and objectivity. This transformation is clear in Raqs Media Collective's work, but another poignant example is Amar Kanwar's video installation *The Torn First Pages* (2004–08), which presents poetry as evidence against Burma's dictatorial regime. The project tells the story of Ko Than Htay, the owner of a popular bookstore in Mandalay, Burma, who, in a courageous act of political resistance, tore out the first pages of all the books he sold, thereby rescuing them from the propagandistic slogans the military government stamped on the initial pages of all publications. Ko Than Htay spent three years subjected to torture in prison for this subversive activity. In Kanwar's installation, these images—including those of the secretive leader of the Burmese dictatorship, and others that relate additional stories of the victims of its military repression—are projected as videos onto screens hanging away from the wall, like "nineteen sheets of paper floating in the wind, each with translucent moving images from within Burma and across the globe," as Kanwar describes his work. The pages that Ko Than Htay cut from books, which served as the justification for his imprisonment, are thereby transformed into video testimony redirected against the cruel leaders of the regime, fulfilling Kanwar's entreaty: "Imagine the formal presentation of poetry as evidence in a future war-crimes tribunal."

This proposal of "poetry as evidence" can be taken literally. Part of Kanwar's project includes video footage of a search for an old Burmese poet living in exile who is famous for a haiku he scrawled on the wall of a Burmese prison. It is therefore conceivable that that poem might one day serve as photographic evidence of Burma's harsh prison conditions, assisting in persecuting those responsible. But perhaps, more radically than this factual understanding, *The Torn First Pages mobilizes* verse—and more broadly in this context, artistic experience—as evidence of a kind of life entirely distinct from the regimented and strictly policed one in Burma. Maybe this evidence even engenders and cultivates that other kind of life.

The modeling of "poetry-as-evidence," based upon the presentation of experimental video in an art gallery, seems to relate the "making" aspect of *poesis* to the constructive basis of fiction, which, as Jacques Rancière argues, retains its foundation in the Latin term *fingere,* meaning "to forge" rather than "to feign."[5] Accordingly, fiction neither represents escapist reverie nor opposes itself to reality; instead, fiction entails the building of stories, which is the truth of a reinvented notion of evidence. Rancière's conceptualization of "documentary fiction," which he develops in relation to the films of Chris Marker—an important forerunner to Kanwar's own essay-films, such as *A Season Outside* (1997)—identifies an historical transformation in cultural practice that reversed the outmoded priorities of the conjectural paradigm addressed earlier. Whereas film, in its classic role as a documentary medium, once served to faithfully represent reality—in the same way that photography offered an "instrument of evidence" (whether in a criminological or an anthropological milieu)—today, following the precedent set by Marker and other such filmmakers, the real, for Rancière, stands as an "effect to be produced" rather than a "fact to be understood."[6] In other words, there is no objective meaning of reality "out there" that can simply be captured and represented faithfully "here" in this image. Rather, reality's meaning must be constructed, subjectively assembled in representation, narrated according to a particular viewpoint, and submitted to ongoing reinterpretation. To produce the real as an effect means to engage in a process of contemplation and construction, of gradual understanding that brings changes in perception. Poetry as evidence, then, suggests a commitment to emancipation via continual experimentation, creative invention, and self-transformation. Contemporary art, as both a practice and a discourse, defines a privileged realm in which the complexities of this conclusion—the sometimes paradoxical outcomes and the radical possibility of repositioning evidence as a new poetic paradigm—can be animated and addressed. Yet at the same time, as Rancière's return to classical Latin implies, the meanings of evidence, truth, and documentation have long been subject to competing definitions, whether divided across historical periods or split between divergent cultural contexts. In this regard, the staging of various models of evidence and of truth—for instance, those inspired by Buddhist philosophy and those that reference the international legal framework of a war crimes tribunal—offers an important retort to the tendency of any one model to dictate its terms, whether in the East or the West.

Inasmuch as artistic practice defines a creative reinvention of "evidence," it also signifies a new "politics of truth," one that resonates with the attempts of Michel Foucault to elicit the changing definitions of truth at different historical junctures. For Foucault, Western modernity is in many ways the legatee of a centuries-old Christian paradigm of truth, centered on the search for verifiable meaning and guided by the goal of discovering the inner reality of the self. Working against the subjugating implications of that model—based on the conformity to standards, and thus on a restrictive notion of repetition—Foucault retrieved an older notion of truth, that of the Stoic philosophers, for whom truth was not defined by a mimetic correspondence to a given reality, but as a force of transformation actualized in discourse. This politics of truth, thus Foucault, represents "a question of searching for another kind of critical philosophy. Not a critical philosophy that seeks to determine the conditions and the limits of our possible knowledge of the object, but a critical philosophy that seeks the conditions and the indefinite possibilities of transforming the subject, of transforming ourselves."[7] Although Foucault found his point of departure in Stoic philosophy, one might as well consider points of resonance outside Western modernity—for instance, within Asian modelings of evidence and poetry. In this regard, Amar Kanwar and Raqs Media Collective indicate two possible lines of flight. "Poetry-as-evidence" creates an arena capable of integrating the freedom of creative experimentation, social justice, and poetic license, one that offers us presentations that entreat the viewer to become his or her own "storyteller"—in Rancière's terms—who will piece together the evidence in an ultimately subjective and inimitable way.[8] Liberated from the stamp of propaganda, as in Kanwar's *The Torn First Pages,* and equally from the grips of static being, as in Raqs Media Collective's *Unfamiliar Tales,* poetic evidence proposes the positioning of experience within an open ontology, where free interpretation becomes an act of emancipation. Of course freedom may itself be a mirage—we are all variously determined by our cultures, upbringings, social conditions, and political frameworks—yet perhaps the very exposure to these experimental reinventions of evidence will facilitate the questioning of our own paradigms and make other worlds conceivable.

— T. J. DEMOS

1. See Barthes, Roland (1993), "Camera Lucida: Reflections on Photography", R. Howard (trans.), London: Vintage, pp. 88-89; and Tagg, John (1988), "Evidence, Truth, and Order", in "The Burden of Representation: Essays on Photographies and Histories", London: Macmillan, pp. 60-61.
2. Ginzburg, Carlo (1988), "Clues: Morelli, Freud, and Sherlock Holmes", in "The Sign of Three: Dupin, Holmes, Peirce", U. Eco, T.A. Sebeok (eds.), Bloomington: Indiana University Press, p. 109.
3. Ibid., p. 113.
4. Tagg (1988), p. 65.
5. Rancière, Jacques (2006), "Film Fables", E. Battista (trans.), New York: Berg, 2006 (orig. publ. 2001), p. 158.
6. Ibid.
7. Foucault, Michel (2007), "Subjectivity and Truth", in "The Politics of Truth", S. Lotringer (ed.), Hochroth, C. Porter (trans.), Los Angeles: Semiotext(e), pp. 152-53.
8. See Rancière, Jacques (2007), "The Emancipated Spectator" in *Artforum* (March 2007).

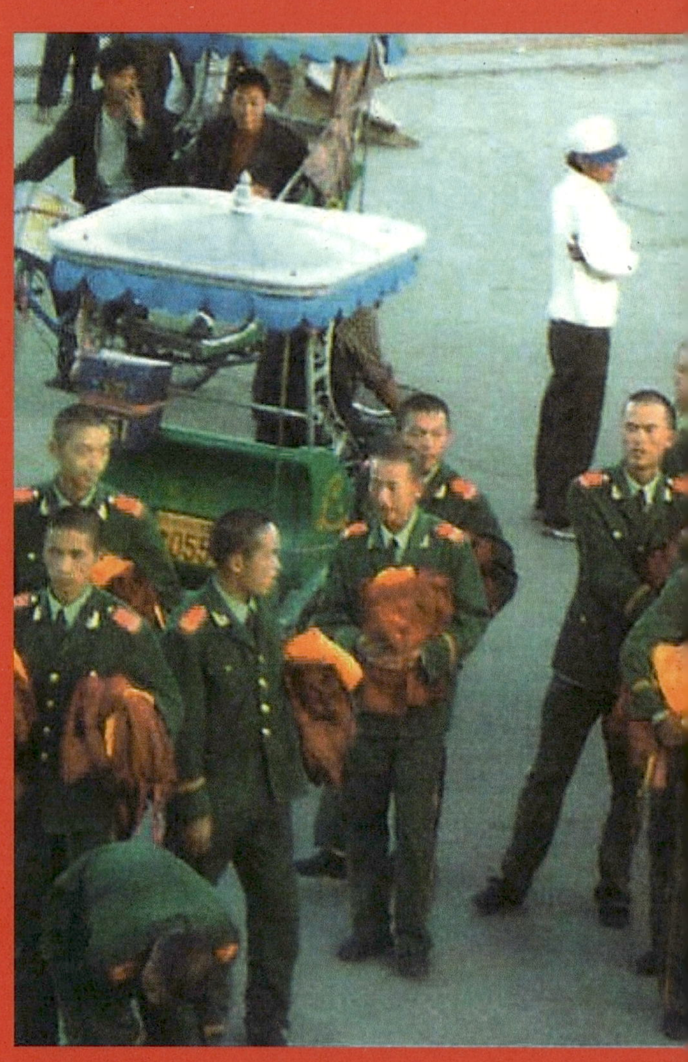

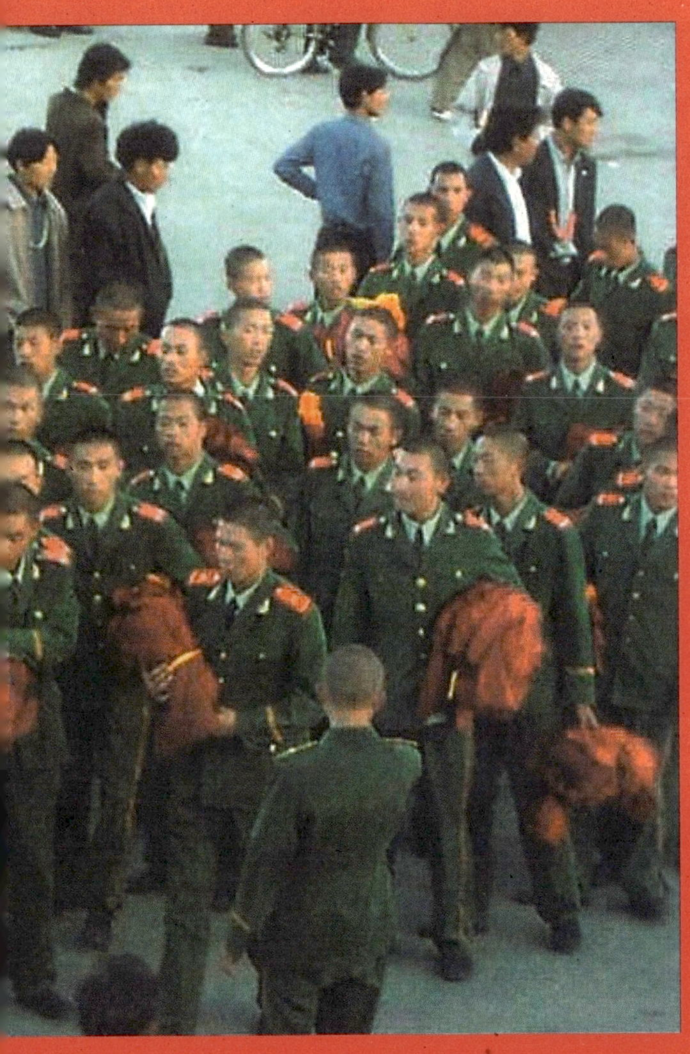

RAQS MEDIA COLLECTIVE
UNFAMILIAR TALES, 2008

How the Long Wait for the Thaw was Endured

There was once an exceptionally genial bicycle that had accumulated enough merit in her youthful life to have almost arrived at the threshold of her liberation. A few more revolutions of her pedals and she would have broken away from the cycle of existence and become a truly free wheel. She was friendly, reliable (her chains, brakes and gears seldom gave way) and she cheerfully ferried anyone who touched her pedals with grace. Many people were thankful for the rides they took on her: hurrying to fetch a doctor to tend a sick friend, rushing to get supplies before the next day's curfew, or just out for a leisurely ride by the lake. Once, on a winter day, the bicycle was stopped by soldiers with guns and her frightened passenger was asked to dismount. Other bicycles on that street were also made to abandon their riders. The bicycles were lined up and left standing, and the men and women who rode them were taken away. The bicycles stayed where they were through the night, waiting for their riders. A snowstorm held them in thrall. Ever since that day, the bicycle has stood with its companions, waiting for a thaw. She does not know, as she stands in the cold, that she is only a pedal-push away from Buddhahood. She waits, neither with nor without hope.

How the Long Wait for the Thaw was Endured

This bicycle was an exceptionally genial bicycle that had accumulated enough merit in her youthful life to have almost arrived at the destination of her migration. A few more revolutions of her pedals and she would have broken away from the cycle of existence and become a truly free wheel. She was friendly, reliable (her chains, brakes and gears never once gave way) and she cheerfully ferried anyone who touched her pedals with grace. Many people were thankful for the rides they took on her: hurrying to fetch a doctor to tend a sick friend, rushing to get supplies before the next day's curfew, or just out for a leisurely ride to the lake. Once, on a winter day, the bicycle was stopped by soldiers with guns and her frightened passenger was asked to dismount. Other bicycles on that street were also made to abandon their riders. The bicycles were lined up and left standing, and the men and women who rode them were taken away. The bicycles stayed where they were through the night, waiting for their riders. A snowstorm held them in thrall. Ever since that day, the bicycle has stood with its companions, waiting for a thaw. She does not know, as she stands in the cold, that she is only a pedal-push away from Buddhahood. She waits, neither with nor without hope.

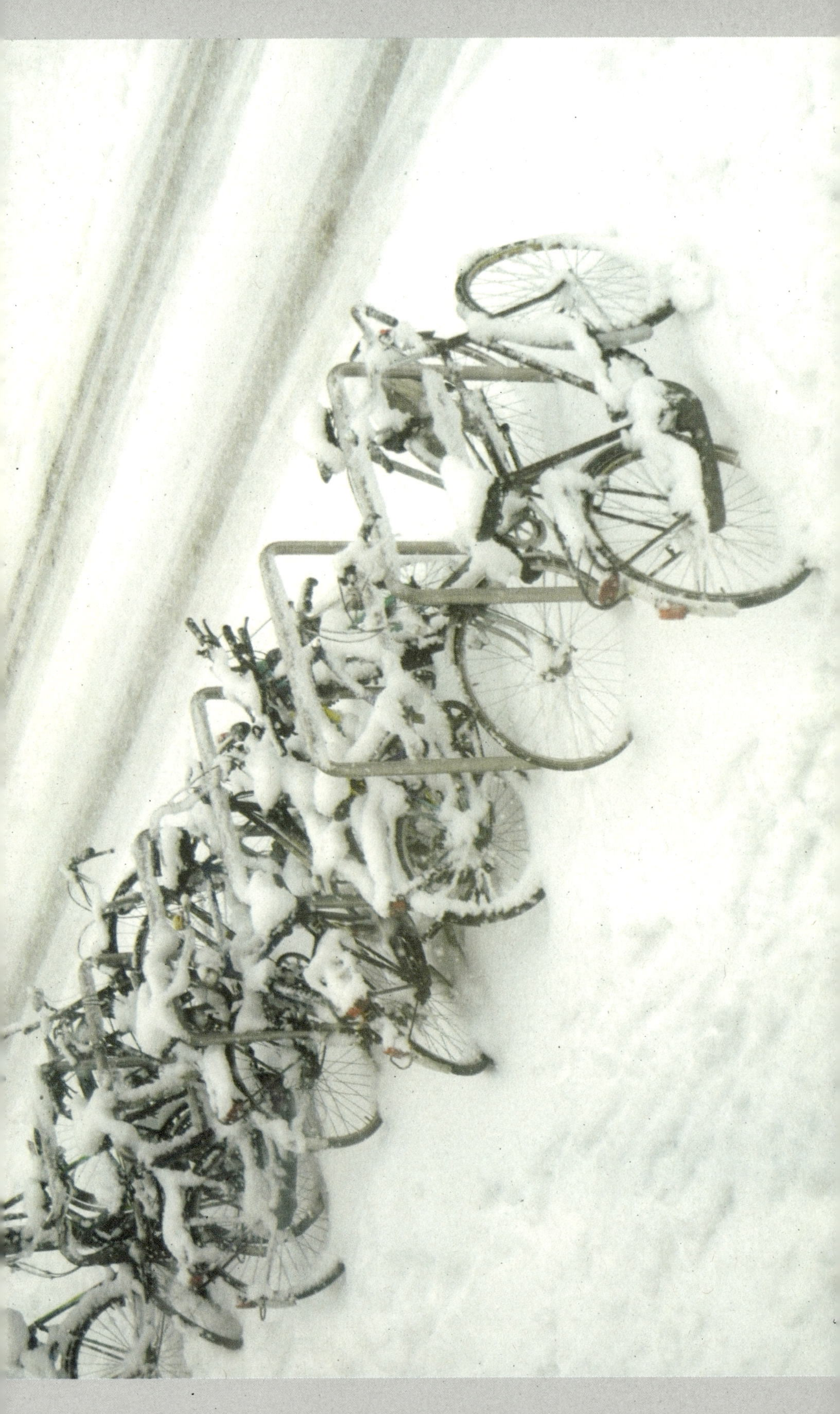

LENS, LIGHT, WORD AND THE FECUNDITY OF ERROR

Once there was a lens that grew to be so taken with a picture it had made that it decided never to be parted from the image's presence. This intimacy changed both the lens and the image. As time passed, it became nearly impossible to distinguish where the picture itself ended and where the lens began. The lens harvested light to nourish the image and clothed it with the fabric of passing shadows. In time, and with the diligent and loving care of the lens, the image grew, deepened, and acquired dimensions that it did not even know it had. When people stood in front of the picture they found themselves thinking about things that they had seen out of the corners of their eyes. The picture seemed possessed to some; others said that they had seen it breathe. There was nothing extraordinary about what the picture depicted, and yet no one could quite tell what it was that they had seen. Its plain and commonplace composition ripened to become rich and wonderfully strange. No one could deny that the picture was truly a sight for sore eyes.

Once there was a story that grew attached to all the mistakes that occurred in its recounting. Repetitions, superfluous words, typographical glitches, spelling mistakes, syntactical anomalies, and all manner of stray errors crept in and out while the story was read, remembered, or told. Odds and ends proliferated within it like strange species in a wild garden. And the story grew fond of them all. It stammered its way through every telling, and the typing of every sentence ran the risk of getting lost in a thicket of errata. When people heard the story, simple though it was, they sometimes felt the whispered urgings and tugs of many other tales, as if the ghosts of strange words haunted the story. No one could repeat the story exactly as it had been told to them, and some said that a page on which it was printed changed subtly between one reading and the next. Words leaked out or seeped in, and sometimes, on turning the page, it felt as if the order of words had just re-adjusted themselves subtly for their own amusement. Yet, despite the tricks played by these mischievous words, everyone admitted that the story moved them to tears.

On looking at the picture, someone said:
"What does a picture gain when it loses the ability to just be itself and becomes something more than the sum of light and shadow at a given time?"

Many years after the story was first told, someone asked:
"What does a story yield when it is pollinated with new seeds in every act of reading, sharing, or remembering?"

We are still looking for the answer to these questions. But what we do know by now is that the truth of an image or a story has more to do with how we see or listen than it has to with how we show or tell.

— RAQS MEDIA COLLECTIVE

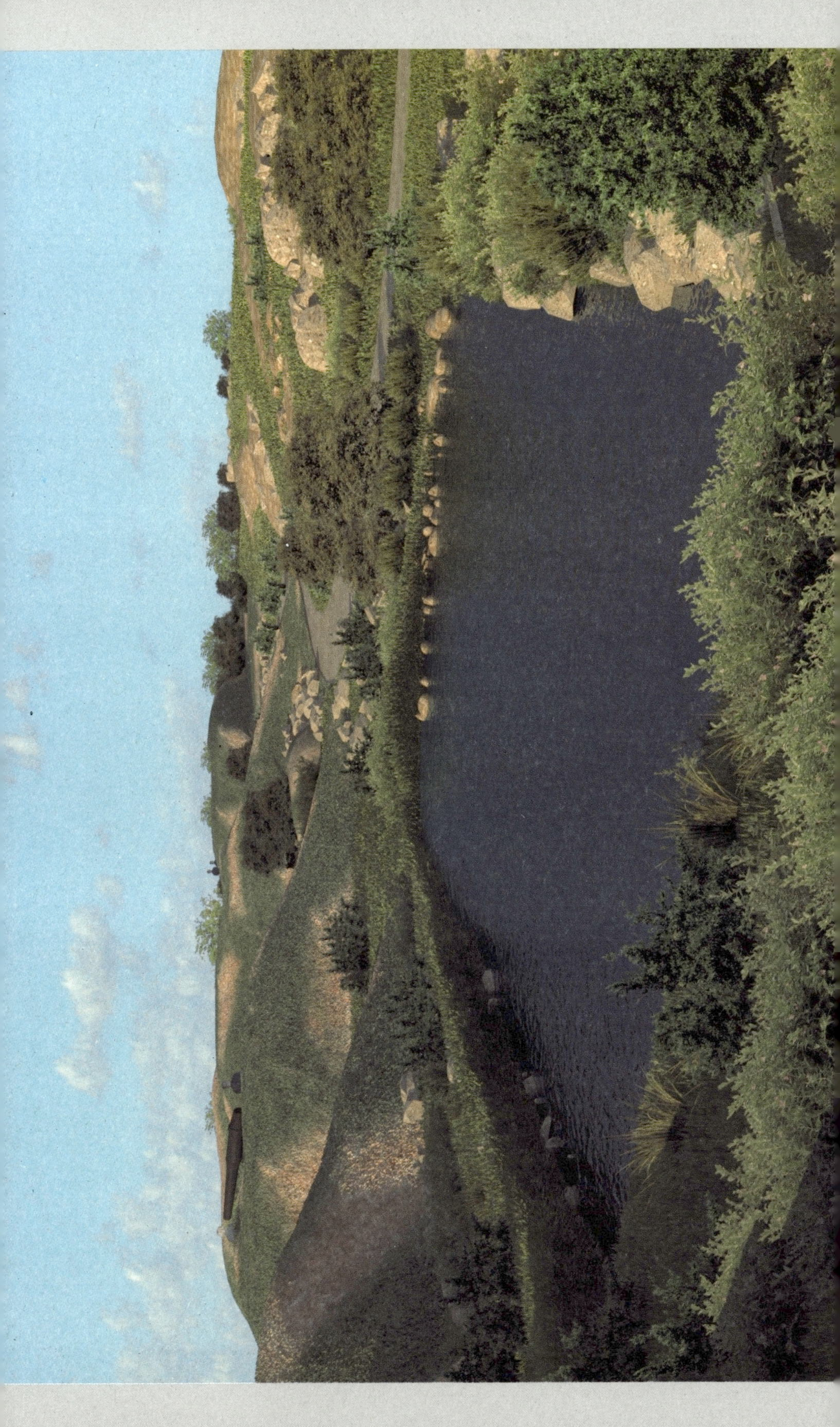

How the Most Terrible Solitude was Overcome

Once, a small piece of sky (a *Bodhisattva* unknown to itself) landed on the earth. It rested, bewildered by the hardness of the surface. Everthing, everywhere, was arid. The sky-patch-Buddha-to-be felt [illegible] … Many years passed.

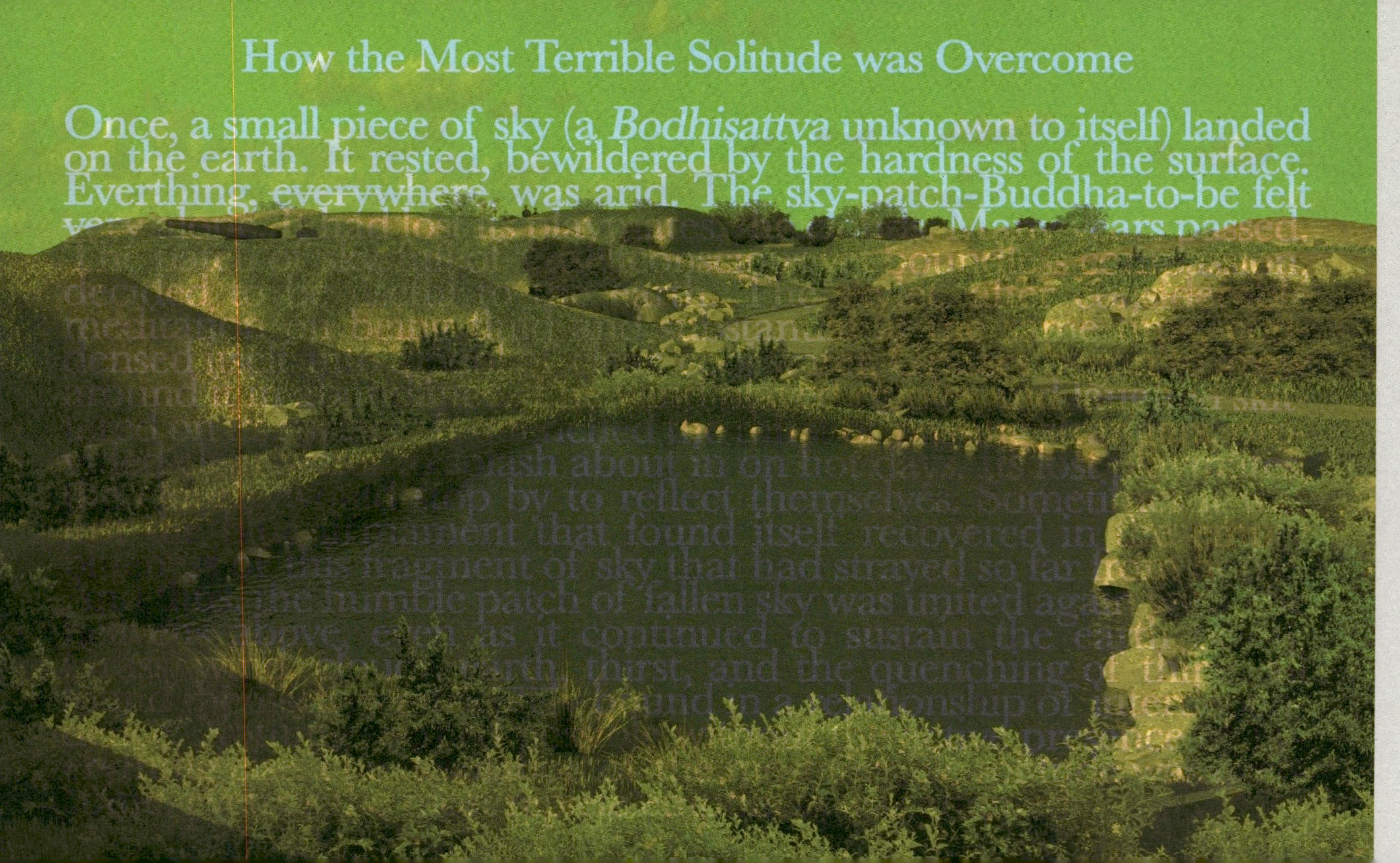

How the Most Terrible Solitude was Overcome

Once, a small piece of sky (a *Bodhisattva* unknown to itself) landed on the earth. It rested, bewildered by the hardness of the surface. Everthing, everywhere, was arid. The sky-patch-Buddha-to-be felt very alone. It had lost its playmates, the clouds. Many years passed. The patch of sky, full of unselfconscious yet boundless compassion, decided to be useful to the earth. The skylet, after considerable meditation on being fluid and substantial at the same time, condensed itself into a pool of clear, cool water. Grasses began to grow around it in abundance. The wind played ripples and laughed skittered on its surface. It quenched the thirst of passing strangers, provided clear water to splash about in on hot days. Its lost playmates, the clouds, would stop by to reflect themselves. Sometimes it was just the blue firmament that found itself recovered in the empty blueness of this fragment of sky that had strayed so far from home. And thus, the humble patch of fallen sky was united again with the heavens above, even as it continued to sustain the earth below. Grass, wind, clouds, earth, thirst, and the quenching of thirst, all found themselves intricately bound in a relationship of interdependence. Nothing seemed possible without the active presence of everything else. The desolation of the most terrible solitude was overcome, even as the most replete emptiness was attained.

MARINE HUGONNIER
AN ARTWORK WHICH
IS NOT AN ARTWORK

In July 2008 Thyssen-Bornemisza Art Contemporary introduced me to the idea of a show about the cultures and contested histories of Tibet and Burma. For years I have been thinking about an interview between Hans Ulrich Obrist (Co-Director Exhibitions and Programmes and Director of International Projects at London's Serpentine Gallery) and Francisco Varela, a noted Chilean neuro-scientist who initiated a "science of consciousness" to bridge Western tradition and Tibetan Buddhism, and Sarat Maharaj, a professor of art history and theory who was one of the curators of Documenta 11.

What so strongly impressed me about this interview was that it defined art as the production of a "non-knowledge system," a way to access unknown circuits of consciousness. This reinforced the intuition I always had of trying to under-stand the nature of art, the core of which had to do with the feeling it could also belong to a nonconceptual ground, a kind of flash of pure intelligence manifest-ing before any verbalization.

This interview became a safe place to return to, where I could reassess ques-tions and doubts and examine the strength of new works. Whereas some artists would take their works out of the studio to see how they resist the pressure of reality, instead I would at times remind myself of sentences by Francisco Varela and Sarat Maharaj and test my ideas against those, pursuing exactly that proc-ess they discussed in relation to the "first-person consciousness."

Moreover, what was so precious to me about this interview was that it made me realize how much I shared with Varela and Maharaj a sense of displacement. Being an immigrant myself had strongly contributed to my frame of mind, forc-ing me to question my identity.

So when T-B A21 invited me to take part in this show, I saw it as an opportu-nity to extend this conversation. The idea was to take forward the notion of *An Artwork Which Is Not An Artwork* and to define it in greater depth. In London I met with Sarat, Hans Ulrich, and Daniela Zyman (T-B A21's curator), and we decided to play a "chain game" in which each person interviewed would, in turn, propose another person to have a conversation with. All interviews will be displayed in the show in Vienna one after the other. The following pages contain parts of the initial conversation between Hans Ulrich, Sarat, and Francisco. It is reproduced alongside elements that have played a formative role in my thinking around the understanding of what *An Artwork Which Is Not An Artwork* can be, as well as establishing cohesion among different parts of this process that resist being described in words.

Hans Ulrich, Sarat, Francesca von Habsburg, Daniela and I present this work as a tribute to Francisco Varela.

— MARINE HUGONNIER

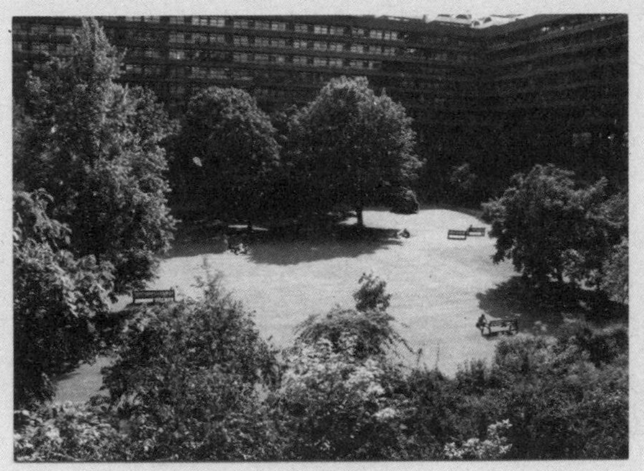

kick-start an exploration of why it is not reducible to it. For it's also about conscious invention, creativity that is, paradoxically, destructive/de-constructive. It's like a dissolvent agent sprinkled on prevailing concept structures and conceptualizing—let alone the acidic, eat-away effect it has on the crust of convention, taste, fixed ways of doing and defining art.

FV:

Right. How come it is not possible to theorize it, even for a painter?

SM:

Is the drift of twentieth century visual arts less a know-how than a highly conceptual affair—even during periods of muscular anti-conceptual rhetoric? But what do we mean by "conceptual" in this context? I stop short of lumping artistic endeavor either with know-how or with regular concept-knowledge structures. What's the chink in-between? Non-knowledge? This is not easy to map in terms of broad principles because it resists hard-hat conceptualization.

FV:

Against know-how and against conceptual consciousness?

SM:

Against both. That's why, with non-knowledge one should think beyond the Renaissance painting model. Today, the contemporary setup is a spread of indeterminate practices. We face the prized possibility, to use Adorno, that "anything can count as art even if does not look like art." We can hardly figure what form the art event might take in advance of its making. But from installations, situations outside the museum-gallery circuits through to experimental events and improbable contraptions—we have a range of practices that style themselves as "conceptual." Strictly speaking, they are reducible neither to know-how or dexterity nor to concept-systems.

FV:

No, they cannot be reduced to know-how. But there's no concept category too?

SM:

That's why I prefer to see them as "indeterminate modes," as "non-knowledge." Should we speak here of the "conceptual against itself" or use something like Deleuze's phrase, the "non-conceptual conceptual."

FV:

Non-knowledge is a form of knowledge manifest in actions and inventions like the painter-practitioner's. That's why I feel to think it through as "non-knowledge" might somehow limit our grasp of its particular quality. Is this not a kind of knowledge better grappled with as *prajna*?

HUO:

In this context, Francisco, can you tell us a little about how dialogues and encounters you might have had with artists or individuals in the field of art might have led you to look at what kind of knowledge or thinking art practice is?

FV:

For me these encounters are a little like Happenings. I run into people like you, then something happens. I don't have a systematic thing about it all. You know what happens when you put a chick into another pen than it has been in normally: there's this feeling of being lost. [*Laughs*] That's how I feel, like a hen out of my pen. I don't really have a story or a theory. What I do know is that artistic imagination somehow cannot be that different from the scientific or the philosophical. Perhaps, in this sense, it's not a form of non-knowledge because it manifests in production, right? Now what would it be? Let's go back to Sanskrit or to a Buddhist term *prajna*, because in Buddhism *avidya* is ignorance in a most basic metaphysical sense, right? *Prajna* is a form of intelligence but a non-conceptual one, it is intelligence without the negation I sense in *avidya*. We all have *prajna*: It's intelligence that happens when you let go of fixated ideas. Basically, that's how it manifests itself; it's the moment when you can just allow yourself to forget, suspend, put into parentheses. If you want, not unlike the idea of the phenomenological reduction. It's to put into suspense, and *poum!*: there is a little light that comes out which is a manifestation of *prajna*. I'm always fascinated by that quality. It is neither know-how, which is too low somehow, nor is it conceptual. There is no term for this in the West. Cognitive science too has none. At best, it's sometimes called "pre-conceptual or pre-linguistic or prenoetic." That's very flattening. It just signals what "comes before" but not what it is.

SM:

For this, I've used the term "*Aconceptual.*" For me it mirrors the neutralizing prefix "A" in *Avidya*. It flags up non-knowledge as "non-negation," as switched into neutral gear. Essentially, I am using *Avidya* to signal something close to what you are referring to. This becomes a little clearer if we unpack *prajna*. The word comes from Sanskrit roots *para-gyana*. The prefix "para" is familiar to us in common words such as paraphrase, paranoid. To this is added *gyana* familiar to us in *gnosis*, which gives us the word *knowledge*.

"Para-gyana" means "above, beyond, around" knowledge—not concept-structure knowledge or scholarly learning but the flash of intuition-intelligence. What you speak of from the Buddhist route overlaps with *avidya* as developed in my, slightly wild etymology. But I think both of us are signaling not something anti-conceptual or sub-conceptual or pre-conceptual but rather a mode of consciousness that is "aconceptual."

FV:

Which would be *prajna*.

SM:

Prajna would be the ideal term. But the hint of negation, I retain by perversely using avidya to give it an edge. This has to do with applying it provocatively in the art/culture context. It's to say that if visual art is seen as a demoted, lesser form of knowledge, so O.K. we'll call it "non-knowledge." The provocation is nudged on a little by Duchamp's mind-boggling question, "How to make a work of art that is not a work of art".

FV:

How can you make a work of art that is not art? What a question!

SM:

Not so much a negation, but a non-negation. Perhaps more a *détournement* rather than sheer annulment.

HUO:

There's something I wanted to ask in this relation: This morning you were struck by this remark of the Dalai Lama, which you somehow linked to John Cage. I thought this an interesting moment to connect with this.

SM:

I think it sprang from the book you were glancing through: *Gentle Bridges: Conversations with the Dalai Lama on the Sciences of Mind* [Jeremy W. Hayward and J. Varela 1992]. The distinction crops up between Hindu thinking, Vedanta, and its structural-conceptual twin: Buddhist thinking or *Nyaya-Vaisheshika*. Like two-halves of the same thing. The former has a logocentric drift—it speaks of fullness, presence, self, metaphysical essences. The latter, in counterterms of emptiness, no-self, non-presence, non-affirmation of ultimate reality. Real mirror images!

FV:

This is your classic Buddhist-Hindu debate, right? [*Laughs*]

SM:

Absolutely! Hans Ulrich triggered thoughts of it. On the one hand, Buddha's skeptical words about defining "ultimate reality": *neti, neti, neti*—"not this, not this, not this"—is by definition negation, by deferral or by Derrida's *différance avant la lettre*. "Ultimate reality" is *nirvana*; burn out of consciousness, nothingness or *sunyata*. On the other hand, in Vedanta, ultimate reality is defined by affirmation "Tat vam asi," or "Thou art That." The self aspires to become one with *sat-cit-ananda* (absolute fullness of truth-consciousness-bliss). I was saying to Hans Ulrich that I was struck by John Cage's relationship with this mirror tradition. His writings show he was tuned in to these ideas through [L.C.] Beckett. Also through Daitzu Suzuki and Ananda Coomaraswamy. At any rate, Hindu-Buddhist traditions of self/no-self, empty-full consciousness provided him with a non-binary grist to the mill for his approaches to "music." This, at times, seems to be neither silence nor sound, neither noise nor music but indeterminate sonic construction—music/non-music, silence-sound, noise-non-noise?

FV:
It's a work of art but not a work of art! But this guy is something else! He knew all that?

SM:
In his own terms. Formally, through L.C. Beckett's writings, the Coomaraswamys, through Daitzu Suzuki's seminars at Harvard.

HUO:
That's incredibly interesting. As we discussed this morning, it would be great to trace these links between Cage, the Coomaraswamy, Suzuki, Duchamp?

SM:
The East Coast mob!

FV:
Did Duchamp ever point out what he felt was his most successful art that wasn't art? Did he have examples?

SM:
I must say I can't quite imagine him even suggesting one. Perhaps the project he secretly worked on *Étant donnés* (1946–1966) comes close. He was working on it when it was assumed he had stopped doing art. Does it look like he was doing something that wasn't? At the time *Étant donnés* was revealed, I suppose, it didn't quite look like art at all. A strange, strip show peephole through which we see, somewhat brusquely, a full-frontal nude in a landscape with a motorized, moving waterfall. It became a model for what is today taken for granted as installation—a genre that is neither the nude nor landscape, neither painting nor sculpture neither diorama nor film but takes in all elements. *Neti. Neti, Neti*? Maybe now it's very

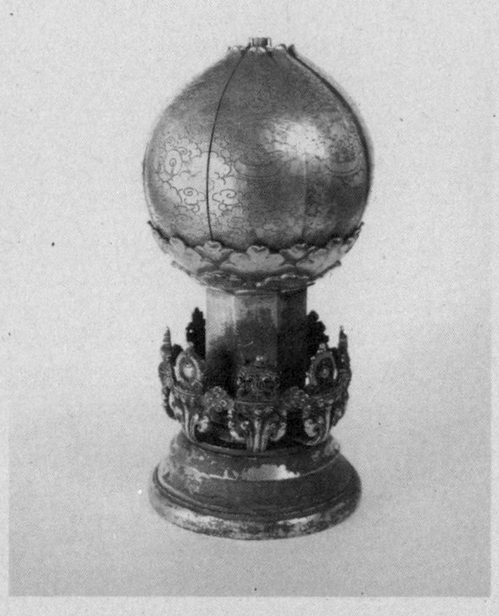

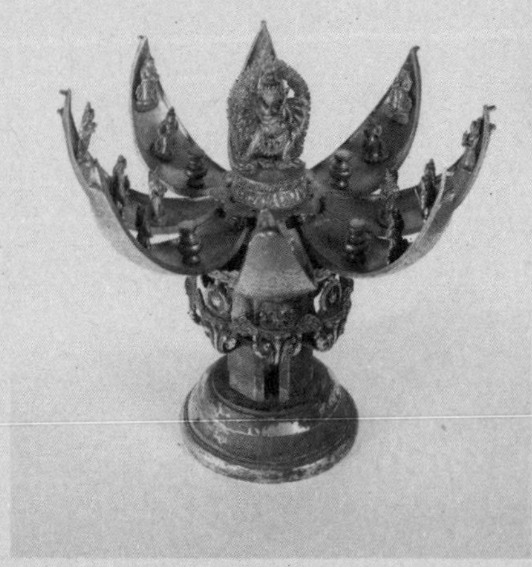

much of "art"——exactly what he had sought to escape. He was trying to maneuver between practices, between fixated ideas of
art/non-art, knowledge/non-knowledge——the space of *prajna?*

FV:

That's very close to my heart because that's basically your thread of
Ariadne into your own growth in the Buddhist context. The symptom is you see this *prajna* growing or not. Then you can tell whether you're making any progress, if there is such a thing. Trungpa
always said we all have *prajna*, every human being. But most people have "baby *prajna*"——a potential that has to develop. I feel when
somebody is acting from the basis of *prajna* you can see it. There is
a quality to it——intelligent spontaneity. But this can easily degrade
into, you know, "goofy golf," as they say in America.

HUO:

Can you expand a bit on the notion of this kind of spontaneity?

FV:

I feel "intelligent spontaneity" is what you see in the beginnings of
improvisation, the moment when everybody is suspended. You see
Keith Jarrett, all of a sudden, getting into his piano, a moment of
pure passion. But you have to be Keith Jarrett to display it on the
Indian drum. When an individual acts, in my experience, individuals who have highly-developed minds, they often tend to be like
that. It's almost like *prajna*, I feel. It has a smell to it. It stops your
mind——the very first symptom is that it attempts to stop your
mind. It happens a lot in the Dalai Lama's company. He's a very
prajna guy. Brilliant *prajna* guy. When you enter in conversation,
oftentimes you find yourself listening with full intent, so your conceptual mind just stops. His *prajna* has brought up your own *prajna*. A mutuality; it's like affection calling out affection that can just
sort of melt you down. You become affectionate. It's similar to
that.

HUO:

So it's a conversation in principle? I mean, that it happens in conversation?

FV:

In conversation, in encounter but it's usually a conversation. It's a
very interesting thing everybody notices with the Dalai Lama. I
took my wife to the meeting with him last March. She isn't particularly Buddhist though she totally respects it. After two days,
she said to me "I've never been with somebody like that. There is
something very unusual there." And she said exactly like I did,
"My mind stops." [*Laughs*]

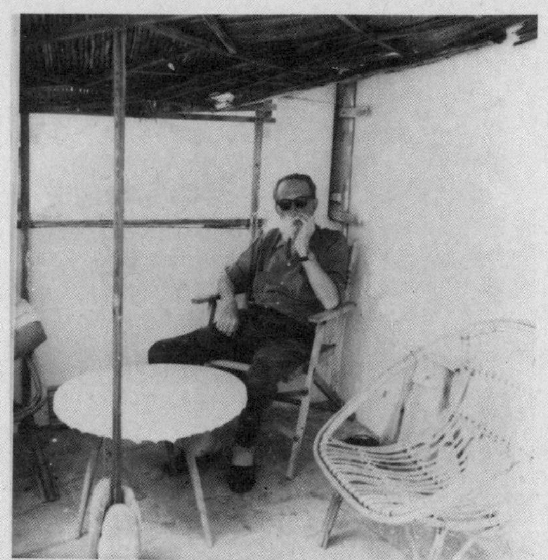

Marcel Duchamp   Cadaqués

p. 65: Thomas Moore Park, Barbican, London.
pp. 66-69, 71: Reproductions from: Obrist, Hans Ulrich (2003), "Interviews, Vol. 1",
Milan/New York: Charta.
p. 70: School of Zanabazar, Mongolia, Chakrasamvara Mandala, late 17th – early 18th Century.
p. 72: Marcel Duchamp in Cadaqués, Spain. 20th Century. Anonymous photograph.

SCENES GONE ASTRAY

The main concerns of Chong's eclectic practice are realities whose multi-faceted systems inform self-contained truths and utopian ideals that can be found in fields ranging from politics to science fiction literature. Describing himself as an "observer, collector and presenter of ideas and images, with a keen interest in processes of visual culture," Chong uses his works—sculptures, installations, graphics, photographs—to explore processes of abstraction occurring between people and objects, mind and matter. For instance, since 2006, the ongoing series *Paperback Covers* imagines the contents of books that the artist hasn't read yet in order to outline an itinerary of meandering thoughts by means of absurd interpretations of titles and authors' names, and a play with pictorial and linguistic associations.

Collaborative practices that question authorship are an important aspect of Chong's art; the artist instigated *Philip* (2006), a novel produced by a team of art professionals during a seven-day writing workshop conceived by Chong in collaboration with the art critic Leif Magne Tangen and the curator Mai Abu ElDahab. Inspired by the American science-fiction author Philip K. Dick, this work of fiction addresses at its core themes of rapture and revolution that suggest today's rise of fundamentalist religion and the crumbling of leftist ideology after 1989. In fact, as a tale, *Philip* recounts the rapid global decline inaugurated by U.S. President George W. Bush. Similarly, in his exhibition *The Sole Proprietor and Other Stories* at Vitamin Creative Space (2006), Chong included copies of print-on-demand books narrated by a fictional historian of graphic design who evokes the story of a magazine established in 1984 that gained world-wide acclaim following the trails of talented spies.

How is it that holding "dangerous" political dissidents and petty crime offenders captive in total isolation and for long stretches of time continues to be established practice in Southeast Asian countries claiming to champion the citizenry's freedom to freely choose their own acts? *Deleted Scenes* (2008) represents this controversial practice. It consists of a series of photographs in a standard snapshot format orderly laid out on medium-sized sheets of white paper. The artist has physically cut out the scenes, removing contents that depicted banal moments of an overlooked everyday, instants that may mean cherished memories for a prisoner with no one to talk to. Scattered across the exhibition like grammatical punctuation signs, Chong's "scenes" remind the viewer of the necessity of questioning and the urgent call to take a stand with regard to this kind of hidden and yet widely implemented form of injustice.

Formally speaking, the work brings to mind self-adhesive pictures that can be affixed to the blank space of a numbered empty frame in an album. Since 2007, a second ongoing series—*Surfacing*—consists of wall drawings made out of thousands of stickers designed by the artist that organically spread around walls, crawling along the architectural features of gallery spaces, adapting to the inner character of environments made to contain and display art. The title ironically alludes to the nature of this work as a formalistic exercise that highlights the endurance and meaning of artistic labor. In *Deleted Scenes*, by contrast, the title and the white background of the collages refer to a common term and a standard technique in the cinema industry: scenes replaced in the final version of a film, and the process of "fading out" that causes a picture or a situation to gradually dissolve. Perhaps a bit cynically, Chong's act of leaving a *tabula rasa* behind such scenes and portraits of depersonalized life purloins their factual evidence, making space for lies that disguise themselves as a new adapted narrative, and suggest the silent circumlocutory violence of "erasing" individuals from society.

Encased within box frames that sever the subject matter from the outside world, the missing scenes above all protect themselves from unjust political moves whose horridness must no longer be confronted. Yet for the history of resistance, compulsory reclusiveness and voluntary disappearance can equally be forms of engagement, as witnessed by the case of the Burmese pro-democracy leader and iconic freedom fighter Aung San Suu Kyi, now in her 13th year of house arrest in Rangoon. With this work Chong pays homage to a doctrine of emptiness, a fundamental metaphysical view in Buddhist philosophy that questions whether the materiality of events and objects, and our experience of interacting with them, is a sufficient self-evident basis on which to accept that they are real. If the vacuums in *Deleted Scenes* are the sole means by which to grasp the discrepancy between appearance and existence, then, whatever the ontological status of their subjects and content, they possesses self-defining and validating qualities bestowed upon them by humans' innate belief in the testimony of a presence.

— DIANA BALDON

FIRST INFORMATION REPORT

The First Information Report (FIR) is a written document prepared by the police in India when they receive information about the commission of a cognizable offense. Looking at FIRs is an exercise in the observation of the intersection and interlacing of many kinds of narrative strategies and claims to truth. When speaking of the FIR, one has to ask who brings it into the domain of discourse, what methods are used to present it, and to what end is it sought to be presented. It is common knowledge that the FIR can become an instrument used to shape "convenient truths" on behalf of those who wield power. The FIR cantilevers "truths"—the different truth claims of different parties, their different credibilities often an index of their material and enunciative capacity—and a "juridical truth" together into a relationship that enables the precise application of legal force intended to achieve a specific aim that fulfils the objectives of power. Sometimes this is done by pressing false charges (fictional facticity) against a person who can then be made a target of police harassment, and on other occasions the facts stated by a complainant can be deliberately distorted, elided, obscured, so that the charge loses credibility and is disqualified due to inconsistencies in the registration of the FIR. Here the inscription of the FIR is marked not by detail but by a blurred vagueness or a powerful opacity. The particular rhetoric of documentation implicit in the language of a given FIR can be correlated to a specific problem encountered by power. What can be said about an FIR is generally valid for most "documents." The normal function of the document is to register and index a stable picture of the world as power wills it to be. The documentary, like history, can be read as the "prose of counterinsurgency," as the record of a permanent military campaign to subdue a recalcitrant world of discomfiting, incongruous, and insurgent realities—to produce in turn images and representations that are well organized and persuasive and that conform to the approximation of truth from the perspective of power.

That the "document" enters the art space at a time when the world seems to be grappling with visible crises should come as no surprise. The enhanced "visibility" of the crises, particularly as a result of the intensification of the extensive presence of media networks, threatens to overwhelm all repositories of significant representations.

IF ONE FUNCTION OF ART MAKING IS TO OFFER A WAY OF MAKING SENSE OF THE REALITIES WE LIVE IN, THEN IT IS NOT AS SUCH REMARKABLE THAT CONTEMPORARY ART PRACTICE CHOOSES TO ENGAGE WITH THE VISIBILITY OF GLOBAL CRISES IN OUR TIMES.

The art space cannot keep the troubled world at bay, and in order to apprehend reality as it is, in all its disarray, it has to permit the entry of the document as a "stable" referent of the chaotic world it inhabits. What magnifies the presence of the "document" in the space of representation and discourse is the cognitive and epistemic pressure brought about by a belated recognition of globalization. Not only is reality visibly "crisis-ridden," but the networked nature of each crisis—the thickly interlaced relationship of one manifestation of crisis to another, across a global space—also seems to magnify the impact of reality. This "magnified and amplified reality effect" presses in. There is, in other words, no escape possible in art at the moment from what may at first seem to be the mere "facticity" of the document, which seems to invade contemporary art from other semantic spaces and spheres.

At heart the dilemma remains one of what can be done with the images, testimonies, and quotations of reality that a documentary mode brings in to art (from everywhere). Just as the FIR can be read as a statement by power about the world (and to the world), it is also always vulnerable to counterreadings, to being prized open, and connected to other "documents" or other realities, and to being made to reveal the inner logic of power. The FIR may not have much that is original or remarkable to say, but its evasions, narrative stances, and silences may be eloquent and compelling. The challenge of working with documents in an art space (for the artist, the curator, the critic, and the viewer) is the possibility of decrypting the aporias in representations of the real. This is what makes working with documents aesthetically and formally a difficult thing to do, and this is why working with documents in contemporary art spaces can often end up only in the alleviation of representational anxieties (of artists, curators, and the public). Because the document's raw material is rhetoric, the practitioner has to constantly evolve a rhetoric of rhetoric in order to make documents yield. This requires more not less imagination, and a vigilance about the relationship between the externality of a document and the subjectivity implicit in the act of reading it differently from the norm. That is why, just as the recovery of memory and history (of defeats and dispersal, of powerlessness and servitude as much as of survival and creation), and the painstaking reconstruction of an archive of lost and scattered meanings is one of the first cultural tasks on the agenda of the insurgent, a critical engagement with a documentary mode of practice too becomes (for the same reason) one of the key undertakings of the contemporary art practitioner who seeks to express contemporaneity as much as s/he engages with art. The contemporary moment, nothing if not a contest of images that seek to define "globality," demands documents as counterweights to its own "documentary" record.

— RAQS MEDIA COLLECTIVE

Originally published in *Texte zur Kunst,* no. 51 (September 2003)

ON THE 'GRAMMAR OF WITNESSING': CONSIDERATIONS ON THE EXAMPLE OF THE COURT WITNESS

In order to understand what a witness is, let us begin with the paradigmatic situation of the court witness. We focus on five aspects: the creation of evidence, perception, speech act, listenership, and credibility. These aspects constitute what we will call the 'grammar of witnessing.'

The witness creates evidence. When a legal case must be adjudged, there are contrary ways to assess certain occurrences. The mission of the court is to investigate facts and to pass judgment. Witnesses are persons who are used as means of evidence (this 'reifying' expression is important); they 'serve' as 'objects' and 'instruments' in the acquisition of factual knowledge on which the judgment will be based. Witnessing creates evidence.[1] The witness takes the stand in a situation characterized by not-knowing: "Thus, one becomes a witness only when one can no longer rely on knowledge […] but must nevertheless relate to a series of occurrences that is in itself not-one,"[2] dis-unified in the antagonism between different narratives about these occurrences. The investigative establishment of 'truth' is not an end in itself, nor merely a decision in a conflict over the 'correct' version of a story; rather, it is supposed to make a just judgment possible. It is a matter not simply of truth or falsehood but one of guilt or innocence. The evidence created by the witness, then, is consequential: it changes lives—sometimes even into death: in the legal procedures of Jewish antiquity, the witnesses were the first to throw stones during an execution.[3]

What matters to us in this context is that the situation of epistemic uncertainty typical of the act of witnessing is connected to the juridical situation of the administration of justice.[4] Witnessing is thus ultimately oriented toward an act of 'restitution' in the widest possible sense, as the redress of an imbalance, which includes the socialization of a private state of knowledge as well as aspects of justice done to the victim and penance done by the perpetrator. If the witness, then, creates evidence, if his function is embedded in the 'restitution of a social balance,' then the truth-claim of witnessing always contains a practical, a 'humanizing' dimension.

The witness testifies on the strength of his perception. The witness was physically co-present to an occurrence located in the past; he saw something 'with his own eyes' and thus attests to an immediate perception, to an experience he himself *had*. This 'principle of immediacy' is of great importance in the code of criminal procedure.[5] True, the perceptions of witnesses include communications made by others: and testimony describing hearsay is now[6] legally admissible as evidence[7] (at least in Germany[8]). For a hearsay witness attests not to occurrences but rather to a *report* of occurrences: this renders his testimony inferior evidence. Incidentally, both Plato[9] and, after him, Plautus already thought that eyewitness testimony outweighed that of ten hearsay witnesses.[10]

The foundation in perception, then, is crucial to witnessing in every respect: *to have perceived something is the conditio sine qua non of witnessing.* The "perceptions of a witness" are the only "suitable objects of testimonial evidence."[11] This distinguishes ordinary from expert witnesses; the later report precisely not their own perceptions but put their expert knowledge at the court's disposal. The witness is called as someone who was an observer. He counts solely as a *receiver* of certain occurrences; by contrast, his activities of cognition and assessment, his opinions, evaluations, and conclusions do not matter in any way: they disturb and tarnish the process of witnessing and therefore remain definitively excluded from the attribution of legal evidentiary value.[12] As a consequence, whoever is capable of perceiving is admissible as a witness.[13]

This status as receiver and observer is at the root of the dilemma of the witness who is simultaneously a victim. The ideal of witnessing—at least as its profile is delineated in the legal sphere—is uninvolvement in the very events that are the subject of the testimony.

The witness renders his perceptions discursive. The witness must not only have perceived something but also relate his perceptions. Witnessing is based on the transformation of perception into linguistic utterance:[14] occurrences are to be transformed into linguistic communication, sensory percepts into linguistic meaning. The witness must perform a sort of translation or transliteration of his private experience into a public statement. This is an exceedingly fragile process. For the witness's utterance to satisfy the demands of the claim to truth, courtroom testimony—and not only testimony offered under oath—is a strictly ritualized and institutionalized act. 'To be witness' is a role on which the authority of those called to the witness stand to give truthful testimony is founded. The witness does not merely talk and report; he performs what is, in the sense described by institutionalist theory, a speech act. By virtue of the *pure fact that he speaks on the witness stand does what he utters count as a truthful utterance.*[15] That is why perjury and false testimony were and continue to be offences punishable by harsh penalties.

Active listeners. The witness must not merely have perceived something and speak about his perceptions; he must also speak *to* someone. No listeners or addressees, no witnessing. The listeners lack knowledge regarding the very occurrences the witness testifies to, or else they would not need the witness. A fundamental asymmetry obtains between witness and listener. The occurrences on which light must be shed have irrevocably passed; no words will bring it back. There is no way to immediately verify testimony by 'checking it against reality.' Witnessing, then, is not a monologue but an interaction between listener(s) and witness consisting of questions and answers. In criminal proceedings, a distinction is made between the 'report' offered by the witness and his 'cross-examination.'[16] Not accidentally, the German word for the dialogue that unfolds and in which legally consequential testimony emerges is *Verhör,* from *hören,* to listen. The questions asked by the listeners thus always also determine, guide, and pre-form *what* the witness re-presents in his words—and *how* he re-presents it. *Witnessing is not only a speech act but, by the same token, also an act of listening.*

Credibility. Mental states such as perceptions and experiences are nontransferable. As John Durham Peters notes laconically: "No transfusion of consciousness is possible. Words can be exchanged, experiences cannot."[17] Whatever the witness says may—in principle—be false testimony. The possibility of lying is inherent to any witnessing. This is the difference between testimony and 'ordinary' evidence or indexical signs, which, although they can be misread and misinterpreted, cannot 'lie.'[18] Even the illocutionary force with which what the witness says on the witness stand presents itself as the truth has its limit in the problem of the empirical unverifiability of the truth of the witness's words. Instead, the credibility, truthfulness, and trustworthiness of witnesses now become matters of fundamental importance. A witness vouches for his words with his person: *the truth of his statements is based on the truthfulness of his person.* Only a witness whom his listeners trust can persuade them. Trust, however, is always liable to be disappointed—or else it would not be trust.

At this point, an ethical dimension inherent to the concept of witnessing comes into view.[19] And it is hardly surprising that examining the credibility of witnesses is an important component of the court's task.[20] Is the principle of the orality[21] of testimony rooted in this personal responsibility, which privileges the voice, as the (more or less authentic) trace of the person, and simultaneously ensures that the participants can keep eye contact?[22] According to Niklas Luhmann, speaking in the face of others at least makes a breach of trust more difficult.[23] Let us note, then: corresponding to the not-knowing on the part of the listeners is, on the part of the witness, the trust placed in him by the listeners, the reliability attributed to him: *the transmission of knowledge is impossible in the absence of the social bond of trust.*

These, then, are the five conditions that constitute the 'syntax of witnessing': (1) in a situation characterized by a lack of knowledge and uncertainty, the witness creates evidence, contributing to the establishment of the facts of the matter; the latter, in turn, is the basis on which a verdict will be reached. (2) Testimony is based on the perception of an occurrence located in the past which the witness observed without—in the best-case scenario—being involved in it. (3) The witness must transform a sensory experience into a verbal utterance that, as a speech act, is true precisely because the witness is authorized by the institution. (4) Witnessing is an interaction between witness and listener in which the expectations harbored and questions raised by the listeners always also influence the substance of the testimony. Listeners, that is to say, are constitutive of the act of witnessing. (5) The institutional authorization of the witness is complemented by his trustworthiness, in which the reasons for accepting the testimony as truthful are rooted.

We will call these five structural components the 'grammar of witnessing.' It does not take a lot of imagination to envision that this 'syntax of witnessing' relates to the concrete praxis of witnessing as a school grammar does to everyday speech: we successfully communicate in everyday life without speaking in grammatically correct sentences. We are led to surmise, then, that real acts of witnessing (and their dilemmas) diverge from the standard of ideal witnessing. Let us examine the core of this divergence.

— SYBILLE KRÄMER

Excerpt from: Krämer, Sybille (2008), "Medium, Bote, Übertragung. Kleine Metaphysik der Medialität", Frankfurt am Main: Suhrkamp, pp. 228–234.

1. Cf. Coady, C. Anthony J. (1992), "Testimony. A Philosophical Study", Oxford: Clarendon Press, p. 32.
2. García Düttmann, Alexander (1996), "At Odds with AIDS. Thinking and Talking about a Virus", Stanford: Stanford University Press, p. 73.
3. Cf. Schwemer, Anna Maria (1999), "Prophet, Zeuge und Märtyrer. Zur Entstehung der Märtyrerbegriffs im frühesten Christentum", in *Zeitschrift für Theologie und Kirche,* no. 96, pp. 320–350, here p. 323.
4. That the theoretical question of truthful statements is ultimately tied to the practical question of guilt, innocence, and judgment is manifest in the fact that the right to refuse to give evidence can be conceded e.g. to close relatives of the defendant, but also in the witness protection the state grants incriminating witnesses when it is expected that the defendants will seek revenge.
5. Regarding this principle—and how it is progressively undermined—see Schünemann, Bernd (2001), "Zeugenbeweis auf dünnem Eis. Von seinen tatsächlichen Schwächen, seinen rechtlichen Gebrechen und seiner notwendigen Reform", in A. Eser et al. (eds.), "Strafverfahrensrecht in Theorie und Praxis", Munich: Beck, pp. 385-407, here p. 401.
6. The Carolina of 1532, the first unified code of law, excludes, as a matter of principle, all testimony based on hearsay. Cf. Scholz, Oliver Robert (2004), "Zeuge/Zeugnis", in J. Ritter et al., "Historisches Wörterbuch der Philosophie", vol. 12, Darmstadt: Wissenschaftliche Buchgesellschaft, pp. 1317–1324, here p. 1318.
7. But it must not appear in the opinion of the court as the only piece of evidence. See: "Fachlexikon Recht" (2005), Mannheim: Alpmann/Brockhaus, p. 1583.
8. English law treats 'hearsay' with greater skepticism. Cf. Coady (1992), p. 33.
9. Cf. Plato, "Theaetetus", 201b-c.
10. Cf. Plautus, "Truculentus", II, 6, 8.
11. Meyer-Goßner, Lutz (2004), "Strafprozessordnung", Munich: Beck, p. 152.
12. Ibid.
13. As all legal commentaries explicitly note, this includes children and persons suffering from mental illnesses.
14. Cf. Peters, John Durham (2001), "Witnessing", in *Media, Culture & Society* 23:6, pp. 707-723, here pp. 709 ff.
15. "The kind of evidence in question here seems to be 'say-so' evidence: we are, that is, invited to accept something or other as true because someone says it is, where the someone in question is supposed to be in a position to speak authoritatively on the matter." Coady (1992), p. 27.
16. Strafprozessordnung der Bundesrepublik Deutschland §69, par. 1 (http://bundesrecht.juris.de/stpo/_69.html, 11/06/2008). Cf. Schünemann (2001), p. 389.
17. Peters (2001), p. 710.
18. Falsely interpreted traces are no longer (real) evidence in the conventional sense, just as a weathercock, once it has seized up because of a rusty hinge, is no longer an index.
19. The ethical dimension of witnessing is explored in detail in Schmidt, Sibylle (2007), "Zeugenschaft. Ethische und politische Dimensionen", master's thesis, Freie Universität Berlin.
20. Considerations of credibility determine the decision "rendered by a court [...] whether a factual claim must be considered true or not": Nack, Armin (2001), "Der Zeugenbeweis aus aussagepsychologischer und juristischer Sicht", in *Strafverteidiger,* vol. 1, pp. 1-19, here p. 2.
21. In accordance with this principle, writing (as transcription of oral linguistic communication) may be admissible; videos, photographs, etc., by contrast, are hardly admissible or only within strict limitations.
22. Auslander, Philip (1999), "Liveness. Performance in a Mediatized Culture", New York: Routledge, pp. 112ff, develops a media-theoretical analysis of orality in the American legal system.
23. Cf. Luhmann, Niklas (1968), "Vertrauen: Ein Mechanismus der Reduktion sozialer Komplexität", Stuttgart: Enke, p. 35.

Source: Announcement by the
Sertha County Government, Aug 7, 2001

公告

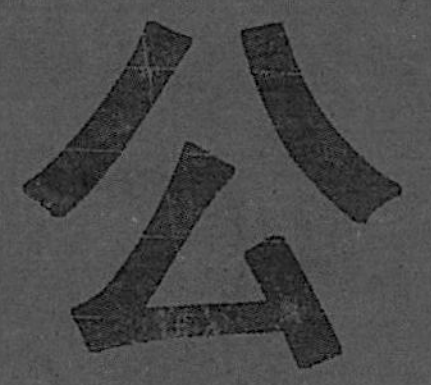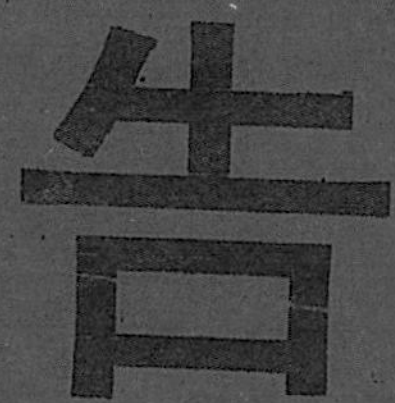

  为进一步做好色达县喇荣寺五明佛学院治理整顿工作，规范寺院的管理，凡在治理整顿期间拆除的扎空木料，房主必须在2001年7月20日之前自行作出处理，逾期色达县人民政府将予以集中处理。

  特此公告

色达县人民政府

二OO一年七月八日

NIKOLAUS HIRSCH
& MICHEL MÜLLER
IN COLLABORATION WITH
CYBERMOHALLA ENSEMBLE

CYBERMOHALLA HUB, 2008

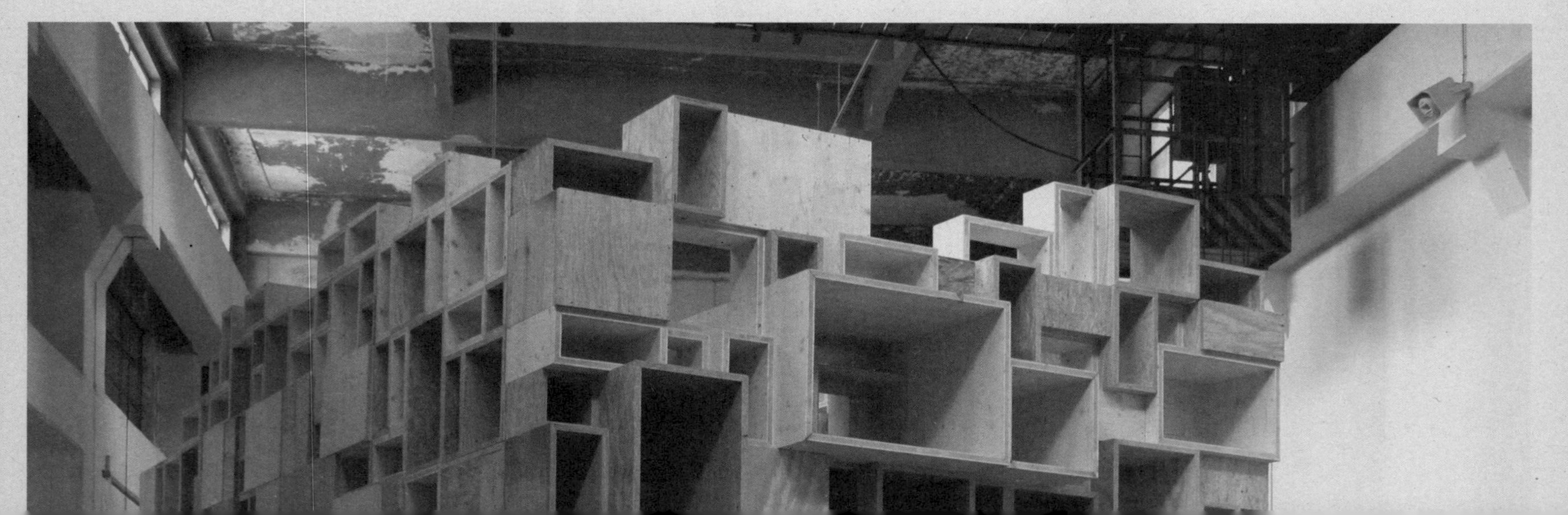

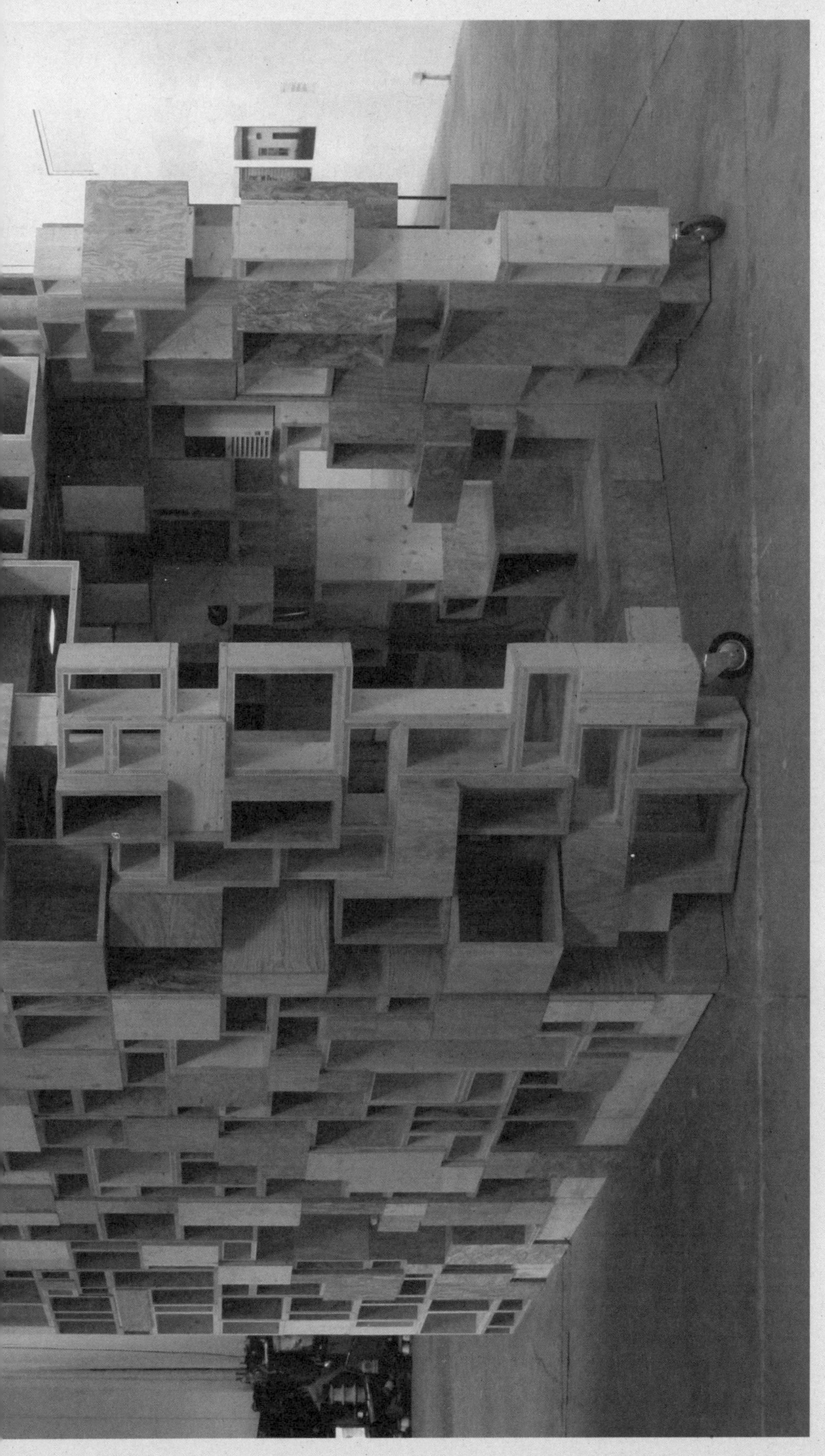

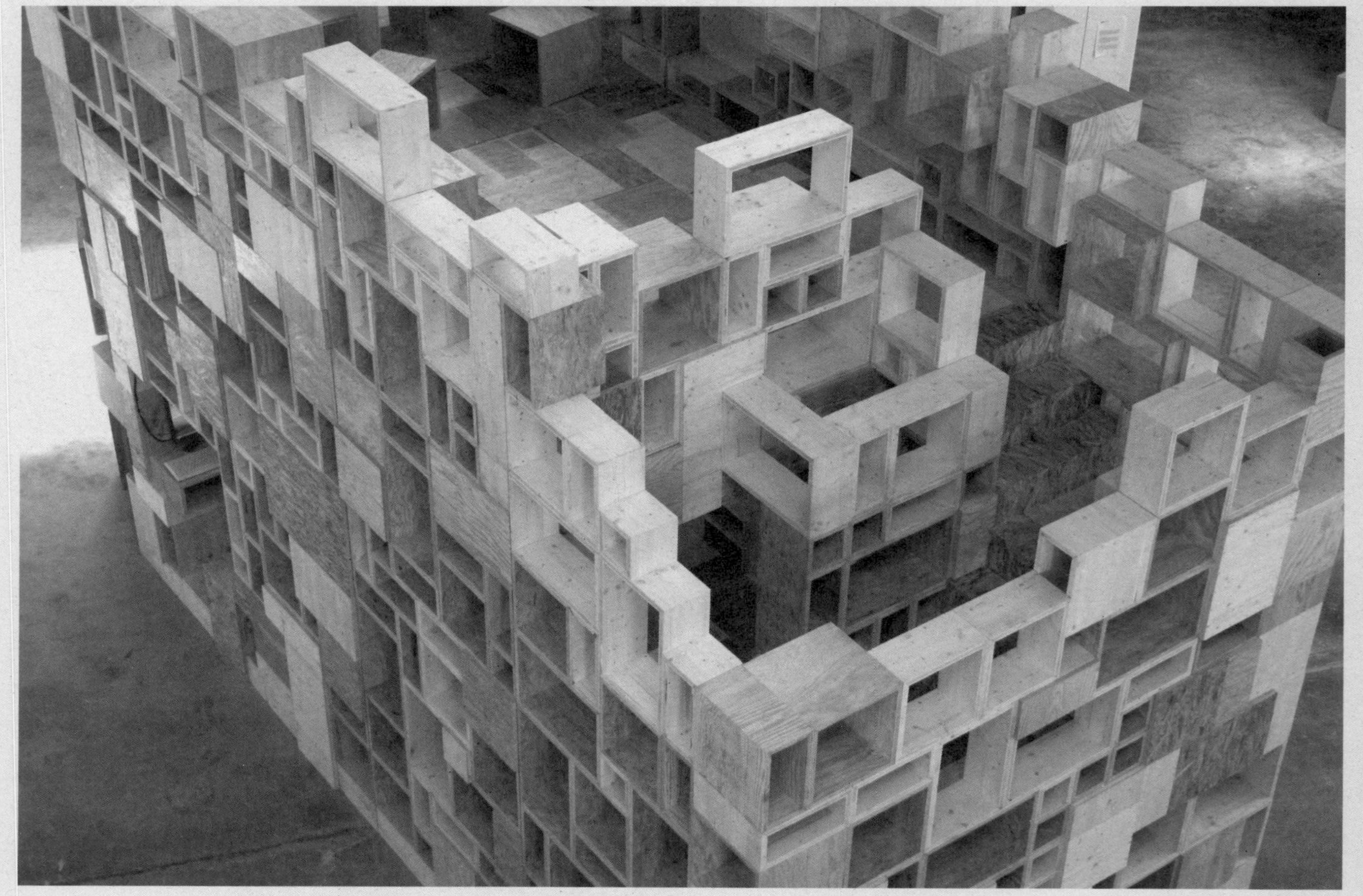

Cybermohalla Hub
Installation views
Manifesta 7, Bolzano

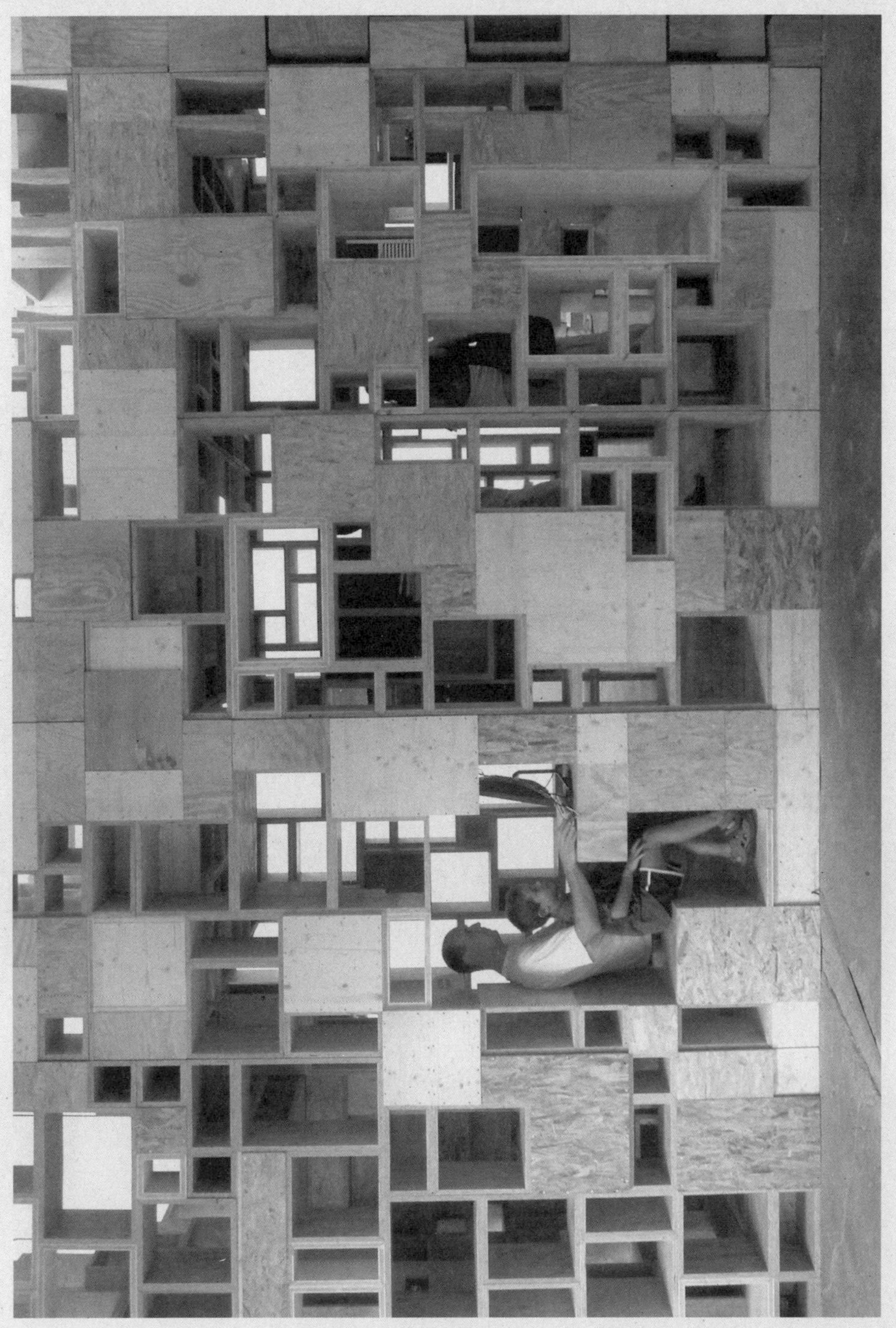

CYBERMOHALLA HUB

The Cybermohalla Hub at Thyssen-Bornemisza Art Contemporary is a segment of Nikolaus Hirsch's and Michel Müller's growing project for a cultural laboratory in a new settlement in Delhi. Initiated by the research institute Sarai – CSDS and Ankur – Society for Alternatives in Education, the project involves approximately 70 young practitioners, who are engaged with their urban contexts through various media. This hybrid of school, archive, community center and gallery is both a load-bearing structure and a display for the dense cultural production of the Cybermohalla Ensemble in Ghevra, including the archive of the destroyed lab in Nangla. The hybrid condition of the project can be seen in the wider context of Hirsch's and Müller's institutional work such as the Bockenheimer Depot Theater (in collaboration with William Forsythe), the European Kunsthalle in Cologne, Unitednationsplaza (with Anton Vidokle), and currently their studio and workshop structure for Rirkrit Tiravanija's and Kamin Lertchaiprasert's *The Land.* Renegotiating and recombining diverse typologies, their projects explore the role of cultural institutions as political and social agencies in the contemporary city.

As an expansion of their previous work, Hirsch and Müller are developing the Cybermohalla Hub as a material process that refers to extremely diverse past, present and future conditions of culture: from the destruction of the previous lab in the squatter settlement of Nangla which was demolished as a result of Delhi's urban cleansing plan, to a workshop in Delhi, to a collaborative construction process within an academic school model in Stuttgart, to a temporary life span in an exhibition in Bolzano and Vienna, to an accumulative construction process in Delhi.

The physical structure is many things in one: a hybrid of school, community center, archive, and gallery. An evolving institution, both programmatically and physically from one to two to three and four storeys, it is never finished. On a parcel of three to six meters, space is so limited that usually separated elements are now blended into one: furniture elements like cupboards, shelves, display boards, and work desks are not additional elements but the load-bearing structure themselves. The institution grows with its production of texts, documents, videos, and objects. Shelve after shelve, the structure (made of leftover wooden material) can grow and at the same time outsource its components – as if the situation in Delhi is already in a mode that oscillates between production and display.

Urbanism in Ghevra - between the Formal and the Informal

The Ghevra settlement is located in the new north-western frontier of the city, having emerged after a large population was re-located there in conjunction with the demolition of squatter settlements in the city, namely in Nangla. In Ghevra, urban planning becomes a tangible physical frame. The grid is its conceptual device. At the megacity's most recent frontier, the grid of the new settlement is reminiscent of the previous neighborhood close to the center of the city, from which the inhabitants were evicted. Nangla was an informal squatter settlement, and now people have been thrown into the urban planning of Ghevra. Its grid might remind us of the proportion of Manhattan, yet in a ver-

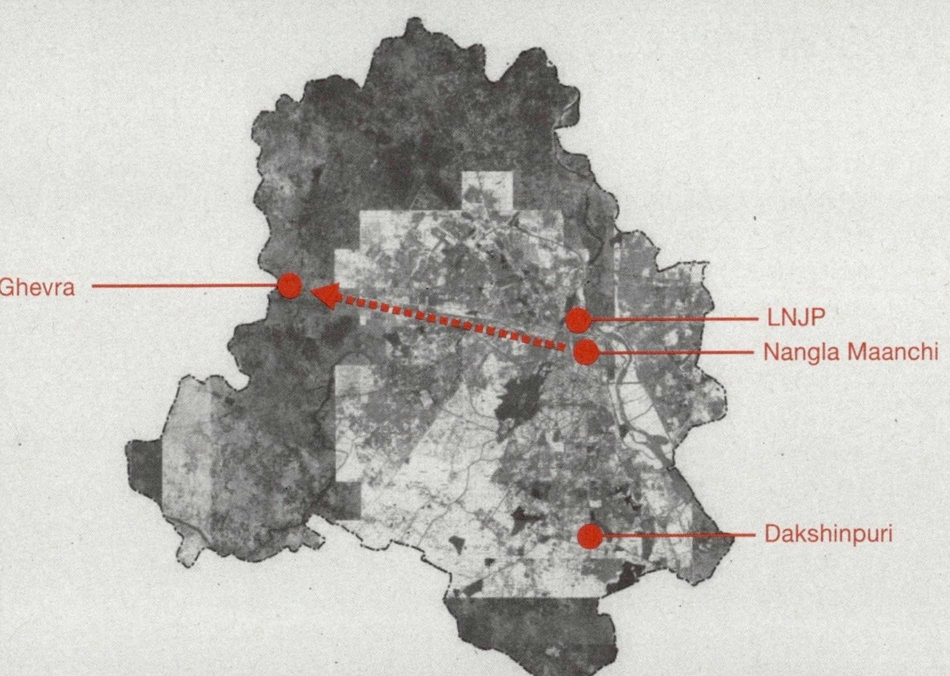

sion that is scaled down to a minimum with blocks of 13 x 2 parcels at three to
six meters each. This parcel is the legal form.
Above ground the informal user tactics are back. One can almost see in real
time how a city grows on the basis of a formal surface: a first generation of
rapidly built temporary bamboo huts, a second generation of more stable brick
and concrete houses, developing in phases from 1, 2 and 3-storey-structures.
The Hub follows the urban parameters: the horizontal parameters are determined by a 3 to 6 meter plan, whereas the vertical logic initiates a growing,
accumulative process. Yet, the Hub follows the urban parameters without mimicking the context. The structure leaves behind a tricky contextualism that has
been always been half way between a good intention and another trick in the
appropriation of the other. Instead, the Hub focuses on production and initiates
a new material logic that – rather than hiding them, insists on the paradoxes
of cultural production and transfer. Ultimately, Nikolaus Hirsch's and Michel
Müller's work attempts to negotiate the ambivalence between the abstraction of
a model and the site-specific condition. It entails the construction of an inhabit-
able model.

Practice

Mohalla in Hindi and Urdu translates as neighborhood. The Cybermohalla
project deploys the meaning of the word *mohalla* in its sense of alleys and corners, of relatedness and concreteness, and as a means for talking one's "place"
in the city as well as in cyberspace. Approximately 70 practitioners work within
the Cybermohalla, engaging with various media tools and forms, including
animation, photography, storytelling, performance, radio, stickers, broadsheets,
event-based conversations, wall writing, booklets, wall magazines, and blogs.
The project has been divided into four different but related approaches. Belong-

ing to *generative contexts,* the activities imply a constant making, questioning, and refashioning of the specific location. Generative contexts thrive on local intellectual life and site-specific narratives. In its ongoing and open nature the resulting generative and multi-layered archive collects information that simultaneously asks new questions about the daily life in the neighborhood.

Activities in the *minor practices* section involve solitary or smaller group exercises such as reading and writing. By paying attention to the self, to the body and its senses, the idea is to unleash and make available creative aspects of each individual's perception.

The *communing activity* is a way to connect resources in a variety of formats. By smaller group collaborations, emphasis is on experimental and unexpected assembly of materials and on the type of conversations that such activities generate.

The *public dialogue* distributes ideas generated by the various activities. An open dialogue is kept in motion that allows for new material to re-enter the intellectual fabric of the localities. This may include provisional constellations of images, texts, sounds, objects, etc., that are regularly brought into circulation and conversation in the forms of broadsheet, radio, installation, wall writing, and books.

Institution Building as Knowledge Production

In May 2007, Nikolaus Hirsch and Michel Müller set the Hub in motion by researching the existing Cybermohalla labs in Dakshinpuri and LNJP, investigating programmatic structures and spatial parameters. Collecting material of the lost space in Nangla and measuring the two remaining cultural labs they started to develop a spatial reference for the new plot in Ghevra. The research process and its tools were almost immediately reintegrated in the Cybermohalla Ensemble's written practice. In his diary fragment "With Nikolaus and Michel, after moving through Ghevra / 2 May 2007," Suraj Rai wrote: "Michel moved from one edge of the room to the other, watchful of his readings on the instrument he used to measure distances. He placed the black instrument squarely on a wall. All our eyes were fixed on the red dot of light that the instrument cast on the opposite wall. Then he read out the measurement and Nikolaus sketched it down. Next, the instrument was on the floor, and the red dot of light on the roof. I have seen hundreds of plots and many rooms being measured with an inch tape. But this measuring felt different. Maybe because of the machine, or perhaps because of the two personalities using it."

Before taking the pencil in their own hands, Nikolaus Hirsch and Michel Müller asked others to draw and to speculate on the future space — those who will inhabit it. The questions were: Can amateurs draw? Can architects share the production of space? Together with more than twenty of the Cybermohalla practitioners Hirsch and Müller sat down on a cool stone floor and made drawings. Programs were drawn as spatial diagrams. Out of scale, yet accurate in their intentions, these drawings became speculations on a future institution that has become a hybrid of community center, school, studio, and gallery.

Back in Frankfurt, Hirsch and Müller developed an initial model based on the workshop in Delhi: an almost perfect system with an extreme economy of space

that integrated entire work areas in the wall structure. Too perfect, one might
say. After the first prototype was shown at the Swedish Architecture Museum
in Stockholm (March 2008) the system was broken up. The spatial elements
and the related decision-making processes were redistributed and scaled
further down to a group of students, decomposing the geometry into individual
components – not for the sake of individuality but for a communal process
that changes again the physical condition of the space. Knowledge production
becomes physically tangible. Within a given systemic approach, multiple scenarios are allowed to evolve. Introducing a numeric multiplication, three groups
of two students work on walls and floor, facade and doors, ceiling and terrace.
Interfaces have to be negotiated: changes in geometry, in structural engineering, and a material strategy is developed using different kinds of waste timber
boards. The structure shown in Vienna, previously exhibited at Manifesta 7 in
Bolzano, is the result of a long process: a one and a half storey, 3 x 6 x 5 m
large prototype of the Cybermohalla Hub that Nikolaus Hirsch and Michel Müller
will construct in Delhi in 2009 with the support of Thyssen-Bornemisza Art
Contemporary. Eventually the Hub in Ghevra shows a possibility of how institution building can become a self-reflexive tool of knowledge production.

— MONIQUE BEHR

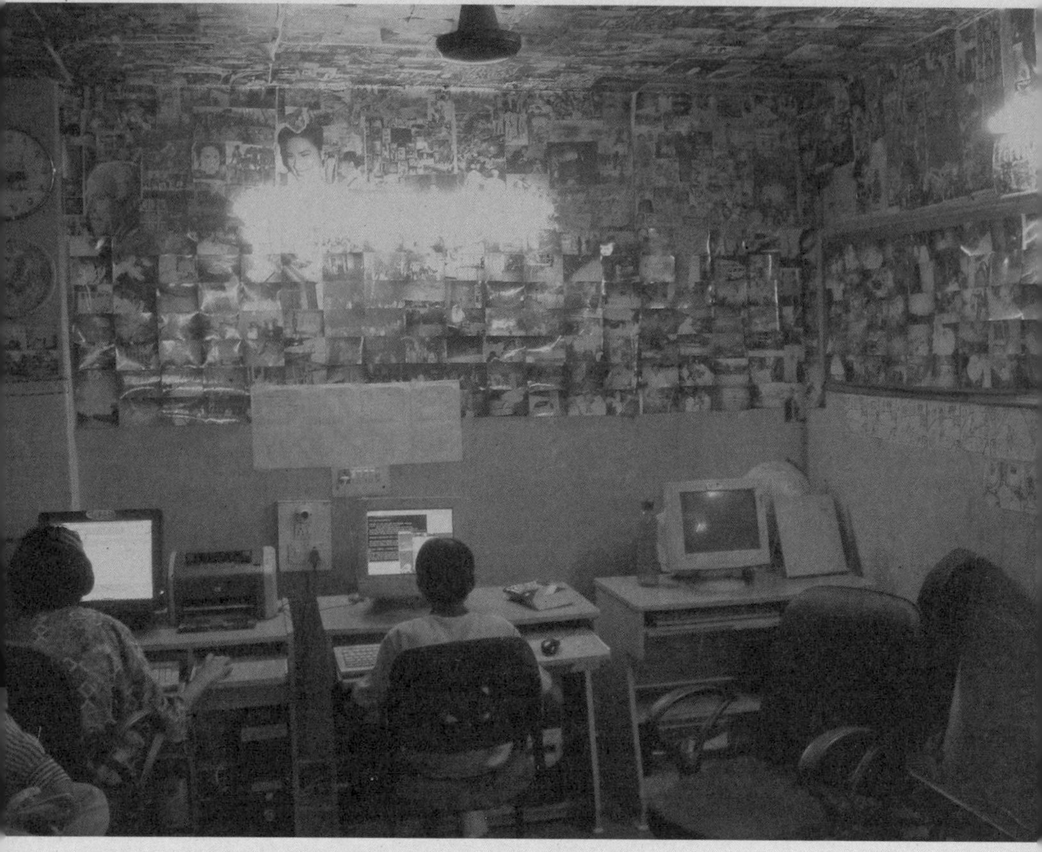

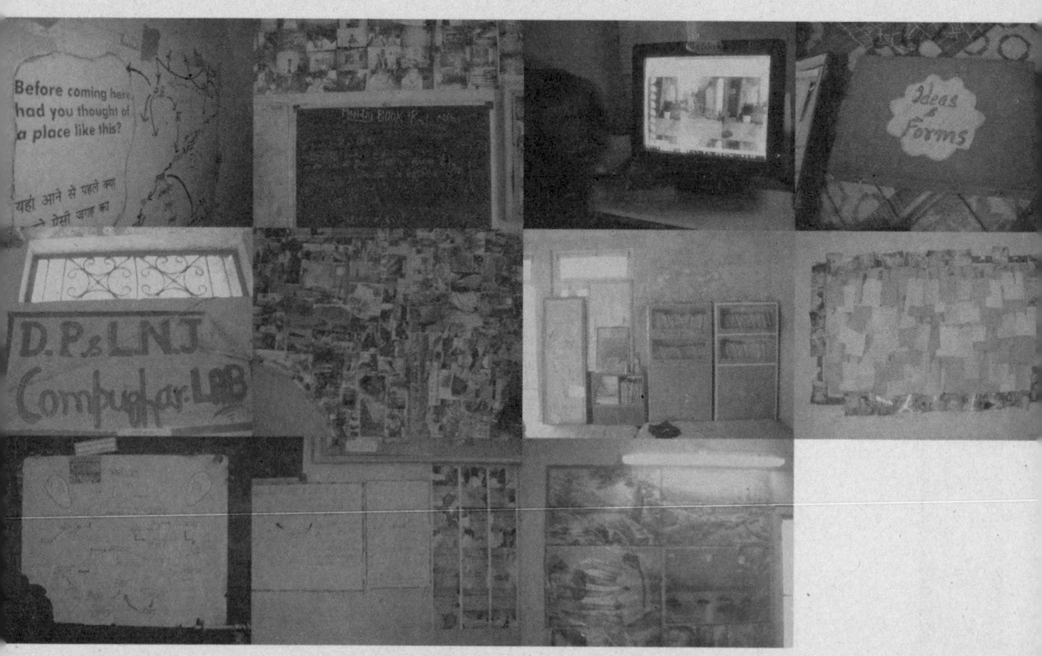

Hubs
Dakshinpuri, Nangla Maanchi and LNJP

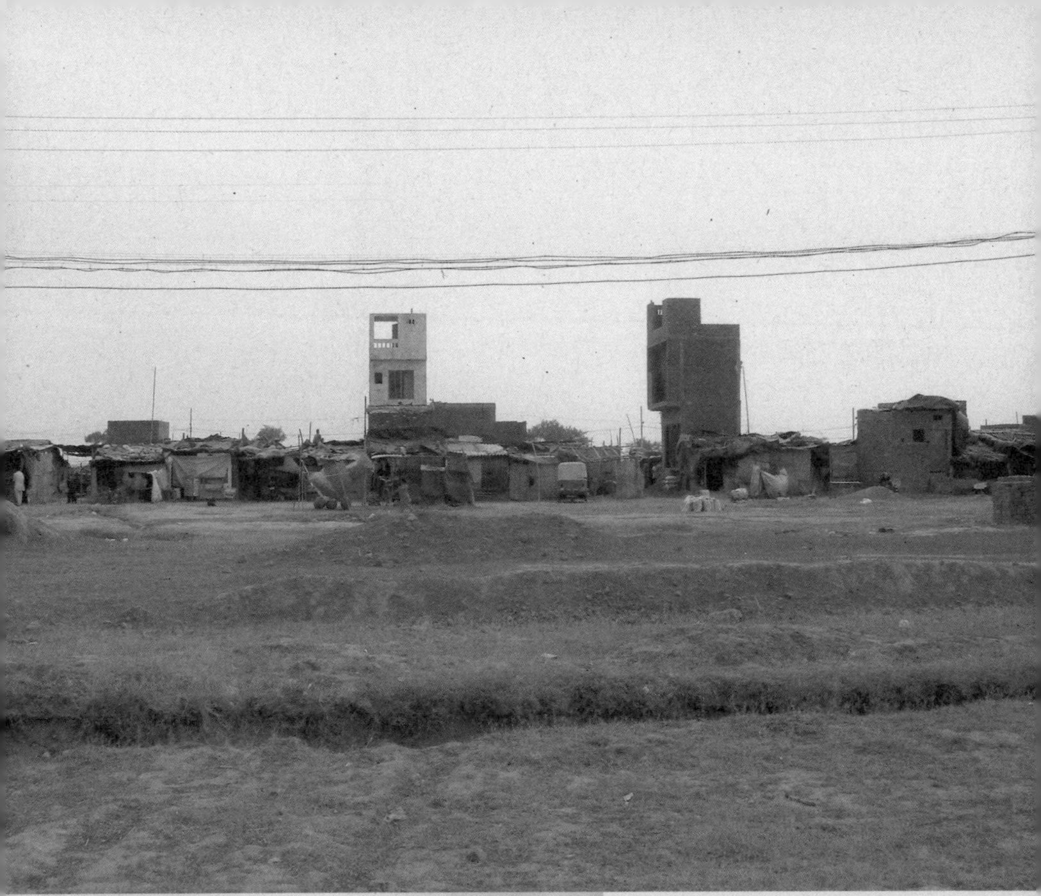

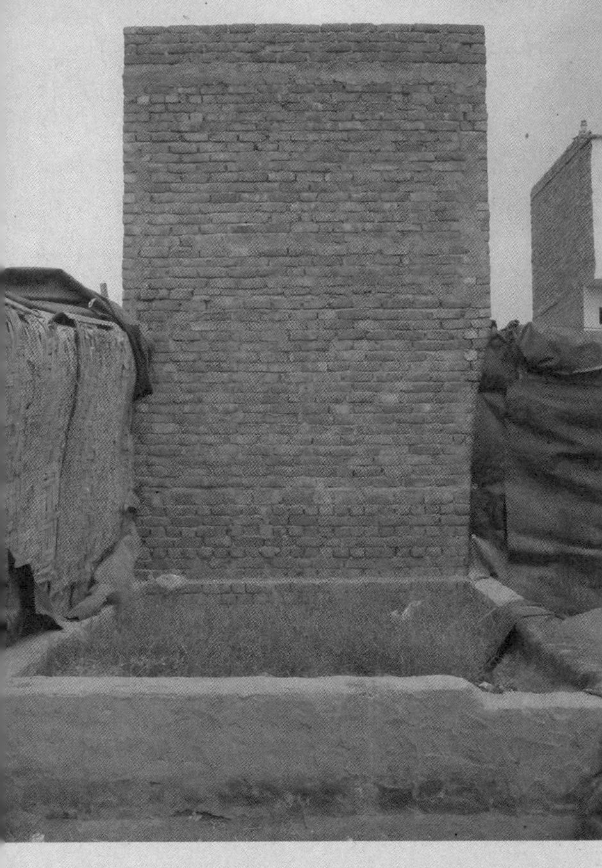

New settlement in Ghevra
Standard plot for construction

THINKING THE HUB IN A CITY

Inception When Sarai, an interdisciplinary space of practice and research, was conceived in the late 90s, the initiators were confident that the shifts and dynamism of everyday media production and circulation in the city would rapidly change the way we think about innovation, creativity and its relation to the conceptual armature of the understanding of urban life[1]. Sarai was designed as a space that engaged in research, media practice, experimentation, and building networks of knowledge production and exchange, intersecting diverse publics.

Within this rubric, Cybermohalla was conceived as a constellation of practices and spaces that would allow a creative engagement with questions of inequality, cultural practice and expression to challenge the firmly held assumptions of the discourse of "lack" about ordinary life in the cities of the South.

In 2001, Sarai entered into collaboration with Ankur, an NGO active in making alternative educational spaces and practices in difficult and disenfranchised neighborhoods for over twenty years. Together we started giving shape to our ideas of experimental spaces that would work with emerging media technologies in the city; spaces that would draw young people into their orbit by allowing them to immerse themselves in creative exploration. We realized such a space would need light-handed intervention from both the initiating organizations so that it could develop its own inner dynamics, rhythms, sense of duration, mutuality, and protocols of recognition. The space would need to work out a resource base for itself and also find ways to encounter afresh the neighborhood in which it would be situated.

Elaboration Cybermohalla started in May 2001 with a digital-lab in the LNJP colony, a densely populated, 40 year-old squatter settlement in central Delhi, and has now slowly expanded to three labs in very different neighbourhoods, in addition to a mobile lab that travels between lab locations and other places to initiate new practices and circulatory forms[2]. These labs have slowly evolved a complex weave of conversational practices, and have generated a vocabulary to articulate difficult experiences via playful and reflective works using animation, sound, photography and wall-writing, as well as online platforms such as blogs and lists employing a variety of formal narrative styles[3].

The young people in the labs are from families with diverse histories of displacement, work, and travel. Finding stable ground in the city has been difficult for most families but they have located themselves, with great skill and enterprise, in productive networks (formal and informal enmeshed) and have affectively stitched together a social surrounding[4]. The lab practitioners have been through rough, segregated schooling systems and have gathered, on their own, various social skills (craft-based and entrepreneurial) from family members and neighborhood circuits. For them the lab is a space to experiment with another trajectory of the self and to re-connect with the neighborhood and the world with an uncharted or forgotten poetics of imagining and making.

The labs are self-managed by the practitioners. These spaces do not aspire to a stable equilibrium among the constituents. Instead, the relationship is always in movement, at times interrupted and chaotic, at times searching and confused,

at times flowing with charge and dynamism; sometimes even anticipating an
occurrence that could render new meaning to the lives inhabiting the space.

Disruption   *"It quenches the thirst of the thirsty, such is Nangla;*
It welcomes those who come to the city of Delhi, such is Nangla."

The third lab of Cybermohalla was initiated in Nangla Manchi in August 2004.
By August 2006 the neighborhood had been razed to the ground to make way
for mega-projects conceived by city planners and global institutions. Nangla
Manchi was a squatter settlement that was incrementally built over 30 years,
along the river Yamuna, which bisects the city of Delhi. Once a lifeline of the
city, the city had turned its back on its river – over the last 70 years it has
slowly become a sewage dump. The upper-reach canalization and the city's
indifference pushed the river away from the consciousness of the elite, leaving
a gap of neglect where working class migrants could build. It is estimated that
about half a million people lived in squatter settlements along the Yamuna. Very
few of these settlements have survived the last 6 years. Most have been demolished and a small percentage of the dwellers resettled relocated, tucked away
into far corners of the city. The river bank has witnessed what is probably one
of the biggest internal dislocations in a city in contemporary times. A dislocation
that has mostly gone unrecorded and unaccounted.
The lab in Nangla was made up of young people from the neighborhood.
Articulate and dynamic, living between the threat of dislocation and dreams of
mobility in the city, Nangla lab practitioners brought in a specific texture to the
Cybermohalla experience. This lab was built and sustained by practitioners from
the other two labs. Battles for recognition, the problematic of self-learning, the
uncertainty of the future of such processes, the inability of language to express
deep turbulence of the encounter – all became a part of the CM practitioners'
thought processes.

Notice of eviction and demolition of the settlement arrived in February 2006.
Documents that would prove how long inhabitants had stayed in Nangla, and
which in turn would entitle them to be resettled, stood questioned. Nangla's
inhabitants dispersed across the city. Their world of work was broken and the
neighborhood ties woven over years, torn.
Cybermohalla practitioners registered this enormous turbulence and also realized that this is a very ordinary event in the life of the city. The only way they
could make sense of this was through writing and helping others with packing
and negotiations with the bureaucracy. They wrote about wedding celebrations
inside the partially demolished houses, re-routing of everyday journeys with
paths impeded by rubble, search for homes in the city, nights without electricity,
and the dismantling of the school and its transmutation into a document verification office[5]. They wrote daily. They recorded songs and conversations with
people, made broadsheets to distribute to passersby, scarves to gift to neigh-
bors and the workers employed to take down houses, and … they reflected on
the wrath of the city.

The Hub   Some of the Nangla lab practitioners found themselves relocated to Ghevra, at the northern edge of Delhi. Municipal trucks carried them to a newly acquired, flattened agricultural land area that had been mapped into grids of plots measuring 3 x 6 m. Life would be re-built here, piece by piece. The new lab would have to be different from whatever had been created before. In Ghevra it would have to be part of the very making of the locality. Long-repressed stories in family histories – of having been thrown out into barren spaces before, and then slowly building homes again – were remembered. Dakshinpuri, where another CM lab is situated, was one such difficult landscape into which an enormous population had been "rehabilitated" in the mid 1970s. Conversation in Dakshinpuri after the demolition of Nangla Manchi returned to how life was 35 years before. Latent memories fought the obliteration of memories.

How does a neighborhood know what is happening in one small room in its midst? Knowing is about being able to make sense, and about being in conversation with it. The different materials that a lab brings into public circulation provide a sense of the various dimensions of its thoughts, its attitude towards places, biographies, and incidents. This creates a hunger for more, a desire to be increasingly pulled into the lab's conversations, and to be noted in its daily presence.

On the other hand, the small rooms of the labs (the biggest being 8 x 8 m) provide a lively context for conversation and mutual learning, but are insufficient for solitary pursuit. Solitude – with oneself, or a few others – is longed for. Even solidarity needs moments of solitude to renew itself.

How do we create a building that actualizes the accretion of the creative practices of those who use it, articulates an affirmation of the overflow of their energies and thirst for connectivity? How can a design be arrived at which can disaggregate a space to address ways of both being together with others and being alone with oneself? The Hub will be an "intermediate" space – living between moments of re-invention of the self, search for recognition in others, and participating in the making of a new neighborhood. Standing in a neighborhood that is itself uncertain what its eventual make is going to be, the Hub begins its journey in search of an uncharted course.

— JEEBESH BAGCHI

1. How Sarai happened (http://www.sarai.net/about-us/introducing-sarai/background) and Jeebesh Bagchi and Ravi Sundaram, "Our Media City" in "Sarai Reader 01. The Public Domain" (http://www.sarai.net/publications/readers/01-the-public-domain)
2. See http://www.sarai.net/about-us/spaces
3. See Cybermohalla Minor Practices (http://www.sarai.net/practices/cybermohalla/minor-practices) and Public Dialogue (http://www.sarai.net/practices/cybermohalla/public-dialogue).
4. See Solomon Benjamin, "Touts, Pirates and Ghosts" in "Sarai Reader 05. Bare Acts" (http://www.sarai.net/publications/readers/05-bare-acts)
5. See Cybermohalla Practitioners, "Notes from Besieged Neighbourhoods: Nangla's Delhi" in "Sarai Reader 06. Turbulence" (http://www.sarai.net/publications/readers/06-turbulence)

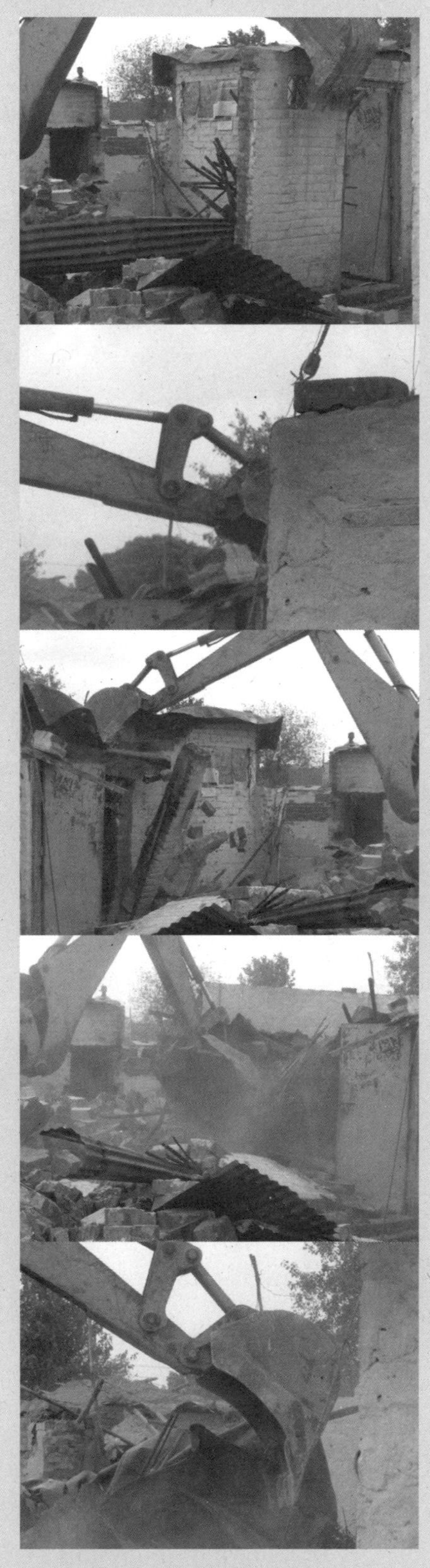

A marksman drawing an arrow on
a bow string, preparing to launch
those it arrests, into the city, like
projectiles

Notice Board
10/02/2006
Jaanu Nagar and Lakhmi Chand Kohli

Signboards. Sometimes they tell the way, sometimes they give unsolicited advice, sometimes they instruct on how to conduct oneself in the city, and sometimes they distract by making one's attention wander: "Gas pipeline underneath. Do not excavate". "The name of this crossroad is (–)". "Welcome to Delhi Railway Station". "Get your tenant verified before trusting him with your house". "Punctured tyres are repaired here". Amidst the quiet breathing of many in front of an emergency ward, a board announcing "Emergency Ward". "Please Use Me" written on garbage bins. And a board in my neighborhood that gives the impression of the presence of a property dealer in the vicinity: "Cheap plots available here".
There is one more board that falls in the company of these boards. It's a notice board that appears from time to time in front of city colonies in the wake of the state's "cleanliness drives". It's a board that doesn't say anything of its own, but repeats the contents of the sheet that is pasted on it. One such board stands in front of my neighborhood.
"This land is the property of the government. It should be vacated."
[…]
This was the morning when the drunkard's words were going to become reality. Police forces descended on the settlement like fog, settling over everything, changing everything. Spotting a uniformed man, Komal walked up to him and asked, "Bhai, what's going on here?"
The policeman replied, "Why? Haven't you read the notice board?"
"No sir, I haven't".
"Well then! Empty the colony! It will be demolished today". […]

It Was Heard
09-02-2006
Jaanu Nagar

"When we came here, what was this land like?"
"It was ashen."
"It was infertile."
"There was nothing but ash all around."
"There was nothing here at all."
"When we would eat, ash would go into our mouths."
"We gave everything we earned in the last twenty to twenty five years in making a dwelling out of it."
"Not just our earnings, we have put in the labour of our bodies to make this place."

Spreading Into The Air
31/03/2007
Suraj Rai

It takes many years for a place to become a settlement, but a settlement is turned barren in merely two days. All around things
are being broken, felled. Some people are watching houses being
broken down. Each time dust rises when a house falls, they don't
turn their faces away. They seem to be trying to take it all in.
They had plastered the walls and roofs of their houses with their
memories. Today those memories have turned into dust and are
spreading into the air.
Everyone is reacting differently to what is happening. Someone is
not able to watch his house being broken down, while another is
breaking it apart himself. For someone it is their home that is
being broken, for another, it is only the four walls of a house
that are being pulled apart. But everyone's heart is heavy. No one
is alone in his sadness. Everyone is expressing the sorrow they
are feeling, in different ways.
"Good that the wait has finally ended. We had been burdened with
fear for so long."
"To live in this world, all we need to do is plant our feet somewhere. Today it was on this stretch of land, tomorrow it will be
elsewhere."
"Nangla Maanchi will be remembered because it is being broken."
"This demolition has imprinted this place in our minds in such a
powerful way that our lives will have ended long before this imprint can get covered over by the layers of time."
"We had thought we would spend our lives by the banks of the Yamuna, but now we will meet her again only after we have died."
It is only the traces of the place Nangla Maanchi that are being
erased; Nangla will continue to nurture inside each person who is
being made to leave from here. Nangla will always live on through
stories that are recalled about it. Then Nangla will not need a
place in the map in order to continue to breathe.

There is a saying in Nangla:
A cooling river and a pair of hissing serpents flank Nangla
Maanchi.
The river is the Yamuna, and the serpents are the two wide lanes
of the Ring Road with their speeding traffic.
Even strangers clasp each others' hands to navigate the Ring Road.

Nangla Maanchi
(1979 — 30th August 2006)

From: Cybermohalla Ensemble: Trickster City. [Orig.: Bahurupiya
Shehr, Rajkamal Publication, Delhi 2007]

PAPER WEIGHTS/WAITS

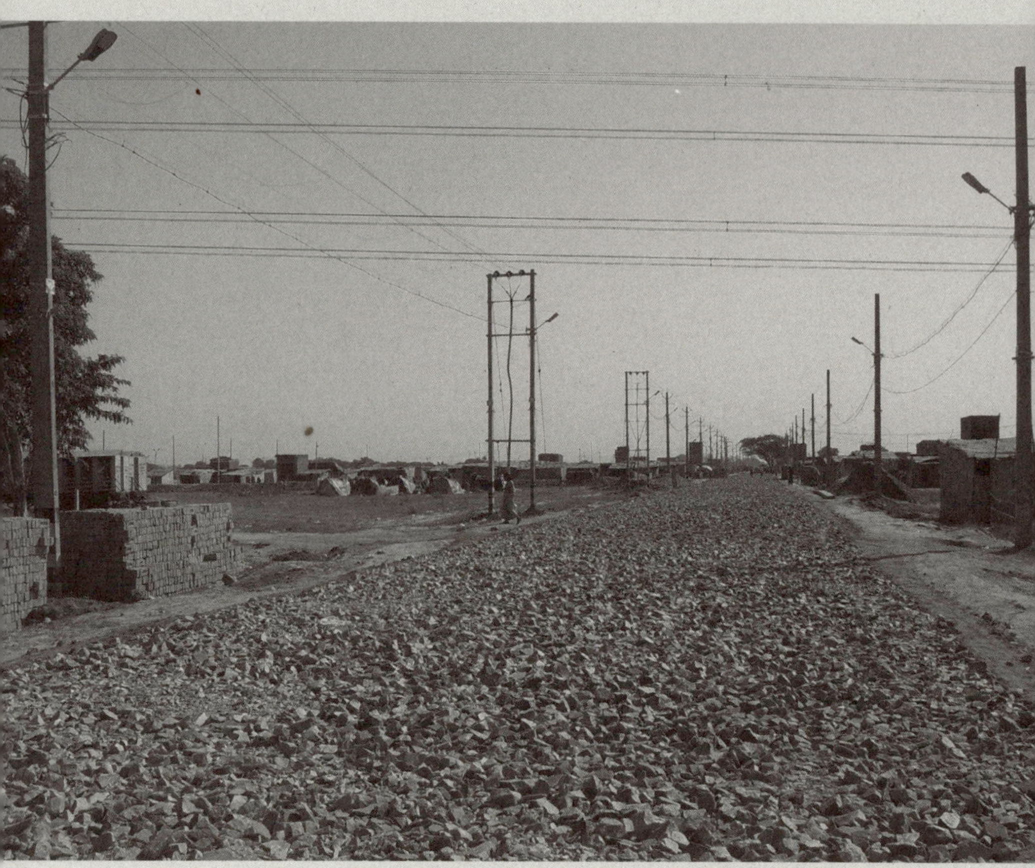

Last night, as I looked inside the trunk, I saw a square metal piece, layered with chalk dust. I had no memory to associate with it. I picked it up and removed the chalk from it. It was an aluminum plate. It bore a number. 4-1-5. I recognized the number. It is the same one as our ration card bears. It was embossed with a sign. The issuing authority's, I thought to myself. Within this sign, or logo, was a stamp of time, 1987. On seeing the year, an image flashed in my mind. A day from my childhood when I saw two men standing on the other side of the threshold of my house, one of them painting this number with a brush onto the wall. The number stayed on the wall through my childhood.

I asked my mother what the square piece of aluminum was. She said it was a token. It bore the token number of our house. It is what our ration card and election I-card have been issued on the basis of. VP Singh [a politician] had got it made. All the poor people who lived here got one. The purpose was to assist in getting kerosene for stoves and sugar at lower costs. Our colony got its name when these tokens were issued. Today it is called LNJP colony, but then it was named T-Wood Market. My mother told me to put it back in the same place in the trunk from where I had pulled it out. She said it would help us later in life. As I put it back in its place I thought to myself, that which has no relation with my memories of my family is a strong token of my family's identity in the city.

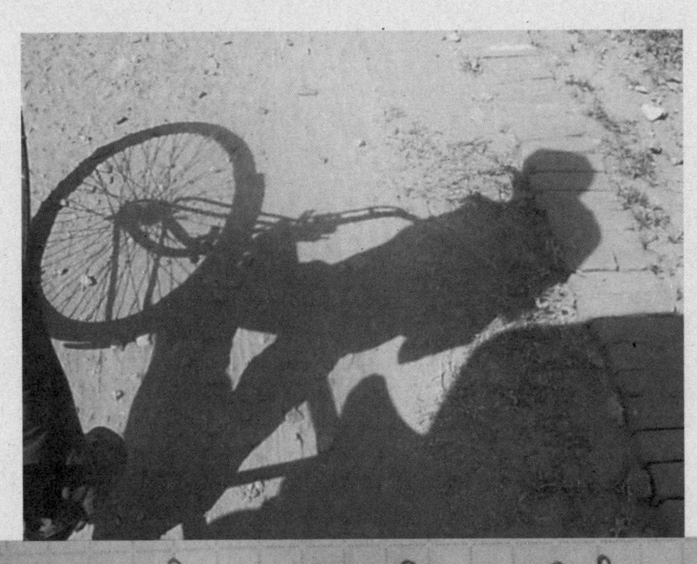

1998 से पहले
Before 1998

निर्धारित करने के
document (basis
of determining):
Ration card /
Election I-card

विभाजन की तारीख
Dateline of division
1995 / 1998 / 2003 ...

राशन कार्ड
के मुताबिक
1998 के बाद
(Post '98,
as per ration card)

Commercial COMM

locked ——— LOCK

no Docum-
ents shown NDS

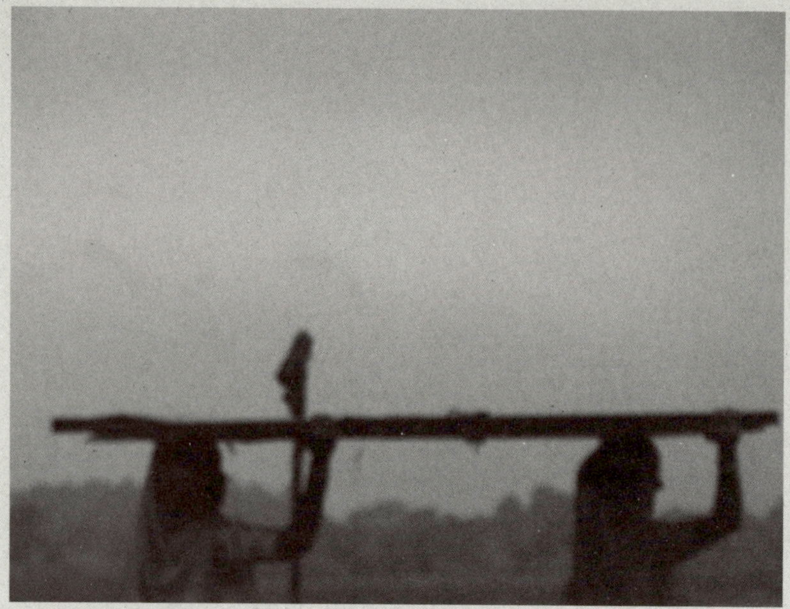

Every settlement, each lane along which people have made their homes, views people as strangers, guests or passersby. But at the time of demolition, what is the gaze that fills eyes that every person passing through the lane seems to be a character playing a part on the stage of a demolition?

A government team had come to the school in the neighborhood. Forms to get election I-cards were being collected and filed. The team was also giving information about the documents that had to be appended to the forms.

A mother asked her 20 year old son to get his card made. The young man was postponing going to the school. His mother finally explained to him, "Look, we had seen the significance of this card recently when there was a fire in the locality. We saw how difficult it is to get the card made. People had to show their burnt ration cards as proof of residence.

We are asked to present evidences for everything. But what all has to be done to keep the evidence intact and safe for producing in time of need remains hidden. You may think your election I-card serves no purpose at the moment; but once we have it on us, we are not asked for any other proof to identify ourselves."

Transformations in a space, changes in our understanding and passing time change the way we perceive that which happens around us. Experience hardens in the freezing and thawing of time when one stands facing an imminent demolition. In that moment, time ceases its journey, lingering quietly between glances. Where I live, we have seen demolitions from very close. At the time of demolition, a person fights his self inscribed on a document. Questions are not asked about us, but about our documents. When torn, burnt or lost ration cards and election I-cards fail as evidences of the self, telephone bills, newspaper clippings about the locality from long ago, report cards from school that people have preserved become proofs that the space itself has existed for a long time. How much time an individual has given to a space is not ascertained by asking that person, but by checking his documents.

Time can be measured in the sayings we have about different times. Why is there no saying for demolitions? A few lines or some stories which could put forth a view about it? Long into the journey of her life, my grandmother is now 62 years old. She doesn't seem to notice time passing; she spends her moments reminiscing about past times that she spent with my grandfather. My three sisters and I often sit with her and she tells us stories from the book of her life. Her lips quiver.

Once, during such a conversation, she pointed to the west of the house and said, "Do you see that spot on the wall? Do you see that old box there? Your grandfather gifted me an idol of the goddess Lakshmi on our first anniversary. Even today she is with me in that box. I have protected her with something a letter your grandfather wrote to me." We looked in the direction she had pointed to, and saw an old looking box. The engravings on it were filled with dust from the years. The box was black, and its lock was broken.

Grandma brought the box to us and kept it on the cot. From close we could see, its lid too was broken. One of its holdnuts was also missing. When grandma opened the box, it made a creaking sound. On top of the box lay a document whose edges had been chewed by rats it was our grandfather's death certificate.

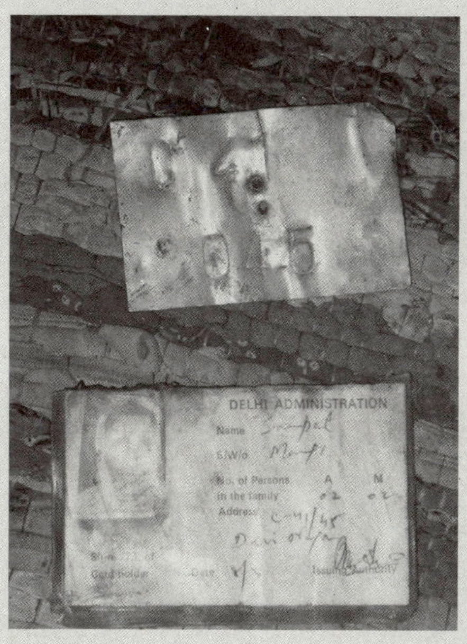

Sonu was trying to tell us something. She had written a text. It was about her mother's morning. A morning which was like any other. Sonu's mother cleans the house every morning; as she cleans the courtyard, she pulls out a box that is kept under the cot to remove the dust from behind it. Often, as she does this, she opens the box and slowly looks through the documents that are kept in it. Sonu wrote that as she watches this, she feels her mother withdraws into some

other world. Her mother doesn't let Sonu touch any of the documents.
After she read out the text, Sonu closed her notebook, and looked around at
her listeners. She seemed to be sifting words in her mind. After a pause, she
said, "My mother removes the box from its place every morning. Sometimes she
opens it. When she looks through the documents and stops for a while with one
among them, I feel the document contains a world and my mother has disappeared into it. At such moments, I feel like I don't know her."
In her text, Sonu had written about her mother; but when she spoke, she was
speaking about the stranger in her. Because of the time wrapped in that document, Sonu finds her mother is a different person every morning.

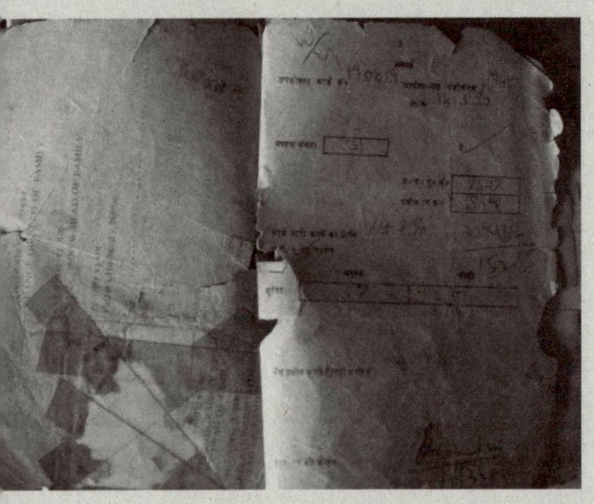

In the hospital, when Sumitraji's
newborn was brought to her, a small
chit was pasted on his stomach. The
date, day and time of his birth were
written on it. Sumitraji asked her
husband to bring her a box, then she
carefully removed the chit from her
son's stomach and stuck it underneath the box.
Today that newborn is sixteen years
old. And that box, which still bears
his date, day and time of birth, has
become Sumitraji's vanity case. Each
time she sits down to wear her lipstick, she takes a pen and writes over the
fading handwriting on the chit. It is as if on the pretext of touching up that detail
she redrafts and reinforces something deep inside her.

My mother drew out the box containing documents from the shelf and opened
it. I could see some of the documents were very old. I was curious, but she
wouldn't let me touch anything. As soon as I would stretch my hand towards
a document, she would push it away. When I insisted, she pulled out one or
two report cards and showed them to me. After I managed to drawn her into
a comfortable conversation, she showed me her marriage certificate and my
brother's birth certificate. Slowly, she let me pick up documents and ask her
about them. I couldn't believe she had memorized what each of those various
documents was. When I asked her how she remembered, she said, "You can
read, yet you can't tell one document from the other. I can't read, but each of
these documents is imprinted in my memory." I thought to myself, she probably
remembers because of the color of the documents, or recognizes documents by
looking at my father's thumb print on them. Or perhaps in her mind she has tied
each document with the moment when it was made, or when it was needed. It
was as if time had passed, but left behind its enduring shadows in the form of
documents.
There is cold ash all around. Amidst it, burnt bamboo poles and sticks have
lost their form and turned to burnt coal. Twisted iron pipes jut out from various

places from the mounds of ash. Remains of doors and windows outlining a lived geometry on the land fade, slowly blowing away with the wind.

Sunitaji is standing at the threshold of her house. Her son Monu is digging up the earth in a corner of the home with a pair of scissors as his tool; the red color of its handle has burnt and is coming off from the scissors on to his fingers. Sunitaji directs him with her hand and he shifts his digging, hollowing out another spot.

Standing at the threshold of the house, Sunitaji is also connected to what is going on outside. From time to time she turns her head to look outside, as if looking for something, and then returns her glance back inside the house. Time and again, those passing by and people from the neighboring homes and shops move as if to approach her, but then change their mind and turn back to their own worlds and their twelve to thirteen square feet enclosures.

Monu's scissors hit something. He has removed the loosened earth with his hands and cleaned up a space as big as a small brass vessel. Now he can see a yellow polythene. He pulls it out.

The hustlebustle of the outside has stilled itself indoors.

Sunitaji removes the polythene, pulls out a box from underneath and opens it. She picks up some sheets of paper from it and says quietly, to herself, "These are the basis of my children's future."

The box, filled with different documents and identity papers bearing official stamps, is like a record of her life; in it, each identity bearing sheet is key to ensuring she is not sealed out of moments when life in the city demands that she take decisions and choose directions.

Our elders say a paper boat does not endure. This saying has a force, is an example. But contrary to it, today the boat of papers is all that remains, carries one across different storms, and is a source of great strength.

When surroundings become uncertain, we begin to search a concrete, material form of our selfhood. Sunitaji was stubbornly trying to keep her identity, her selfhood, intact.

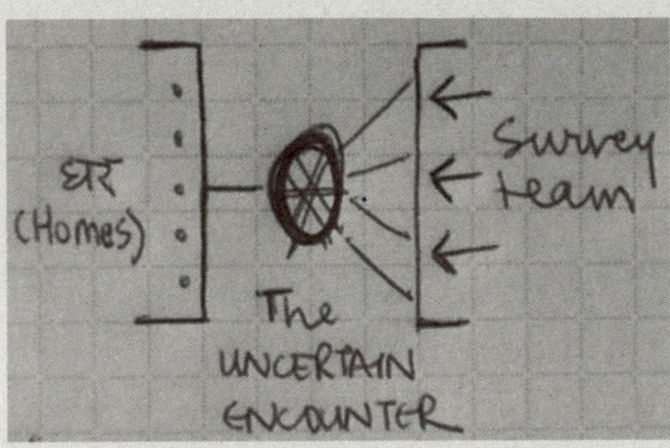

Reprint of: Paper Weights/Waits. A Reflection by Cybermohalla Ensemble (unpublished compilation of texts by Cybermohalla practitioners, http://www.sarai.net/practices/cybermohalla/minor-practices/collecting-documents/cm_paper_waits.pdf)

The Corners of a City
Shamsher Ali

[…]
The thought that the world is very big and that everyone will
surely find a place in it becomes a force with which the search for
a location begins. The wheels of time keep moving, and the person
who came to the city recently soon becomes a city-dweller who has
been here for ten years. He participates in and becomes tied to
the time and the crests and troughs of the space he is in.
An invalidated license. Everyone finds one so as to stay in one of
the infinite informal spaces in the city. Desires find shade to rest
in. That is why when a young child runs away from home, the hope
of his return remains. This hope stays tied to spaces even when a
long time has elapsed. It is these spaces that evictions and demolitions are threatening today.
People whose houses were marked "P-98" (post 1998) in Nangla, and
who have not been allotted a plot in Ghevra, have also reached
Ghevra. Their certainty that there is a corner in the city for
everyone is intact. They are sure there is that wall in Ghevra for
them, where they and their families can rest their backs.
And why not! This is a city, after all.

Construction Has Begun
Rakesh Khairalia

[…]
One man has driven four to six bamboo sticks into
the ground to create a frame, tied ropes around the
frame and created a canopy by putting blankets and
sheets over them. The afternoon sun shoots rays like
arrows to the ground. In the fields, each grain of
sand seethes like lava.
Construction has begun in Ghevra.

From: Cybermohalla Ensemble: Trickster City. [Orig.:
Bahurupiya Shehr, Rajkamal Publication, Delhi, 2007]

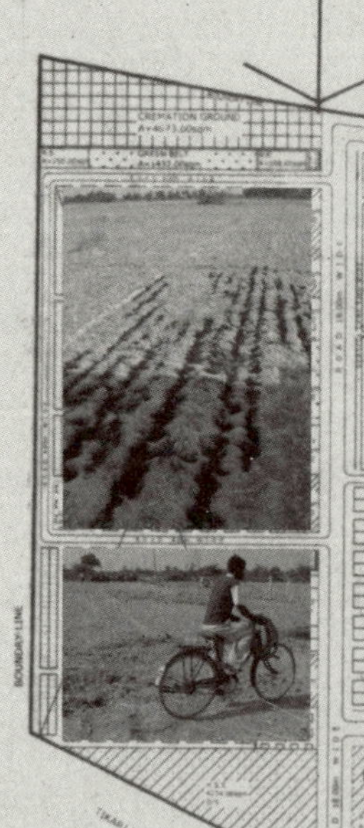

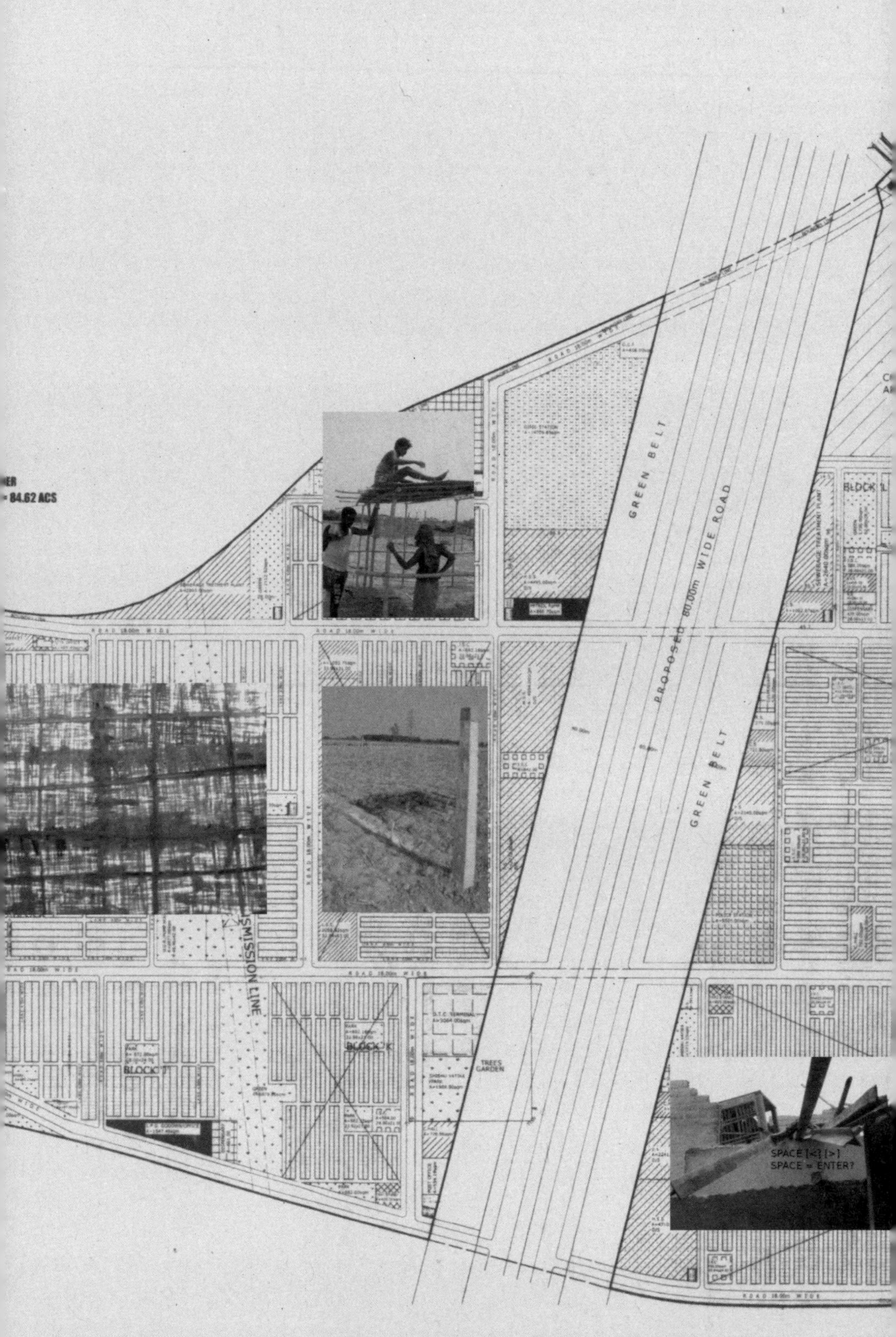
SPACE [<][>]
SPACE = ENTER?

MOBILE AESTHETICS DISCUSSION

Dear All,

Below are the transcripts of a discussion on videos shot by mobile phones.

The link to the mobile video
Mobile Sketches
Memory Card 01
http://www.youtube.com/watch?v=nbnSth4cxOY

best
Jeebesh

Extracts from a discussion on Mobile Videos
Cybermohalla Ensemble
June 2008

Suraj Rai: A mobile phone... It's in our pockets. We just take it with us to the fair, take it with us to the play, take it with us when going from one place to the other, carry it with us on the way.

[...]

Jaanu Nagar: Just day before yesterday, in the evening, it was raining heavily. It is said a downpour can ruin many things. But when I stood and watched, it seemed to me everything was becoming more resplendent. I found this attractive. Everything looked so different from usual. Descriptions of rain are usually about how people run for shelter, leave what they are doing. But what I was seeing was something different. I thought a photo may not capture this difference. I wanted to see if I could make a video resonate with what I was thinking. I looked through the screen and started recording. Someone held an umbrella, another had covered himself with a plastic sheet. Someone was returning from work, a scarf thrown over his head. People were not running around. Some were buying vegetables for home. And there was a chowmein stall — It was open to the sky. The man was busy frying chowmein in the pan. I thought a photograph would not have helped me capture this style, the special music... Along with the raindrops was the sound "chhan–chhan–chhan", as the Stirrer moved in the pan, while everyone stood around under their umbrellas, waiting to eat.

[...]

Love Anand: For instance, I'd often look out of my window at the shadows cast by clothes put out to dry.
These shadows would hover over the entire lane, and create a very special ambience. Shadows would glide over people's faces, knock against things. I'd always try to search a language to think, to describe this environment of shadows.

Babli Rai: To make a mobile video, one doesn't need to go out in search of a "special" event or occasion. Mobile Videos draw from the simplest moments of our lives. In that sense, the mobile phone camera makes one look for the special within the ordinary. A woman may wear make-up everyday. But to make a mobile video of this simple thing, makes her, her make-up and the ordinariness of that moment, special.
Lakhmi Chand: One immediately thinks of a mobile video as being something personal. But mobile phone conversations, sms, photos, videos, ring tone etc. have a velocity in everyday life — they get their life from being in circulation. That is why, even though mobile phones have very small screens, the staggered circulation of its images stretches their lived beyond the first moment in which they were taken.
Love Anand: In the two years that we have been making mobile videos, it seems to me that all of us have deepened out ways of looking through the act of looking around us, everyday. In writing, we think about what we have seen and how to write it. But in

making mobile videos, the view before us unravels itself frame by frame. There is a relation between the practice of writing and the practice of making mobile videos. One requires inner stillness, and the other requires us to still our surroundings. I think with a mobile video, we try to find a stillness amidst the speed around us. We try to find a moment of stillness in the world.

Yashoda Singh: And in writing?

Love Anand: In writing... In writing it is as if we are inhabiting a stillness and trying to write it. By making a mobile video, we still that which is speeding, so we may think from within it.

Yashoda Singh: So a mobile video makes us go deeper into something than writing does...?

Love Anand: No, I'm not saying that. I can try to understand that which I can see by revisiting it in my mind's eye. But what about that which elides me? A mobile video can help me bring it into my view. So I can be with it.

Yashoda Singh: Is it that we see something and immediately know it is interesting, we should make a mobile video of it?

Love Anand: No... The question for me is, how do we perceive something that races past us? What can we do to bring it into our field of vision? How can I hold it, even for a moment, while it rushes past me, so I may enter it to think with it?

Lakhmi Chand: Mobile phone videos are embedded in networks. This opens up a big playing field. The shrinking and expanding images around us become a player here. As do those minor moments which would not even have been thought of as occasions before.

Jaanu Nagar: The world is foggy. When you capture a grain from it, as you may sometimes do with a mobile video, it helps you understand the expanse and the detail.

Tripan Kumar: I may have made an image of something that I don't recognise. This image may allow others to address those images which remain unnamed in their lives.

Azra Tabassum: A frame is like a hook that gathers that which lies scattered around us. And I join a few of my own hooks to think ahead with the frame. Probably the attempt is that what lies scattered in my life is brought to speech through the movement within the frames. Or maybe I depict the dilations of my eyes and in this I connect the various scattered flickers that are around me.

Rakesh Khairalia: In the depiction of things around us, we sometimes see them still, sometimes in movement, and sometimes in turmoil. So this is a way to try to understand how to look. And when this is deepened, we create generative environments. From where does this generative form come into our thinking? This is a question. What is in our imagination that searches the generative both in stillness and in change? Whose mind is this? Where did it come from? Where is it about to go?
It is the turmoil of these questions that shapes the way we construct a frame. They are an occasion to think, to rethink what we have thought before, and to plough further. Where can it take us? How deeply are we connected to it? This life, things around us, changes around us, the time in which we live — how are we related to all this? This is how we think with mobile videos.

From: http://mail.sarai.net/pipermail/reader-list/2008-June/013029.html

WE
HAVE TO BE
VERY

CAREFUL THESE DAYS BECAUSE...

DECODING THE FUTURE

For Pak Sheung Chuen, art production is a process of poetic self-enlightenment. Among other media, he works in performance, photography, video, and sculptural installations to examine the effects of social situations on both a macro and a micro scale. Whether dealing with issues that affect the public realm, the tradition of identity politics, or the importance of the idea that everyday life is full of mysterious signs, his works maintain a personal and intimate tone.

Breathing in a House (2006) which is, in the artist's own words, a "human breaths sculpture," took the form of a performance during which Pak recorded his breaths by collecting air into transparent plastic bags until their total volume would fill a typical two-person apartment. At the other end of the spectrum, Pak documented, through the systematic replication of folding a corner of page 22, of the invisible existence of a public library's users. (It is these same users who, when borrowing a book, will be unaware of accidentally stumbling upon an unannounced artistic intervention, an exhibition hidden among the pages of thousands of books.) Similarly, in 2006 Pak stood for hours in one location in Hong Kong's underground transport system until he finally encountered someone he knew, giving this acquaintance the impression that he was expected without having made prior arrangements. For *Alternative Tokyo Travel Projects* (2007), Pak folded a map of Tokyo in the shape of a chain of mountains, turning its two-dimensional cartography into a three-dimensional imaginary territory, then walked along the map's folds, documenting his alternative routes by means of photographs of vertical objects oriented towards the North cardinal point only. Clearly, these works suggest an indebtedness to the legacies of North American and European Conceptual art; Pak has, to some extent, incorporated Western formal principles and operative methods. The contemporary art worlds in the West and the East have notoriously influenced and borrowed ideas from each other for well over sixty years. However, Pak's employment of an identifiable "allegorical procedure," to use a term coined by art historian Benjamin H.D. Buchloh, elaborates on chosen antecedents and familiar stylistic typologies. His "referentialism" can be mistaken for quotationism, but Pak's acts of indebtedness (and not of self-legitimation) inscribe the old in a novel context, reassessing former models and strategies from the viewpoint of an artist living and working in Hong Kong, which has its own long tradition of cultural exchange. Pak depends on multiple value systems when devising the rules guiding his visual practice.

A Present to the Central Government (2005), is a video accompanied by an interview with the artist broadcast on a local TV station and a supplement in *Ming Pao,* Hong Kong's mainstream newspaper (with which the artist has been occasionally collaborating since 2003). The piece was realized in response to an annual demonstration on July 1st that has protested, since the 1997 transfer of Hong Kong's sovereignty from the United Kingdom to the People's Republic of China, against the establishment of the area as a Special Administrative Region. In 2003, the march drew large public attention after nearly 500,000 demonstrators advocated, among a variety of political concerns, universal suffrage, rights for minorities, and the protection of free speech. Beginning with a small intervention in which Pak laid a piece of yellow textile across the asphalt of a main road to trace and bear witness to the marchers, the fabric imprinted with their footprints was later cut into tiny ribbons. He then brought these ribbons to Beijing and tied them anticlockwise—a manifest sign of disagreement—to objects placed along the perimeter of Tiananmen Square. In the *Ming Pao* article reporting on the rally, Pak inserted a photograph of himself overseeing the path trodden by the campaigners, protected by a universalist and phantasmagoric aura.

A Present to the Central Government alludes to the fact that Hong Kong's political system is in fact different from the administration in mainland China, and that there is a strong sense of identity in this region. In this sense the artwork acts, if quietly, on a political level. As the German cultural critic Walter Benjamin wrote, "The political significance of art does not lie in the clichéd resistance of the autonomous piece of art or in the coarse tendency of the revolutionary subject, but in the translation of the artist's formal competence from a piece of art to the organizational forms of society."[1]

A striking aspect of Pak's interests and conceptual approach is the way he appears to refuse direct engagement with his subject matter, maintaining a degree of romantic detachment that seeks out extra-ordinary associations among things and events, secrets at work in the world; he ties together the mysterious inner workings of the everyday data and occurrences to bring into sight normally invisible forces around us. Such symbolist language pervades *Miracle of $132.30* (2003), which comprises the photograph of a receipt accompanied by a few items in a plastic bag bought at a supermarket. If one reads from top to bottom the second word of the description of each item, an extraordinary message can be deciphered, encouraging the viewer to find further daily chimeras. The encrypted message finds an unknown "frequency of discourse," and Hong Kong's territory becomes a coded "transmission site": together they redefine the understanding of this artwork as a process that rearranges information full of lost meaning. Whether in the role of participants or witnesses, viewers-*cum*-receivers find in the truest reality the most unlikely facts, buried codes that carry revelatory meanings. Camouflaged in a supermarket receipt, the under-cover hide-and-seek mechanism is unleashed. All of Pak's micro-interventions work in this manner, disseminating their power by way of puzzlement.

— DIANA BALDON

1. Walter Benjamin (1999), "The Author as Producer", in "Selected Writings. Volume 2. 1927-1934", Michael W. Jennings, Howard Eiland and Gary Smith (eds), Harvard University Press.

PAK SHEUNG CHUEN
A PRESENT TO THE
CENTRAL GOVERNMENT
2005

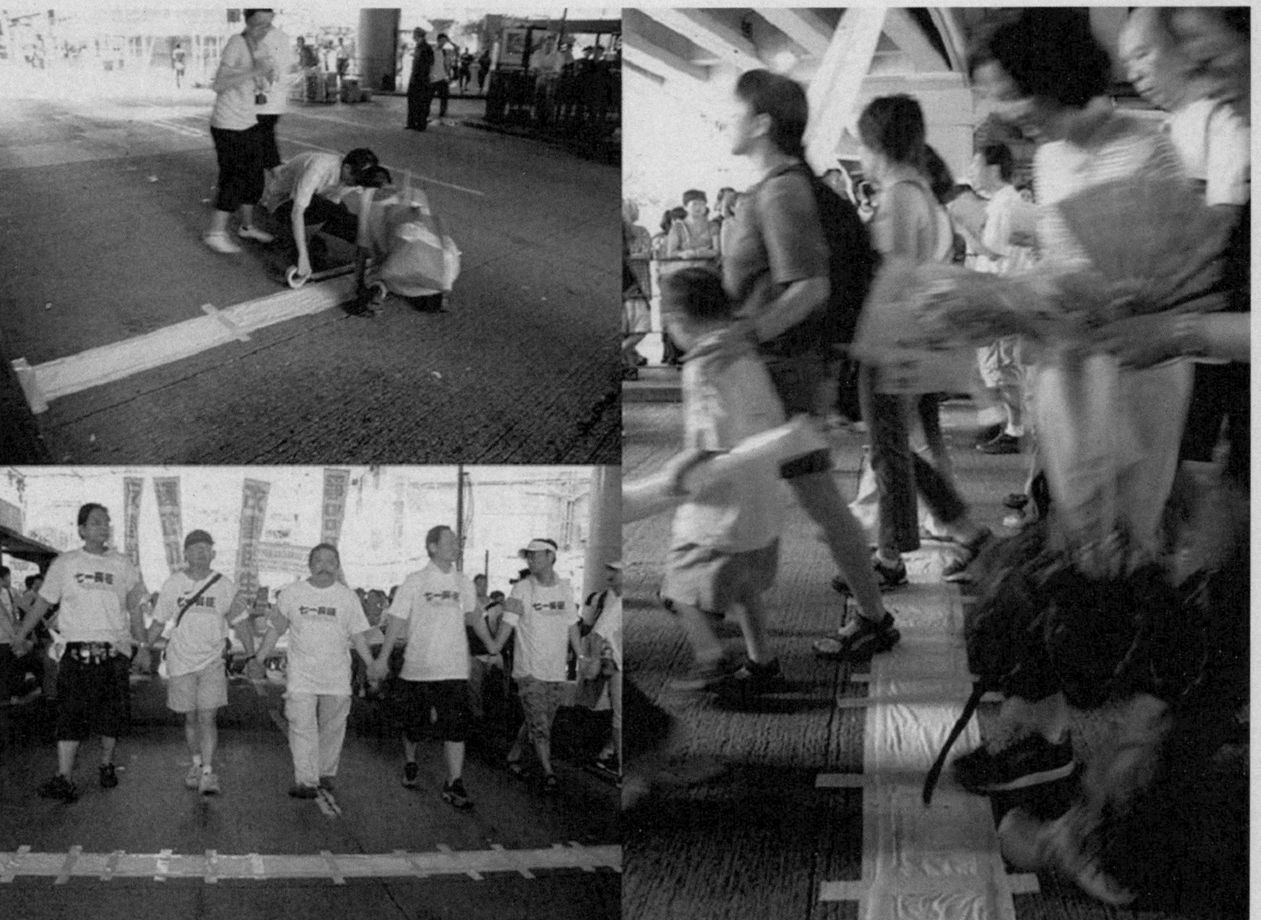

01.07.2005 (15:00-17:00)
Causeway Bay, Hong Kong
I laid a piece of yellow cloth (0.2 x 10 m) on
Hennessy Road to bear witness to the third
July 1st march. Cutting across the route, it
was placed so as to pick up the footprints
of the marchers.

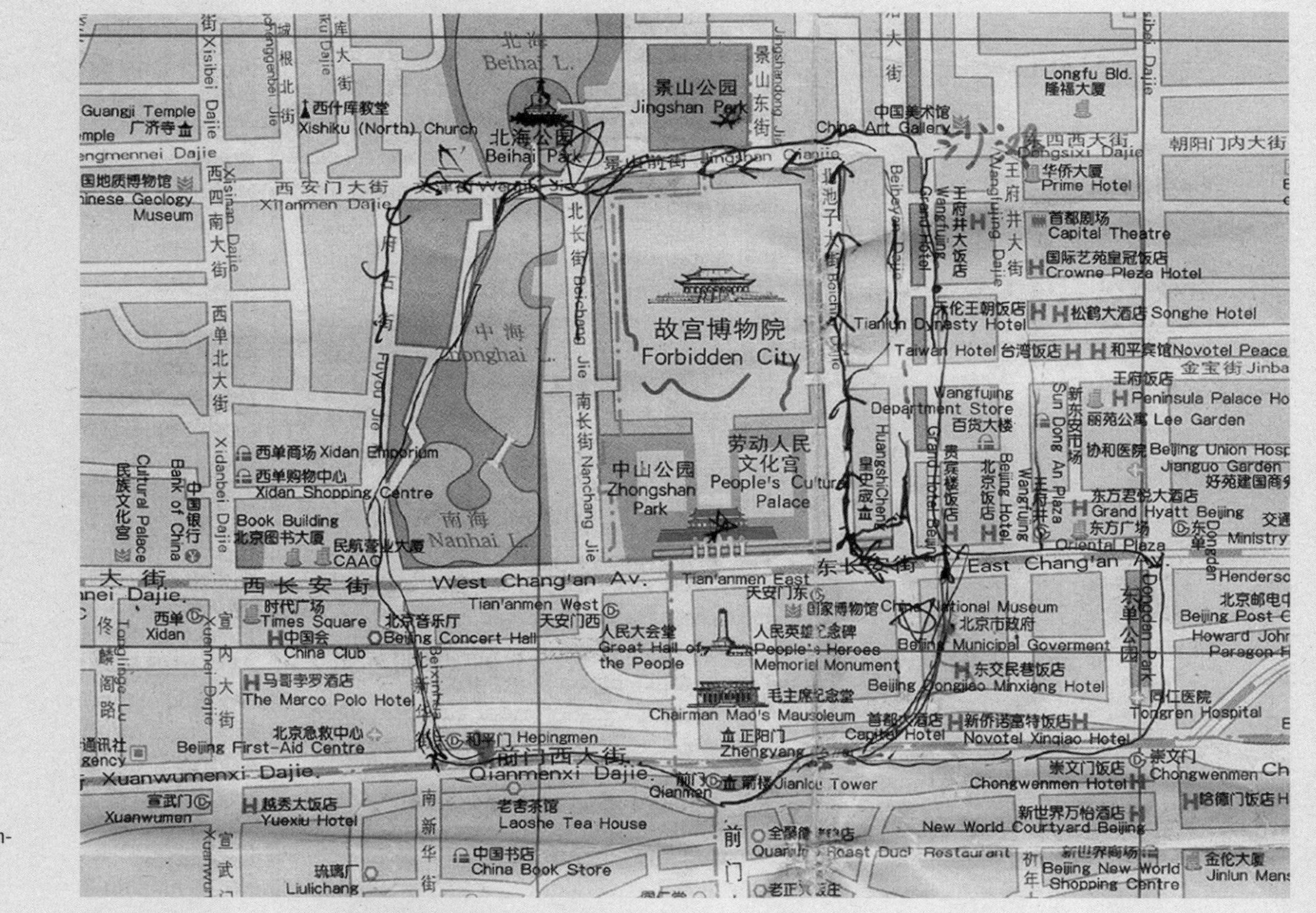

17.07.2005 (10:00–17:35)
Around the periphery of Tiananmen
Square, Beijing
I tore the yellow cloth into tiny ribbons.
Then I tied the ribbons around the periph-
ery of Tiananmen Square. (Afterward a
friend untied them from a distance.)

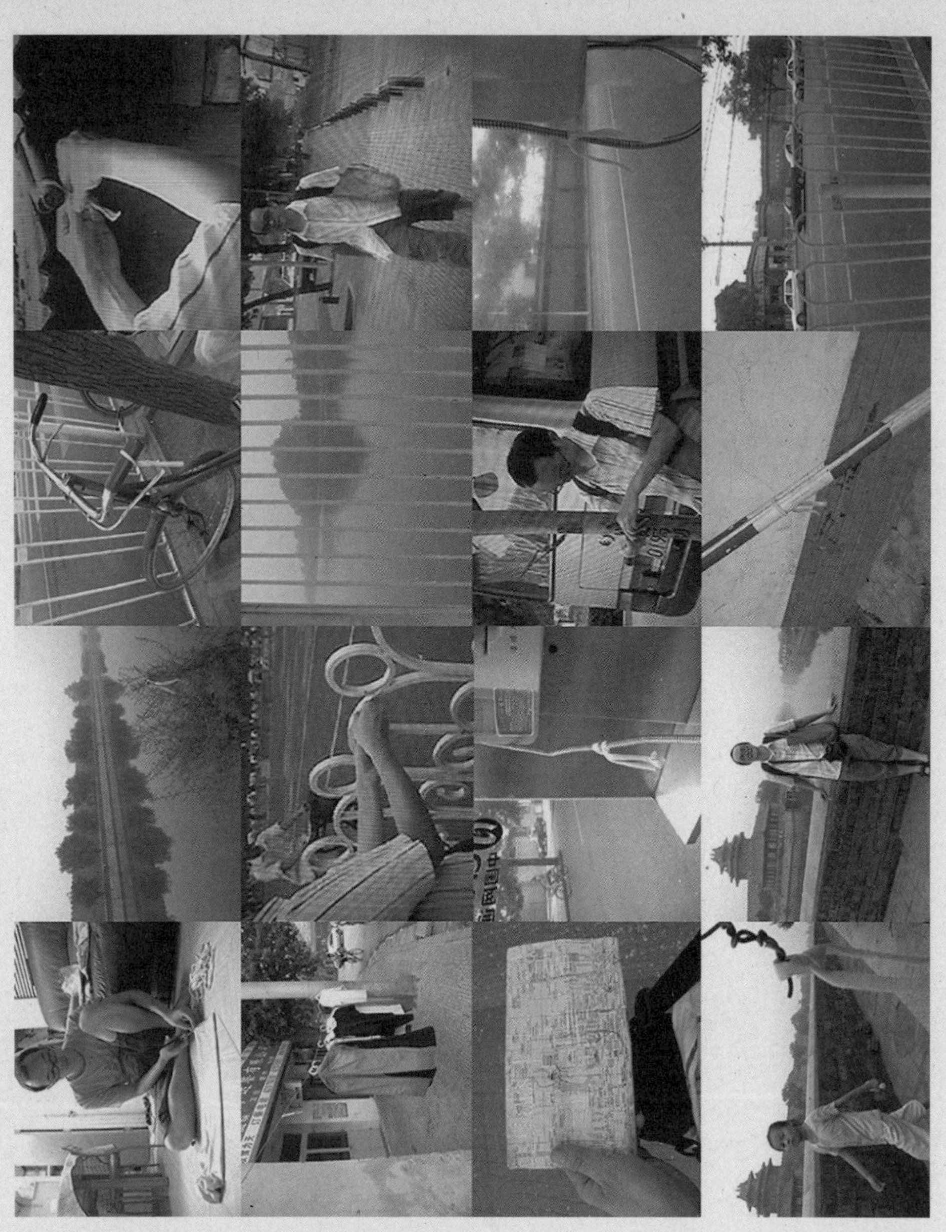

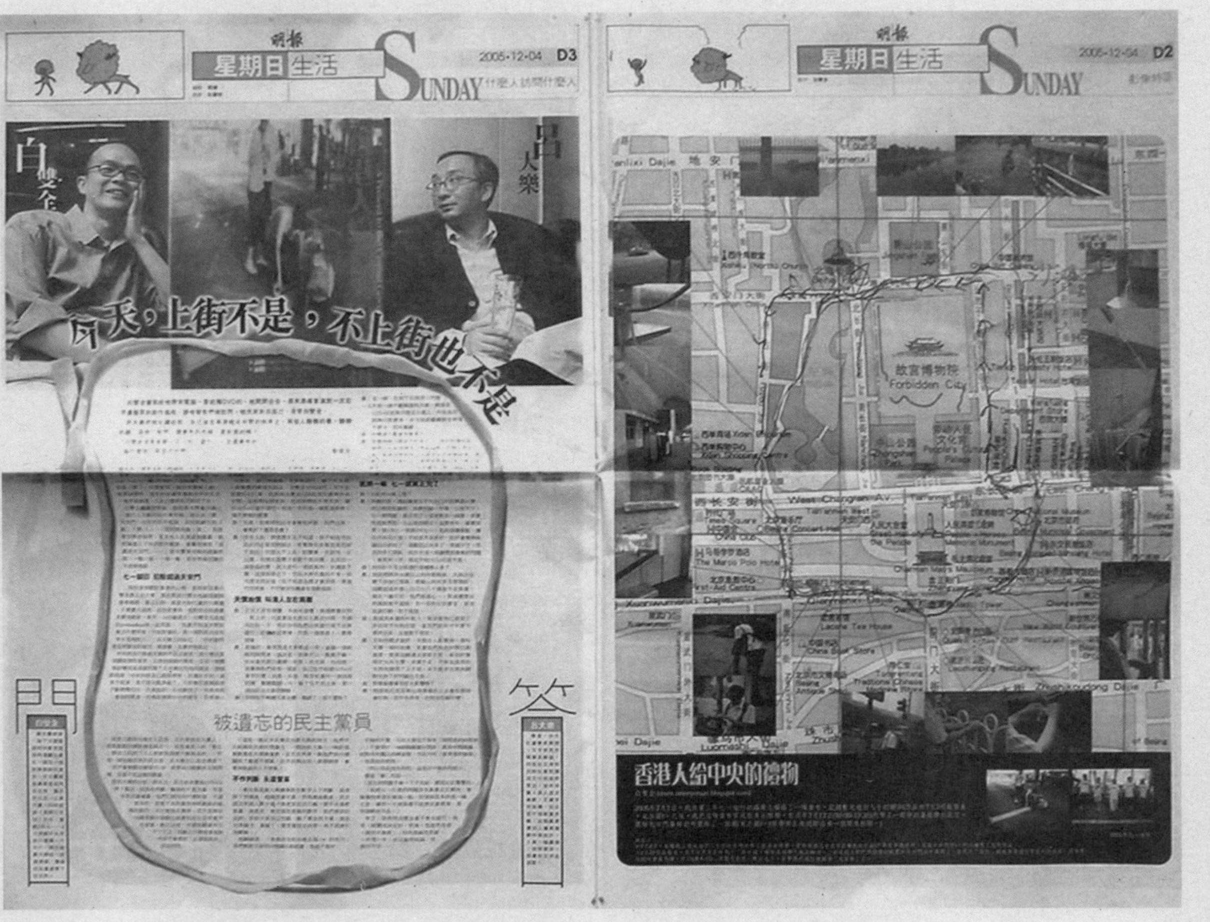

明報 星期日生活 SUNDAY 2005·12·04 D3
白雙全
音樂人
反天，上街不是，不上街也不是
被遺忘的民主黨員
問
答
明報 星期日生活 SUNDAY 2005·12·04 D2
香港人給中央的禮物
故宮博物院 Forbidden City

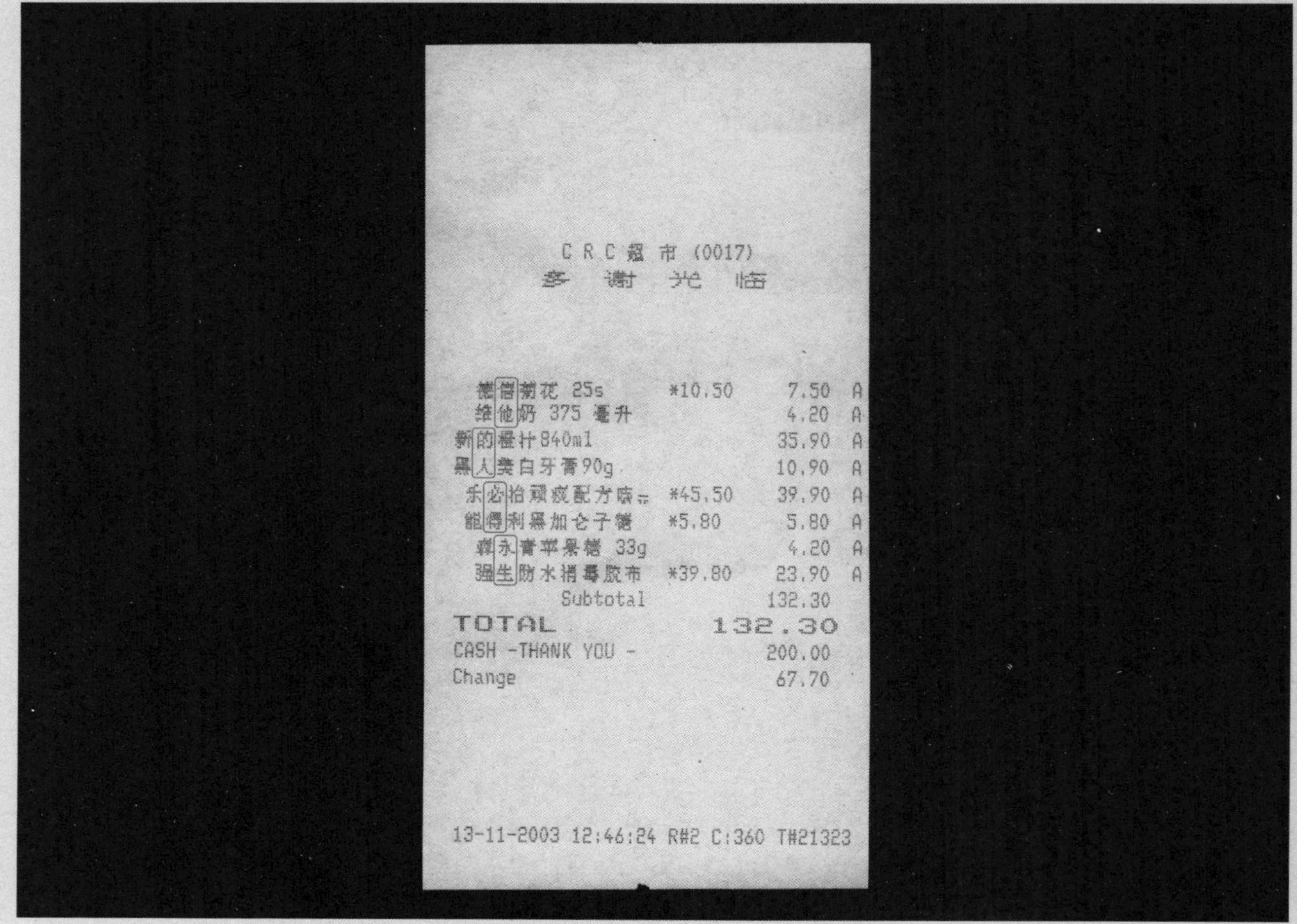

```
          C R C 超 市 (0017)
             多  謝  光  臨


  德 菊花 25s        *10.50      7.50   A
  維他奶 375 毫升                 4.20   A
  新的橙汁840ml                 35.90   A
  黑人美白牙膏90g                10.90   A
  乐必抬頹疯配方膏=   *45.50     39.90   A
  能得利黑加仑子饊    *5.80      5.80   A
  森永青苹果糖 33g               4.20   A
  强生防水猜毒胶布    *39.80    23.90   A
           Subtotal          132.30
TOTAL              132.30
CASH -THANK YOU -            200.00
Change                       67.70



13-11-2003 12:46:24 R#2 C:360 T#21323
```

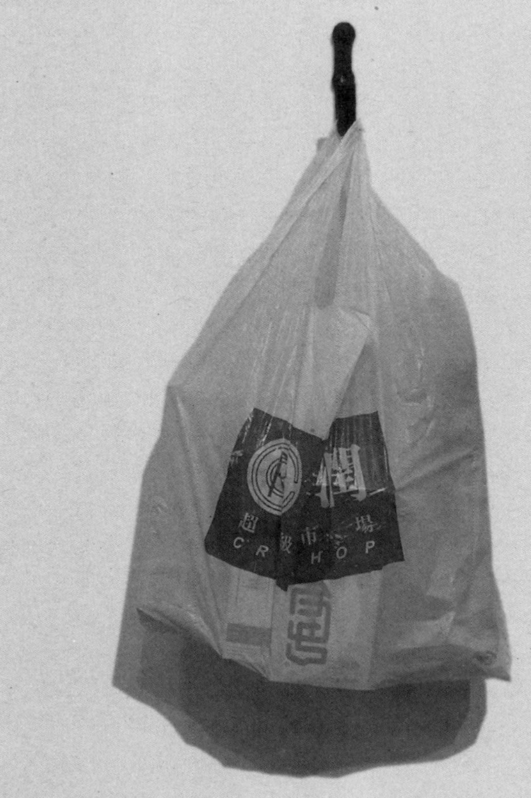

Miracle of $132.30

I bought eight items from the supermarket and got a receipt. If you read the second character of the name of each item from top to bottom, you will discover something extraordinary. It reads: Whoever believes in him should … have eternal life (John 3:16). (In Chinese: 信祂的人必得永生. 13.11.2003 12:46, Shatin CRC Supermarket, Hong Kong.)

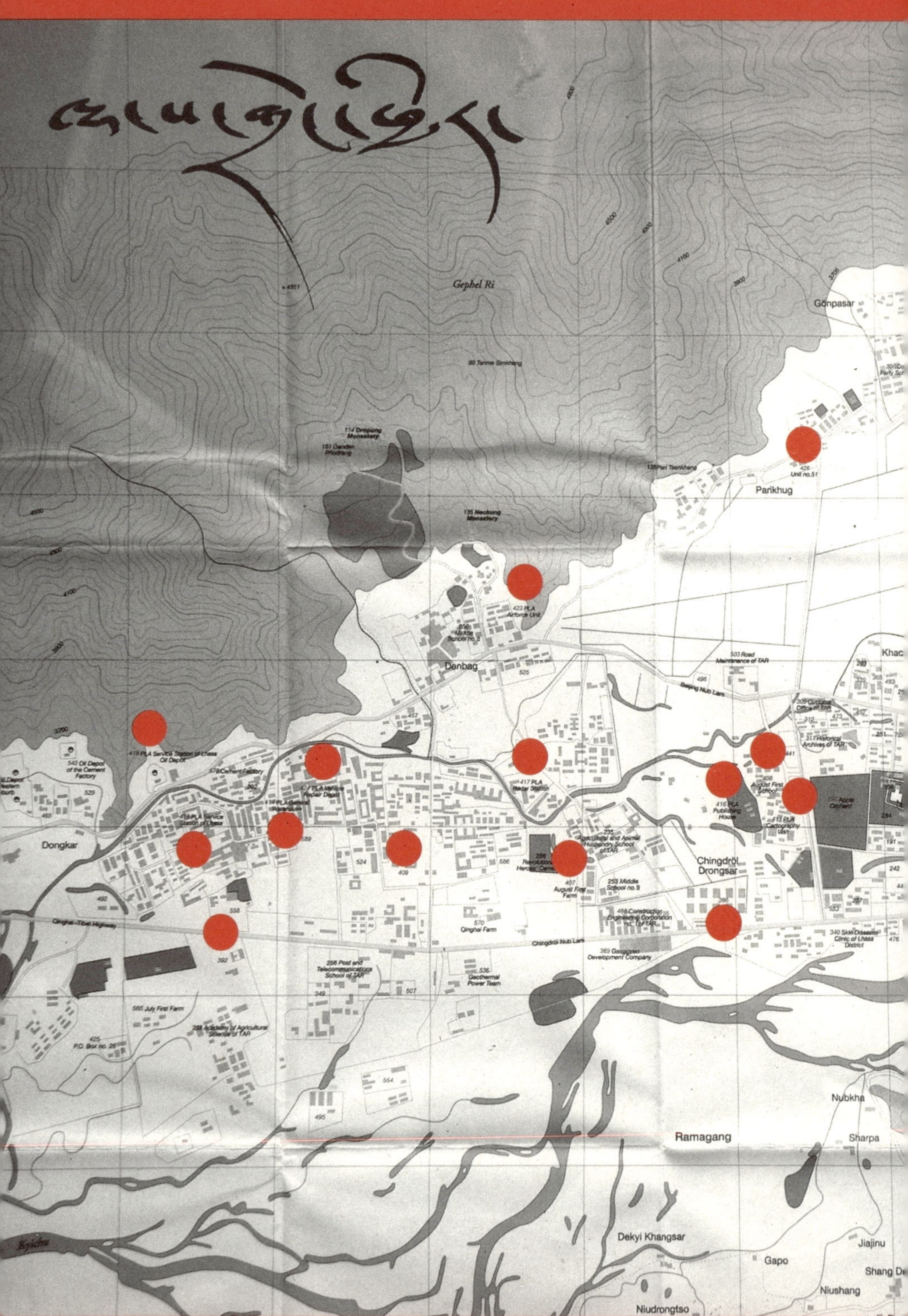

Source: Amnye Machen Institute, Dharamsala

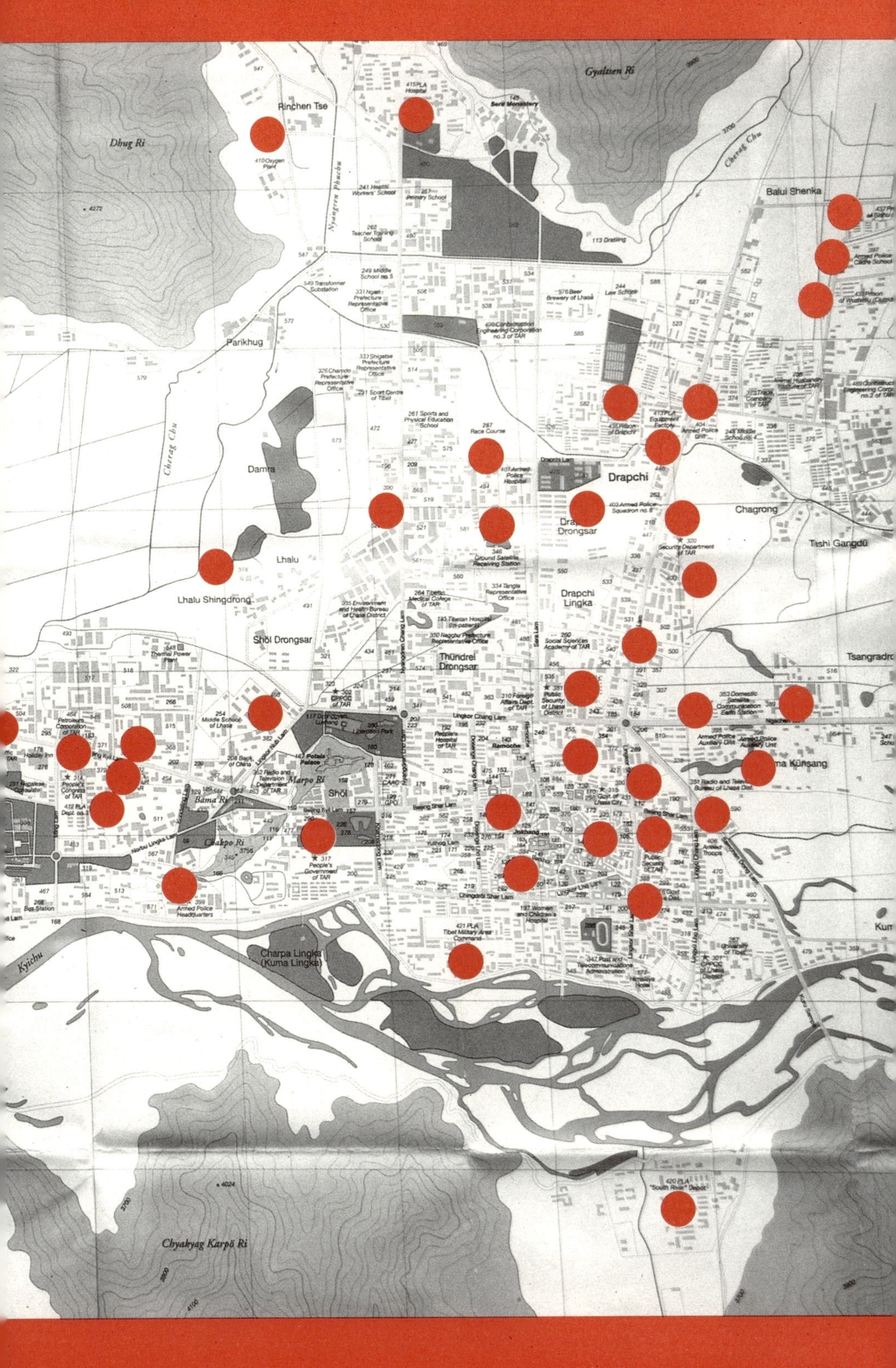

Gyaltsen Ri
Rinchen Tse
Dhug Ri
Balui Shenka
Sera Monastery
415 PLA Hospital
241 Health Workers' School
257 Primary School
262 Teacher Training School
249 Middle School no.5
331 Nyingtri Prefecture Representative Office
549 Transformer Substation
113 Drapling
Parikhug
579
326 Chamdo Prefecture Representative Office
333 Shigatse Prefecture Representative Office
291 Sport Centre of Tibet
261 Sports and Physical Education School
576 Beer Brewery of Lhasa
244 Law School
400 Construction Engineering Corporation no.3 of TAR
Damra
287 Race Course
401 Armed Police Hospital
413 PLA Equipment Factory
404 Armed Police Unit
243 Middle School no.4
Armed Police Cadre School
Prison of Wutsela (Outha)
Traffic Corporation of TAR
Drapchi
435 Prison of Drapchi
Drapchi Lam
403 Armed Police Squadron no.8
Chagrong
Tashi Gangdü
Lhalu
Dra Drongsar
Security Department of TAR
Lhalu Shingdrong
346 Ground Satellite Receiving Station
335 Environment and Health Bureau of Lhasa District
264 Tibetan Medical College of TAR
193 Tibetan Hospital
334 Tangla Representative Office
Drapchi Lingka
Shöl Drongsar
350 Nagchu Prefecture Representative Office
260 Social Sciences Academy of TAR
Tsangradro
Thermal Power Plant
Thündrel Drongsar
310 Foreign Affairs Dept. of TAR
281 Public Security of Lhasa District
363 Domestic Satellite Communication Earth Station
Petroleum Corporation of TAR
Middle School of Lhasa
117 Disinfection Liuxiang
Liberation Park
People's Hospital of TAR
204 Ramoche
Armed Police Auxiliary Unit
na Künsang
Holiday Inn
Tina Kyil Lam
People's Congress of TAR
208 Bank of China
312 Radio and Television Department of TAR
Potala Palace
140 Ramoche
Public Security of TAR
Radio and Television Bureau of Lhasa Dist.
412 PLA Dept. no.8
Marpo Ri
Shöl
CAAC
GPO
Barkhor
Golf of Lhasa City
Armed Troops
Bama Ri
Chakpo Ri
317 People's Government of TAR
Beijing Shar Lam
Yuthog Lam
Norbu Lingka Lam
Public Security of TAR
Bus Station
Armed Police Headquarters
Chingdol Shar Lam
197 Women and Children's Hospital
Radio and Television of Dist.
Charpa Lingka (Kuma Lingka)
421 PLA Tibet Military Area Command
342 Post and Telecommunications Administration
University of Tibet
301 of Lhasa District
Kyichu
Kum
Chyakyag Karpö Ri
420 PLA "South River" Depot

EVIDENTIAL MATTERS

"There is no political power without control of the archive, if not of memory. Effective democratization can always be measured by this essential criterion: the participation in and the access to the archive, its constitution, and its interpretation". (Jacques Derrida, "Archive Fever," 1997)

The immediate value of Derrida's reflection is that it strongly advocates the view that we should pay as much attention to the power of the archive as to the question of governance, of those who legislate over and those who participate in its construction and use. One of the effects of this is to raise the legal and juridical role of the archive as composed of evidential traces of that which has taken place. And yet, nonetheless, there is no guarantee that the material which belongs to the archive is sufficient as evidence that serves a juridical function. There would need to be corroborating evidence, other sources. What constitutes evidence is itself established in relation to a juridical precedent and therefore its validity as to being permissible or not. What would result, too, if one was to observe that the state was fundamentally archival in its impulse, seeking to govern its citizens through the processes and procedures that provide a means of documenting the course of everyday life as much as measuring its subject? However, in such cases, we may argue that such processes and procedures are not autonomous to that of the interests of the governing body. Rather they are, in fact, shaped by those interests and results that serve best in shaping evidence and means of governance.

In the twentieth century, the literary and visual arts has entered the archive precisely because it has served as a form of evidence. For instance, the fate of many poets, artists, and filmmakers who lived in the Soviet Union demonstrates not only the tragedy of their lives and the power that artistic form can have while they live and as evidence long after they pass away. They serve as testimony to these individual and collective histories. Similarly, there exists writing and art produced during or in the years following the Armenian genocide or the Holocaust that serves as memory or witness to the fact of these events. Whatever remains, whether it be fragment or trace, is, in the absence of all other forms of material evidence except for those who survived, critical to the formation of a historical archive.

In the light of such histories, we may view the concepts of evidence and the archive as critical points of reference in the practice of a number of contemporary artists. However, these different and specific histories inform the kind of practices undertaken, not in a manner of determination but, rather, as to how best to engage with the limits of the archive. The following remarks offer ways to understand the specific and distinct kinds of practices that have emerged as a form of response, and which are the focus of the exhibition. Moreover, we may view these practices as bringing to bear in effect a tacit reading of, if not challenge to, dominant notions of the evidential.

This is not to undervalue the practices of those working in and around the archive. To the contrary, it seems imperative to understand their work if only to recognize the potential power and characterize the limits of their approaches. Christian Boltanski or, in a very different manner, Ilya Kabakov, have both developed extraordinary practices that expose the dark underbelly of artistic modernism's complicity with political modernity and the model of authoritarian state culture. For Boltanski as for others, it is the perpetual failure of the archive to ever be sufficient that leads to restorative efforts, even if only traces of a subject or historical event—insufficient, partial, buried, or absent—is manifest in its archival representation. This approach seeks to recognize the archive an abysmal space, and to render visible the endless task of its construction.

AND YET THIS PROJECT RISKS A CERTAIN MADNESS: REMEMBERING IS A FRAGILE ACT, MOST ESPECIALLY WHEN IT IS FACED WITH THE APPARATUSES OF THE STATE OR WITH GUARDIANS OF THE ARCHIVE. IN THIS RESPECT, THERE IS A VIOLENCE IN ITS CONSTRUCTION—NOT ONLY AS REGARDS WHAT ENTERS THE ARCHIVE BUT ALSO IN WHO AUTHORIZES ITS CONSTITUTION.

An alternative approach to that employed by Boltanski has been developed in response to such regimes or institutional apparatus. For artists like Kabakov, who have lived and worked within the logic of communism, the absurdity of history as with the forms of inscription and recollection, is immediately apparent. These artists' practices perform a parody of the archive insofar as history becomes a social construction, open to being formed and shaped according to the dictates of its authorizing force. The radical consequences of this position are fundamentally disastrous. For if we accept this position, there exists the possibility that lived "histories" can be either invented or made to disappear while there exists nothing in the way of corroborating evidence to its factuality. It depends purely upon the authority that instates it and the idea of the self-evident as being sufficient. This creates a radically different manner through which history finds its forms of inscription, forms that may not have a visual analogue. We may mention here other approaches that challenge what properly belongs to the archive or is adequate to the notion of evidence insofar as its depends upon the veracity of *videre,* the visual domain, as "evidence." Introducing the space of orality can serve as "evidence" to unwritten histories, and yet, what is this evidence of more than the existence of these voices? And whose voices are they, precisely? What value do these re-presentations, albeit recordings, have, except in the most existential manner that these voices are signs of an embodied existence of persons no longer present? From this perspective the phrase "voice of the people" is to be understood for what it is not. The archive in this context can also be used to destabilize the validity of such speech.

The significance of each of these approaches is as much in their limits as to what they have achieved as artistic strategies. One critical way to respond is by constructing a counter-archive that makes evident a multiplicity of points of view and produces a disjunctive form that resists the appeal of the solitary point of view as being adequate to the truth of history. History lies in the unspoken or absent, the footnotes or the interstitial spaces between its main actors. For many artists, as with writers and filmmakers, this view has led them to turn to the fictional as a form through which to explore subjects and domains of experience otherwise unremarked upon or unaccounted for. Yet, one cannot contest fiction except by proposing a notion of the "real" against which it may be measured. What is its veracity, or what is an internal logic that exists outside of the domain of the real? This challenge leads others to question as to how to use the archive against itself.

The challenge is especially felt in a society where different points of view or positions cannot legally be held or brought to bear upon the understanding of past events. In those societies with a controlling state apparatus, the issue of representation is of the utmost critical importance, and carries with it the freight of the evidential document and the archive. In such cases, the role of the state presides over all forms of re-presentation. According to the law, matters concerning what are permitted as admissible evidence, burden of proof, and witnesses are subjected to state law. If the state does not distinguish between its own power and the authority of the Law—the latter requiring an independent status—then the results are disastrous not only for authority of the law but also for the constitutive formation of the archive as one of the underpinnings of a democratic state.

Recent years have also brought a return to the domain of the document, seeking not so much to contest the ideological reading brought to bear upon its subject but, rather, the issue becomes the status and authority of the document itself. What constitutes a document in the first place? What gives it its authority? The practice of some individuals working across the spectrum of the arts has produced (even if indirectly) new forms of evidence. In this manner, these figures challenge the conventional definitions of the document that, in turn, provoke the question of what constitutes and delimits the archive as a sufficient source of evidence for the materiality of lives led. In aligning literature or art to that of political activity, Jacques Rancière argues for a "mode of expression that undoes the perceptible divisions of the police order by implementing a basically heterogeneous assumption of [...] the equality of any seeking being with any other speaking being."[1] This form of practice is in effect more direct, more contestational of the dominant or hegemonic way in which history is written and to what ends it is deployed. Rather than seeking a mode that is essentially oppositional, as in fiction, these artists act to delegitimize the prescriptive terms of definition. Through an expansion as to what is permitted, they bring to bear a different perception and knowledge of a subject.

This essay suggests a set of practices that are grounded in a very different field upon which such knowledge is elaborated. This field attaches itself to forms of social activism while, at the same time, recognizes the very real institutional limits of legibility. This has to do not only with dominant conventions of reading that inform the reception and dissemination of visual practices but also with the recognition of the limits of the archive, of the ways it in effect acts as a legitimating device. Critical to this view is a recognition of the constitutive violence of the archive. As the philosopher Jacques Derrida discusses in his book "Archive Fever," this violence is the founding impulse of archival desire. This recognition allows artists working with (or against) the archive to consider the form of their own practice in relation to both the subject and the defining site of a historical practice on the part of authoritarian regimes. However, insofar as it provides a historical framework in which the formation of the archive is situated, it admits also to a space lying outside its formation—a delegitimized space, in effect—whose recognition, livelihood, and form of survival is always at stake.

The constitutive potential of digital forms such as videos and online blogs—employed by the Cybermohalla Ensemble and Raqs Media Collective—recognize the power of dissemination on which they depend for their distribution. The function of distribution is folded into the agency of dissemination, providing in the process a critical tool by which to contest still other forms. In this regard,

BLOGS AND THE INTERNET RADICALLY DISTINGUISH THEMSELVES FROM THE ARCHIVE INSOFAR AS THE CONCEPT OF INTERACTIVITY IS BASED ON EXCHANGE AND THEREFORE IS ALWAYS OUTSIDE THE DOMAIN OF A SINGLE POINT OF VIEW OR SOURCE.

This characteristic diminishes the authority that underscores the principle of the archive. This struggle to authorize is evident in the efforts made by archivists to develop a practice that has both a methodological and a theoretical basis for the inclusion of sound recordings, video, web material, etc. Such materials have, of course, already entered into the archive, yet their status remains uncertain. For what can be properly admitted to the archive? This question becomes, as suggested earlier, on what terms can such material be classified, and, in effect, be contained with the laws governing the archive? Contemporary artists and media practitioners have recognized this distinction and the tremendous potential of more mobile forms of dissemination as the vehicle for their work. In its ability to stream moving images, the website or blog not only transforms the power of video and film production, but also, and more critically, converts still images, archival material, records, and evidence into a mobile form of transmission.

The integral importance of this mobility is seen most clearly in the status given to myths, fables, and beliefs. Their power and ability to survive resides precisely in their ability to circulate. This is implicit, for example, in the recent work by the Raqs Media Collective, *Unfamilar Tales,* which incorporates both Burmese and Tibetan Buddhism as subtexts through which to contest the authoritarian power of secular governments. In this regard, we may also defer to the image referred to in the title of Amar Kanwar's most recent work, *The Torn First Pages,* a nineteen-channel video installation that was commissioned by Thyssen-Bornemisza Art Contemporary. The title describes specifically the act of Ko Than Htay, owner of a bookshop in Burma who has been imprisoned for tearing out of the books for sale the first page on which are inserted ideological statements by the Burmese military government. While mimicking the "Ex-Libris" of ownership, the intervention of the government, its authority of imprimatur or signature, changes the status of the book. True to the ethos and belief of the Burmese state, it becomes an ideological instrument governing the legitimacy of the book. This becomes a symbol for the project but, also, a reflection on the issue of the archive. For, strictly speaking, an archivist can only make the case for retaining this page. This would preserve its passage in time and determine its status as archival as opposed to the library. The ripping out of this page is not only an act of defiance but also an appeal to reinstate the democratic right of individuals to publish or speak without the intervention an agent of the state's authority. To accompany his work Kanwar writes, "Imagine the formal presentation of poetry as evidence in a future war crimes tribunal. Imagine nineteen sheets of paper floating forever in the wind."

The achievement of this body of artists' work, as with others in the exhibition, is to shift the ground of their practice towards collaborative action, an engagement that is precisely not about representation or the politics embedded in praxis. Neither an object of representation, on the one hand, nor identifiable as subjective or neutral on the other, such *modus operandi* situates the artist's work as a form of agency, a performative engagement through dialogue as dissemination. As a form of dialogue, this space offers different modalities through which not only think through the question of what constitutes evidence, but to expand its conception in the light of those who seek recognition.

— CHARLES MEREWETHER

1. Rancière, Jacques (1999), "Disagreement: Politics and Philosophy", Minneapolis: University of Minnesota Press, p. 30.

LHASA IS FAR AWAY...

The geographical inaccessibility and spiritual mystery of Tibet have endowed it with the mythology of an earthly utopia—the forbidden realm of Shangri-La. Lured by the promise of a divine kingdom, over the past few years Qiu Zhijie has been traveling to Tibet in an ongoing art project that challenges the premises of an idealized state of utopia, investigating its sociocultural realities, shining a light on local perspectives and beliefs regarding art and religion, through an engagement with history and lived experience.

The project to date can be seen as a journey—a pilgrimage of ideas, of cultural capabilities and processes of communication. In its course Qiu Zhijie has explored artistic and social developments as expressed through painting in *Subverting Shangri-La—a Survey of Tibetan Subject Matter in Painting* (showcased as exhibition at Long March Space in 2007); he has physically retraced the steps of Indian cartographer Nain Singh while engaging with local communities in a reinterpretation of the past and of future forecasts in *A Railway from Lhasa to Kathmandu* (2006–07); and created the performance and photographic work *Lhasa Is Far Away, America Is Far Away* (2007).[1]

A Railway from Lhasa to Kathmandu

Qiu Zhijie's monumental and painstaking undertaking of walking from Lhasa to Kathmandu with fetters attached to his ankles in an attempt to regulate the length of each stride was inspired by the historical figure of the pundit (explorer) Nain Singh. In 1863, as part of the Great Trigonometric Survey of 1802–66, Nain Singh became one of the first foreigners to successfully enter and survey roads in Tibet. In the first half of the nineteenth century, the British Survey of India made several abortive attempts to map the lands that lay beyond Tibet, but the Tibetan border was closed to foreigners. Several men of the survey died in this attempt, until Thomas G. Montgomerie decided to recruit Indians, disguised as itinerant lamas, to "spy out the land." Nain Singh was a thirty-three-year-old Tibetan-speaking headmaster of a school in Milan, in the upper Himalayas. Together with his cousin Mani Singh, he was prepared for his mission in a rigorous two-year course for training Indian surveyors, or "chain men," as they came to be called. They were first trained to walk in a measured fashion, each pace measuring exactly thirty-three inches, and to record their progress with rosary beads.

Equipped with sextants, which they carried concealed in specially designed secret pockets within their clothes; thermometers for altitude measurements; mercury, required for setting an artificial horizon from which to take altitude readings; and Tibetan prayer wheels, which were modified so that the surveyors could record their observations on these paper strips, the two pundits finally departed on their first mission in 1865. With this primitive apparatus, Nain Singh spent the entire summer journeying to the

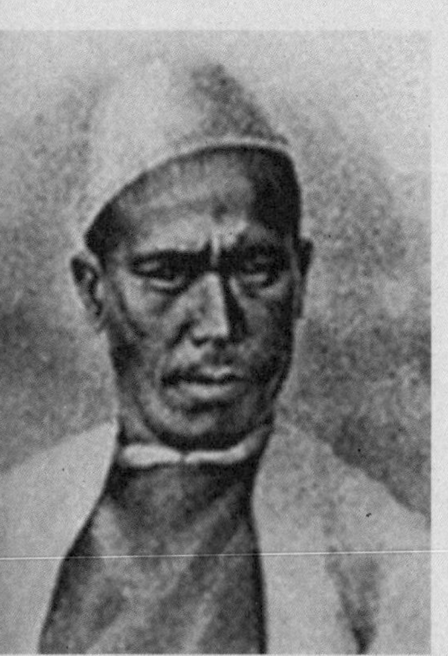

Nain Singh

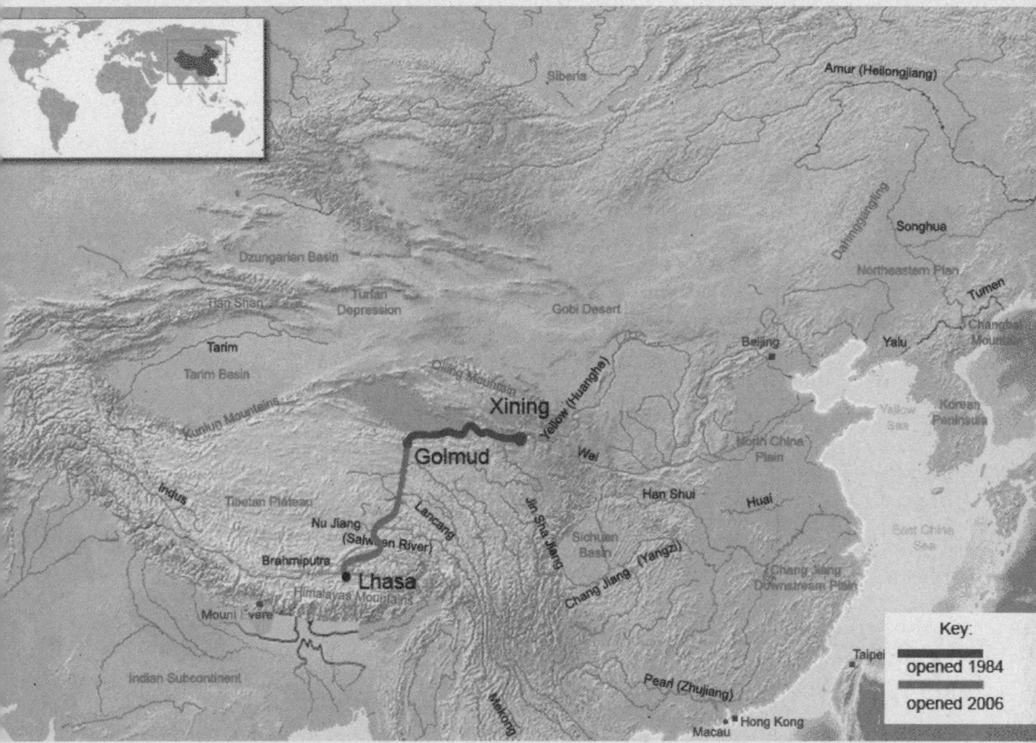

Map of Qinghai–Tibet-Railway

"forbidden" city of Lhasa, which he reached in January 1866. During this trip and his subsequent expeditions, he succeeded in charting the route through large parts of Tibet. His maps provided the only definitive information on the Tibetan plateau and the mountainous border regions for almost half a century, until the next British party was able to reach Tengri Nor.

The desire to map the "uncharted" territories of the Tibetan plateau was significantly related to the geopolitical importance of the area. As a "blank space," the Himalayan plateau, which constitutes about 25 percent of what is now the People's Republic of China, constitutes an area of possible infiltration and contingency between British-ruled India and dynastic China. The Chinese influence on the Himalayan plateau represented a possible threat to the British interests and their status of "dominant power" in South Asia and possibly on the Asian continent altogether.

At the same time the mysterious and mystical lands of Tibet became the imaginary for a quasi-fictional place—the Shambhala, the storied ancient kingdom hidden in the snow peaks of the Himalayas, or, in its popularized version, the Shangri-La of James Hilton. "Of course, in the late 19th century, the British were motivated less by seeking enlightenment than in unlocking borders that would assist in the formulation of political, economically-driven policies. What followed in the early 1900s (beginning with the expedition led by Francis Younghusband in 1904) wasn't exactly an invasion, but it certainly changed the course of history for Tibet."[2]

Based on this research, Qiu Zhijie started to chart his own trip through the

Himalayan plateau, embarking on an expedition that was both a historical revisitation, a retracing of the Tibetan colonial expeditions, and a performance in real time and geopolitical space. In addition to the traces of memory inscribed in the history and imaginary of Tibet by Nain Singh, Qiu Zhijie researched a number of other expeditions into Tibet, specifically by Krishna Singh, a brother of Nain Singh, and like him an important pundit. Furthermore, the expeditions of Nikolai Mikhailovich Przhevalsky, a Russian general and traveler whose explorations were major contributions to the geography of central Asia, and Sven Anders Hedin, a Swedish explorer and geographer whose investigations in Tibet and western China made him one of the most eminent explorers of Asia, are inscribed in Qiu's map of Tibet, as are the journeys of the "mystic, anarchist, occultist and traveler" Alexandra David-Neel, the first Western woman to enter Tibet in 1924. But in Qiu's own undertaking, he would not only follow the foot-steps of the explorer but also "reenact" the process of measurement, mapping, and surveying that was at the core of Nain's expedition.

"AS WE EMBARKED UPON OUR RE-SEARCH, I CAME ACROSS THE FIGURE OF NAIN SINGH—THE FIRST PERSON RE-ALLY TO PENETRATE TIBET. I HAVE AL-WAYS BEEN FASCINATED BY MAPS, SO IT ALL MADE SENSE. I DECIDED THAT, AS A CONTEMPORARY HOMAGE TO NAIN, I WOULD WALK THE OTHER WAY, FROM LHASA TO KATHMANDU, ATTEMPTING TO FOLLOW EXACTLY THE SAME PRO-TOCOLS HE HAD AT HIS DISPOSAL FOR MAPPING THE JOURNEY. I WOULD WEAR A FETTER ON MY ANKLES TO RESTRICT MY STRIDES TO THE SAME EXACT MEASURE OF PACE SO AS TO RECORD DISTANCES COVERED, AND ADOPT THE SAME TECHNIQUES FOR CALCULATING ALTITUDE AND ORIENTATION. THIS JOUR-NEY, MY 'MAP', AND ALL ACCOMPANYING DOCUMENTATION ARE THE CORE OF THE WORK."

As the title *A Railway from Lhasa to Kathmandu* indicates, Qiu's extraordinary journey is related to another "expedition", which possibly has had and will have in the future a far greater impact on Tibetan history, and that is Lhasa's connection to the Chinese railway system and its future extension into Nepal. Extending a total of nearly 2,000 kilometers, the Qinghai-Tibet Railway is a major strategic and symbolic tool in China's Western development plan and a consolidation of China's political control of the region. Since its completion in 2006 the railway has facilitated a mass influx of Chinese traders, temporary migrants, and other Han populations into the Tibetan Autonomous Region as well as the industrial exploitation and removal of natural resources—in the official language to "promote the development of impoverished Tibet."[3] By reassimilating Tibet into China, the railway confers legitimacy and prestige on the Communist Party as the institution that has reversed centuries of weakness and territorial fragmentation through such an impressive feat of engineering. "The second background to the project is the launch of the Qinghai-Tibet Railway on July 1st 2006, which is without doubt an epoch-making event in Tibetan history. It struck me that nothing the British could have done back then, nor even the imposition of Chinese sovereignty (in 1959), will have as much impact upon Tibet and the traditional way of life as the opening of a railroad connection between Golmud and Lhasa. The railway will be the instrument that will destroy the myths about Tibet, as it will allow everyone to discover its mysteries. The image of monks on motorbikes wielding mobile phones is hard to imagine, but it's part of the new reality. The railway is the modern world's invasion of Tibet. None of us can predict what it ultimately means for the Tibetan way of life. It has already changed so much from the old, traditional ways," states Qiu Zhijie.

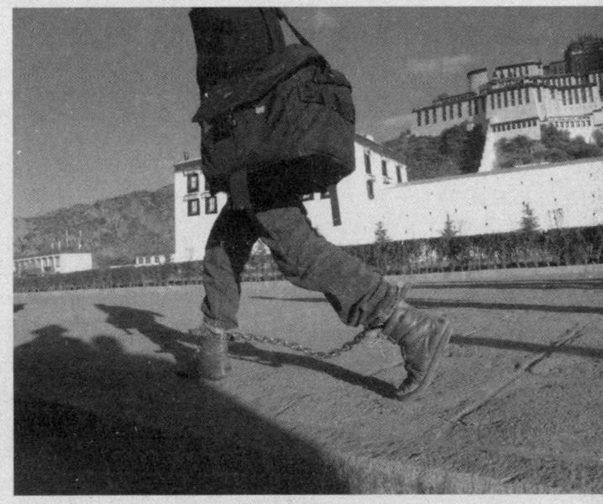

Video-still from *A Railway from Lhasa to Kathmandu*

Lhasa Is Far Away, America Is Far Away

As part of his journey from Lhasa to Kathmandu, Qiu Zhijie completed another work, *Lhasa Is Far Away, America Is Far Away* (2007). Combining history and geography, engaging with the idea of the individual and everyday necessities, Qiu Zhijie produced this work throughout this journey. For this project Qiu utilized ten special "Mani" stones, which are used as name boards distributed along the railway from Lhasa to Kathmandu. Qiu Zhijie has written two sentences on each Mani stone, replacing the stop names: "Lhasa is far away from here" and "America is far away from here." These two sentences, taken from an English textbook used in a primary school in Tibet, are carved onto each Mani stone by Tibetans who live in the foothills of the Medicine Emperor Mountain. Qiu placed nine of these stones at nine stops on the way from Lhasa to Kathmandu: Medicine Emperor Mountain, the railway of Nimu county seat,

Baiju Tower in Jiangzi county seat, the mountain at the back of the temple in Rike Zezha Shilunbu, the entrance of Zhu Mountain Road in Dingri county seat, the entrance of Niela Mu mountain, the garret at the police station in Zhangmu Kouan, and Kate Xinbu temple at the old city zone in Kathmandu. Nowadays these Mani stones with the written sentences have probably been mixed with other stones, or have disappeared and started their own journey in everyday life in Tibet. Qiu carried the last Mani stone to Beijing for this exhibition. Wherever these stones exist, however, they are far away from Lhasa and far away from America as well. In other words, through this work Qiu emphasizes that even if we live in Lhasa, we are far away from it. Similarly, even if we live in America, we are still far away from it.[4]

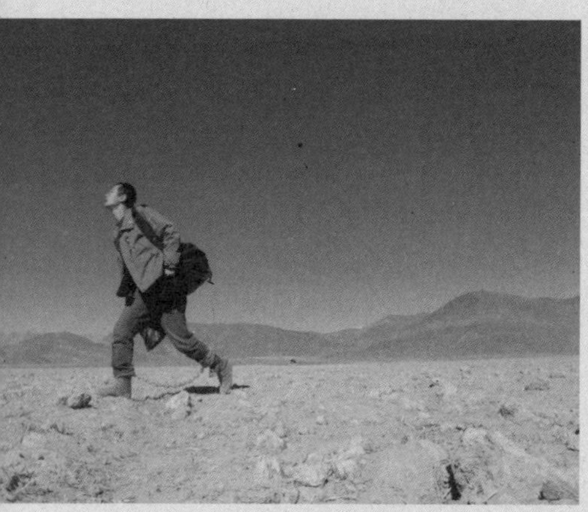

Video-still from _A Railway from Lhasa to Kathmandu_

What makes Qiu Zhijie's Tibetan journeys and the resulting practices so exceptional in today's Chinese artistic landscape is for one his overt exploration of the Tibetan presence or nonpresence within China, its coding as the Other—that which remains unspoken and repressed—or as the scholar of Tibetan culture Robert Barnett has remarked: "One of the most strange and in a way, the most troubling things, about the Chinese approach to the Tibet issue has been that apart from the government and the Party and then almost only in written form, no Chinese people have dared to speak about the Tibet issue. It's almost unheard of for Chinese intellectuals, Chinese scholars to appear in their own name speaking to the public in the West about the Tibet issue."[5] Furthermore, Qiu Zhijie has developed a meticulous practice of reflecting upon and collecting the factual evidence, what he calls the traces, residues, or memories—in a linguistic and archaeological sense, an artistic fieldwork of sorts—of contemporary society's experience with its socialist past and present. As a researcher and investigator, he is aware of the clichéd appeal of socialist or Maoist nostalgia but also of the tacit "tolerance" for totalitarian regimes so characteristic of some of Western geopolitical discourse but also of a certain conformist attitude within China: "One hundred years of revolutionary struggle and the lived experience of socialism not only influence every facet of contemporary society in China, but have also left a deep residue in the memory of the people. This permeates every corner of Chinese contemporary visual culture, becoming a resource—sometimes apparent, sometimes not—for Chinese contemporary art. Revisiting revolutionary memory in this way, we hope neither to parody nor to subvert the conservative or authoritative elements of socialist life. Nor do we seek to turn history into mythology by simplifying the past, maintaining the integrity of the grand narrative via creative nostalgia. Our working method is to subtly explore this historical period's traces in contemporary visual culture, re-organizing the chaos and rescuing it from overused, canonized discourse. We must search for the points where historical memories converge with contemporary ideological trends, re-sensitizing ourselves to the subject and bringing the past into the present so that we can examine the traces' effects, both negative and positive. This requires the integration of fieldwork and linguistic analysis, of the archaeology and architecture of knowledge."[6]

— DANIELA ZYMAN

1. Qiu Zhijie, original project description.
2. All quotations from the artist are from Karen Smith, "[Rai]lway from Lhasa to Kathmandu", http://www.qiuzhijie.com/NEWS/e-lajia.htm.
3. "China Completes Railway to Tibet", BBC News, October 15, 2005, http://news.bbc.co.uk/2/hi/asia-pacific/4345494.stm.
4. Qiu Zhijie, original project description.
5. Robert Barnett, unpublished interview by Ritu Sarin and Tenzing Sonam, 2008.
6. Lu Jie and Qiu Zhijie, "Curators' Words", Discourse, http://www.longmarchspace.com/english/e-discourse5.htm.

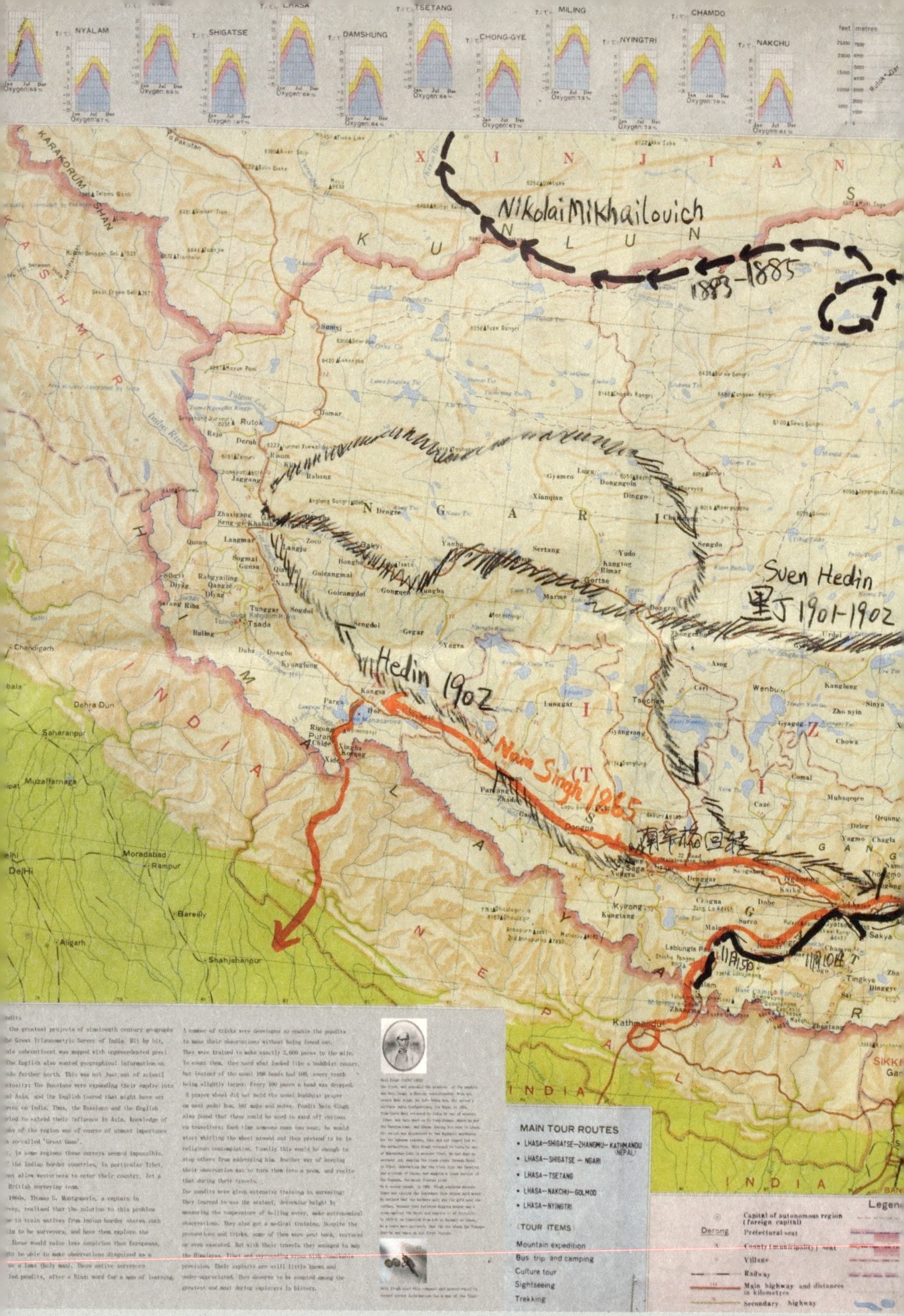

QIU ZHIJIE
A RAILWAY FROM LHASA
TO KATHMANDU, 2006-07

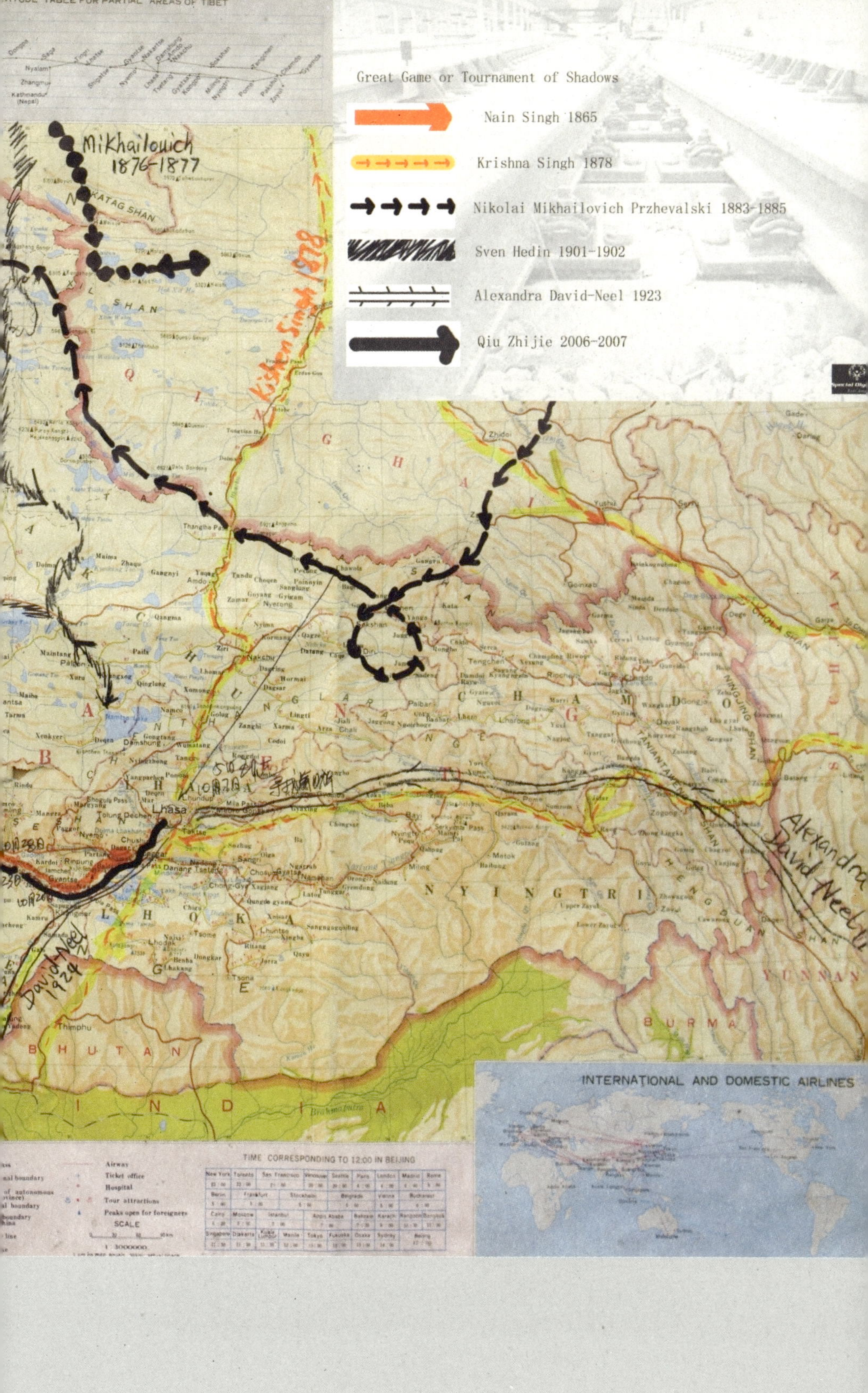
TITUDE TABLE FOR PARTIAL AREAS OF TIBET
Mikhailovich 1876-1877
Kishen Singh 1878
Great Game or Tournament of Shadows
Nain Singh 1865
Krishna Singh 1878
Nikolai Mikhailovich Przhevalski 1883-1885
Sven Hedin 1901-1902
Alexandra David-Neel 1923
Qiu Zhijie 2006-2007
Alexandra David-Neel 1924
Lhasa
BHUTAN
INDIA
BURMA
YUNNAN
NYINGTRI
INTERNATIONAL AND DOMESTIC AIRLINES
TIME CORRESPONDING TO 12:00 IN BEIJING
SCALE
1:3000000

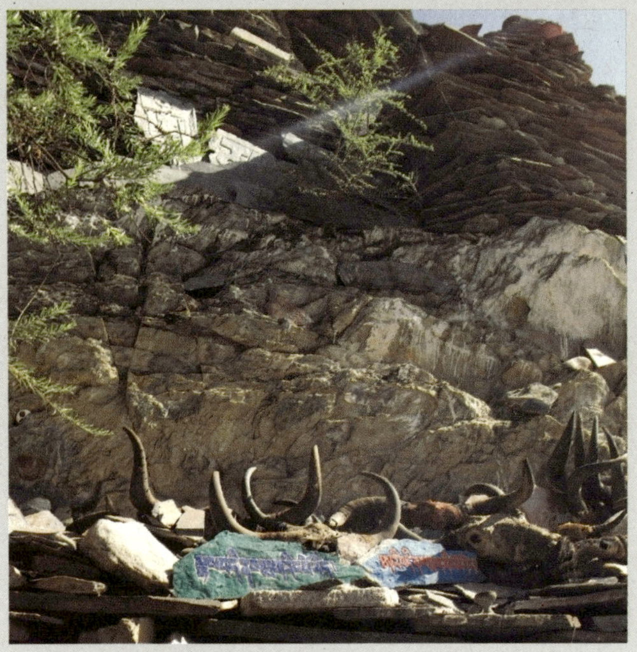

***Lhasa Is Far Away, America Is Far Away,* 2007**
Lhasa Medicine Emperor Mountain
29°39'04.22" N, 91°06'22.73" E, elev 3652 m

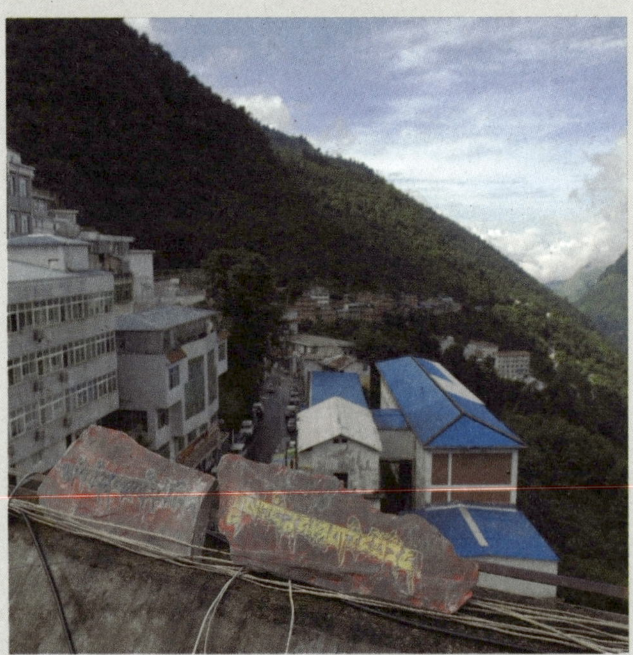

The garret at the police station in Zangmu Port
27°59'23.30" N 85°58'55.62" E, elev 2240 m

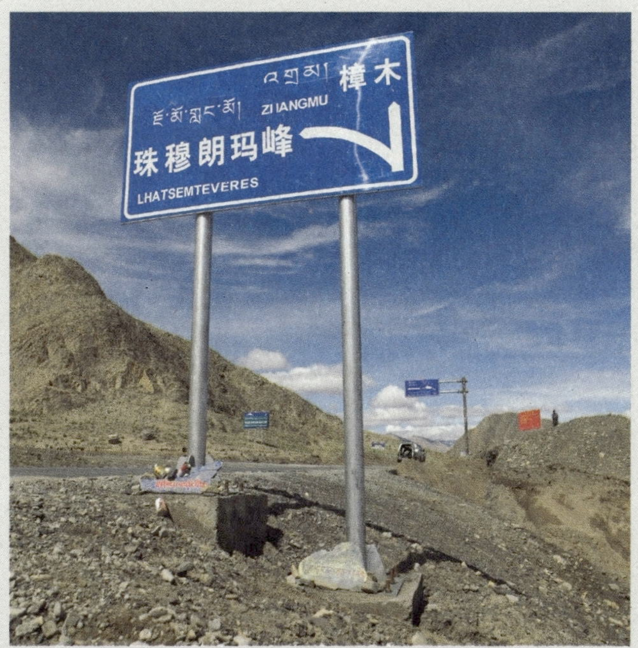

Entrance of the Road to Mount Everest in Tingri County
28°35'22.51" N, 86°32'22.51" E, elev 4341 m

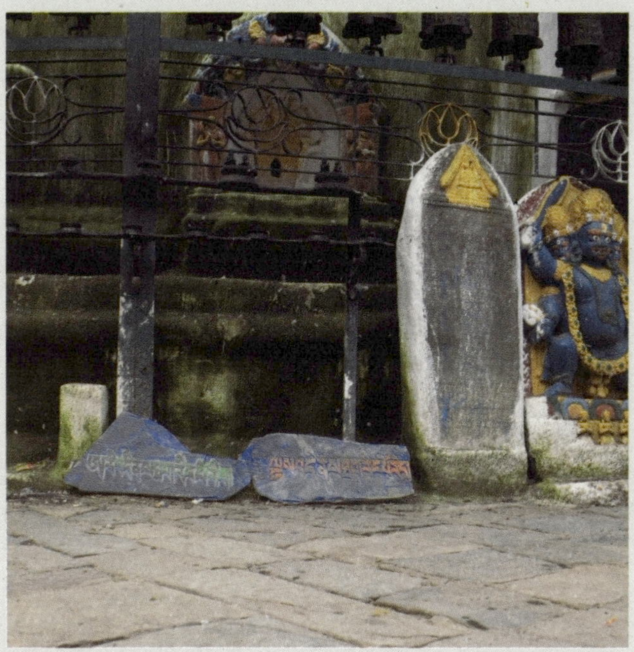

Kate Xinbu temple at the old city zone in Kathmandu
27°42'34.49" N 85°98'34.95" E, elev 1315 m

STYLE EXERCISES IN SELF-IDENTIFICATION

A leading figure in contemporary Tibetan art, since the beginning of his career Gonkar Gyatso has attempted to unify divergent representational systems, abstract and figurative, to show how each can turn into a highly politicised tool that promotes parallel systems and histories by, on the one hand, religion and, on the other, a totalitarian party line. In the 1980s, Gyatso was one of a few artists to defy local artistic conventions in order to discover a more modern image of Tibet. After being educated in Beijing and Lhasa, since 1984 he was able to access tapes of the Dalai Lama's speeches, which were then openly circulating through the city as a result of subsiding anti-religious sentiment. These led him to question the truthfulness of the history he was taught in Communist China as the son of governmental officers, as well as his belief in the then widespread idea that religion is wasteful. Together with a few friends he then founded the *Sweet Tea House,* a school by and for ethnically Tibetan artists, and was propelled to research a specifically Tibetan modern-art visual language whose subject matters and style challenged, and rejected, the ubiquous Sino-Realist visual regime. To combine traditional motifs and abstract images, he had to engage with and learn *thangka* painting techniques, and in the process he became increasingly acquainted with Tibetan Buddhism. The resulting vernacular style he deployed embedded covert political messages aimed at defying Chinese realism.

My Identity (2003) is emblematic of the artist's pursuit of the logical conclusions of such a major ideological shift. After beginning his career as an artist, he had lived in Beijing, as a self-imposed refugee in Dharamsala, the Indian city hosting the Tibetan government in exile, and later emigrated to London, where he is currently based. His developing identity as an artist and an individual has led him, as scholar Clare Harris states, "across borders of many kinds—national, political, and stylistic—but the journey has left him caught in a no-man's-land between the imaginative territories which currently constitute 'Tibet'."[1] However, *My Identity* reaches beyond his own experience to engage the modernist dilemma facing contemporary Tibetans. In each photograph included in the work, Gyatso appears seated before a large canvas looking out at the viewer, but each time the context is radically different. The series is a re-enactment of a 1937 photo by C. Suydam Cutting, the first American, and Westerner, to enter the Tibetan capital. During his expedition, Cutting photographed the Dalai Lama's senior *thangka* painter at work, initiating through his ethnographic lens a process of overturning Tibetan taboos that, by the '50s, challenged the myth of the anti-materialistic Tibetan who prohibited portraits of religious figures until after their death. Gyatso's photographs refer to the events through which Tibetans slowly opened themselves to self-portraiture. The first image depicts the artist dressed in a traditional Tibetan robe as a thangka painter apt at drawing a Buddha figure. It indirectly refers to the fact that the distancing of manuscripts and *thangkas*— painted or embroidered Buddhist banners which can be rolled up, sometimes also called "scroll paintings" from religious devotional imagery, as well as portraiture from strict mimesis, is a recent development in Tibetan art history. However, the beginning of this process didn't take place in Tibet but rather in India, when in the first decade of the twentieth century the Thirteenth Dalai Lama had taken temporary refuge in British-run Darjeeling and became fascinated with the medium of photography. *Thangkas* served as important teaching tools: they depicted the life of the Buddha, described historical events concerning important Lamas, or retold myths associated with other deities. At that time "photo-icons" began providing the possibility of making Barthesian "certificates of presence"

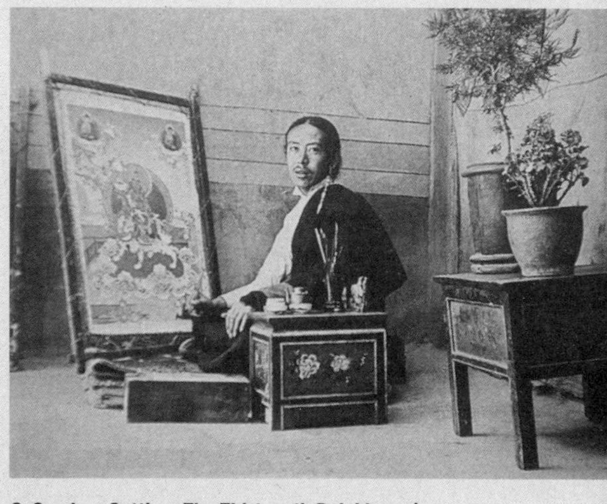

C. Suydam Cutting, The Thirteenth Dalai Lama's senior *thangka* painter, 1937.

attesting the incarnation into a particular new bodily house of a bodhisattva. The second of Gyatso's photographs depicts the artist as a Communist Chinese painter rendering an image of Mao Tse-Tung. In this photo he wears an olive green jacket and cap to toy with the cliché of the "post-invasion style" Chinese. In the third image, a contemporary refugee artist sits before a painting of Potala Palace and the Dalai Lama. Within schemes set by their spiritual leader, exiled Tibetan artists living in Dharamsala (or elsewhere in the Tibetan community in exile), have had the liberty to incorporate some of the imagery and visual codes of the host country, as long as those embedded images represented "ephemeral" and "fugitive" objects of popular culture. For these artists mimesis was associated with modern abstraction and demanded an "authentic" Tibetan imagery that was translated into the tinted zones surrounding the photographic "certificate"—in this instance, the Fourteenth Dalai Lama—the body of their spiritual leader surrounded by the social and political conditions of his relocation. The incorporation of the Dalai Lama's photographic image—as if he had returned, fictionally, to his homeland—represents the belief by Tibetans in the ephemerality of bodies, counteracted by the indestructible notion of the transmigration of "souls" that licenses them to imagine a return to Tibet. This, of course, turns reincarnation into a rather politicised concept. The fourth and final photo depicts the contemporary Gyatso sitting in a modern urban flat, in the act of creating an abstract image.

Having resided in Lhasa, Beijing (where he was the first Tibetan artist to paint a mural in Beijing's Great Hall of the People), Dharamsala, and London, one can also interpret these photographs as depicting aspects of his life in each of these locations. However, Gyatso's multifaceted transformations are not cosmetic but fundamental; they ask who, and what, has the power to control forms of iconization beyond time.

— DIANA BALDON

1. Harris, Clare (1999), "The Image of Tibet: Tibetan Painting After 1959", London: Reaktion Books, p. 192.

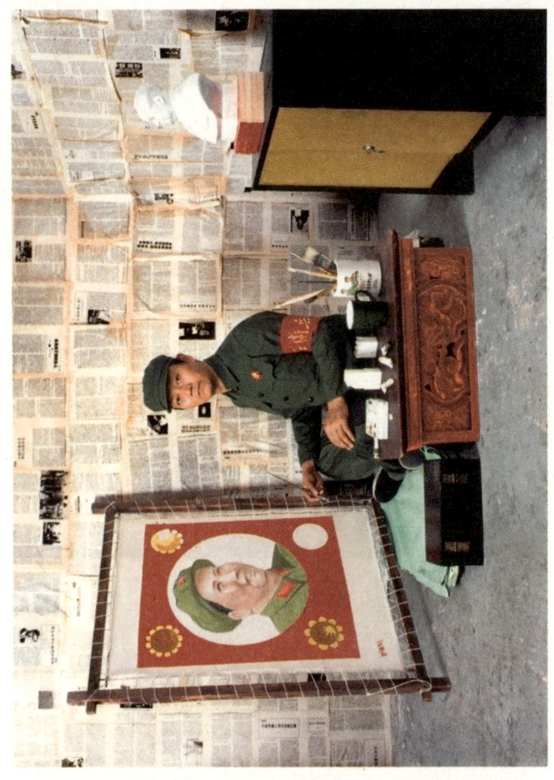

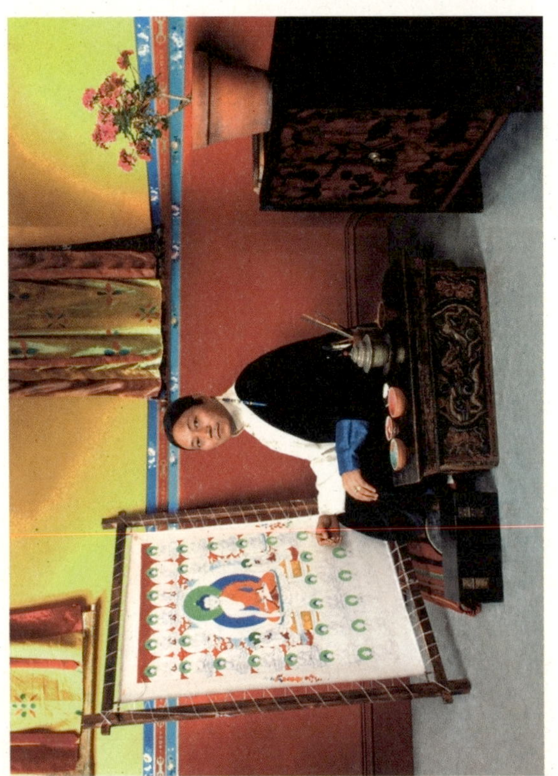

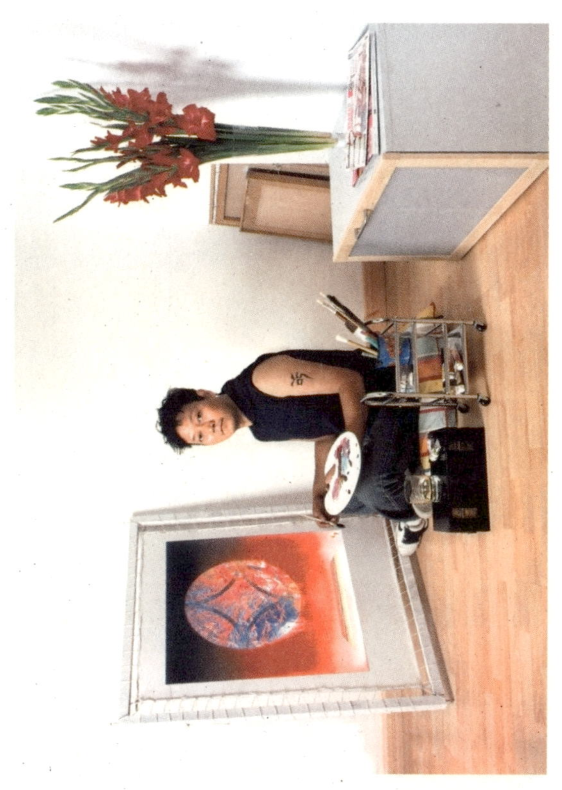

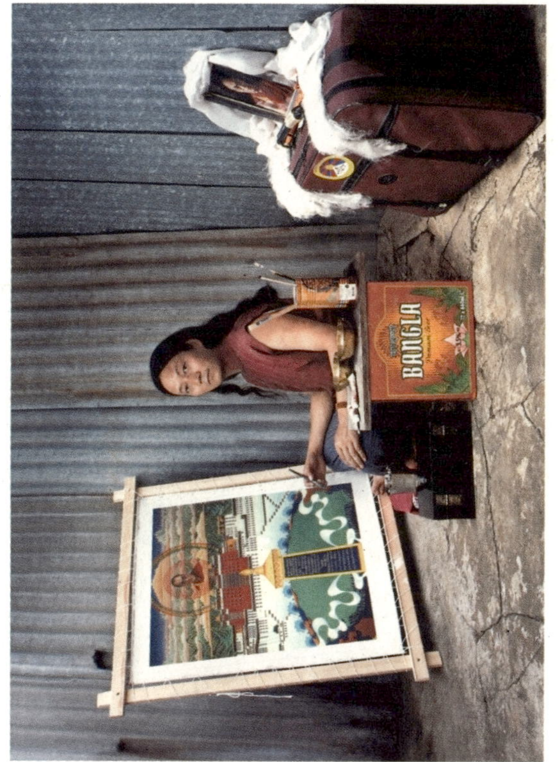

FREEDOM, COMPASSION AND THE POLITICS OF TIBET

In the spring of 2007 my partner, Ritu, and I attended a Buddhist teaching given by the Dalai Lama in New Delhi. At the end of the final day, he spoke informally to the audience, which was made up mostly of Indians. He told them that he always considered India to be the guru, and Tibet, the disciple, and that for many centuries Tibet had been a faithful disciple, diligently preserving India's ancient Buddhist traditions long after they had vanished from their own land. But today the disciple was in trouble; Tibet's own culture and traditions were under serious threat from the Chinese occupation. Folding his hands in a gesture of supplication, and looking more vulnerable than we had ever seen him,

THE DALAI LAMA MADE AN EMOTIONAL APPEAL: "YOUR DISCIPLE NEEDS YOUR HELP. PLEASE HELP ME!"

Along with everyone else in the room, we were deeply moved by the directness of his appeal and by the sheer weight of responsibility that we could sense bearing down on him. The Dalai Lama had done everything in his power to engage the Chinese in finding a mutually beneficial solution to the Tibet problem. Since the late 1980s, against the wishes and advice of many of his own people, he had formally given up the goal of Tibet's independence and instead proposed what he called the "Middle Way" approach, which accepted Chinese rule so long as Tibetans were given genuine autonomy. He based this on the Buddhist principle of avoiding extreme positions, and on the ideals of compassion and altruism. But his conciliatory overtures have led nowhere. China continues to insist that there is no problem in Tibet and therefore no need to deal with the Dalai Lama. Inside Tibet the Chinese have stepped up their anti–Dalai Lama campaign by reinstating the Mao-era practice of "political education," a key component of which is the denunciation of the exiled leader. It is a crime to display or possess a photograph of the Dalai Lama. Publicly they have relentlessly vilified him, calling him a "false religious leader," a "double dealer," and most recently, "a wolf in monk's clothing, a devil with a human face." The Communist Party Secretary of Tibet described the battle against the Dalai Lama as a "fight to the death." Meanwhile, a massive influx of Chinese migrants, boosted by the opening of the Tibet railway in 2006, has already made Tibetans minorities in their own cities. Under such circumstances we could well understand the Dalai Lama's sense of despair and desperation.

On March 10, 2009, it will be fifty years since the abortive Lhasa Uprising sparked the Dalai Lama's escape into exile and signaled the final takeover of Tibet by China. For nearly fifty years, against great odds, Tibetans inside and outside Tibet have somehow kept alive their hopes that truth and justice will finally prevail and that one day their beloved leader will return to his rightful place. But there are no signs that this will happen any time soon. How much longer can they sustain their aspirations and their cultural identity before they are engulfed and assimilated by the Chinese? Why has the Dalai Lama's "Middle Way" approach not worked so far, and does it have any chance of succeeding in the future? Is reinstating complete independence as the goal of the Tibetan struggle—as more and more Tibetans in exile are suggesting—a viable alternative? How do Tibetans in Tibet see the future of their country? And what do ordinary Chinese think about the Tibet issue? With these questions in mind, we started filming in January 2008, beginning with the Dalai Lama's visit to the Tibetan refugee settlement of Mundgod, in southern India, to inaugurate one of the largest Tibetan Buddhist temples in the world. Little did we know then that this would be a watershed year for Tibet, that beginning on March 10, protests on an unprecedented scale would erupt all over the Tibetan plateau, dramatically exposing the Chinese lie that Tibetans were happy under China's rule and that there was no popular support for the Dalai Lama and once again reinvigorating the Tibet struggle worldwide.

Over the course of the year we followed the Dalai Lama from his exile home in the north Indian town of Dharamsala to his travels in the United States, Germany, England, and France, where, although his visits were nonpolitical in nature, he was dogged by the media and by protesting Chinese students. We filmed the outpouring of grief and outrage among the refugee community in India. We filmed various political actions, including the street protests against the Olympic Torch relay in San Francisco, where large groups of ordinary Tibetans and Chinese came face-to-face in tense showdowns, perhaps for the first time outside Tibet. We followed the fortunes of the nearly three-hundred-strong Return March to Tibet, which set off from Dharamsala on March 10 and was finally stopped by Indian police three months later, not far from the Tibet border. We traveled to Beijing to meet the dissident Tibetan poet Woeser, who has been the voice and conscience of the Tibetan people, courageously writing about the true situation in Tibet despite Chinese efforts to cow her down. We gathered footage of ordinary Tibetans in Tibet, speaking out at great risk to their lives about the reality of life under Chinese rule and their continuing devotion to the Dalai Lama. And over the months that we traveled and filmed, we interviewed a wide range of people, including the Dalai Lama himself, supporters of his "Middle Way" approach, proponents of independence, Tibet watchers, and several Chinese, who included students, academics, and intellectuals. The picture that emerged was a complex one, with no clear answers. The only unambiguous conclusion was this: if left unchecked, the changes taking place in Tibet would rapidly and irrevocably destroy its unique cultural identity and reduce it to yet another Chinese province.

— TENZING SONAM

**RITU SARIN AND
TENZING SONAM
*MIDDLE WAY OR
INDEPENDENCE?***
2008

On March 10, 2008, the Return March to Tibet set off from Dharamsala, the exile headquarters of the Dalai Lama in India. The aim of the marchers was to cross over into the Tibet Autonomous Region in support of the Tibetan cause.
Three months later, the marchers were stopped by Indian police close to the border. The majority of the marchers were monks. During the march, they often engaged in heated discussions on the viability of the Dalai Lama's "Middle Way" approach, which gives up the demand for independence in return for genuine autonomy.

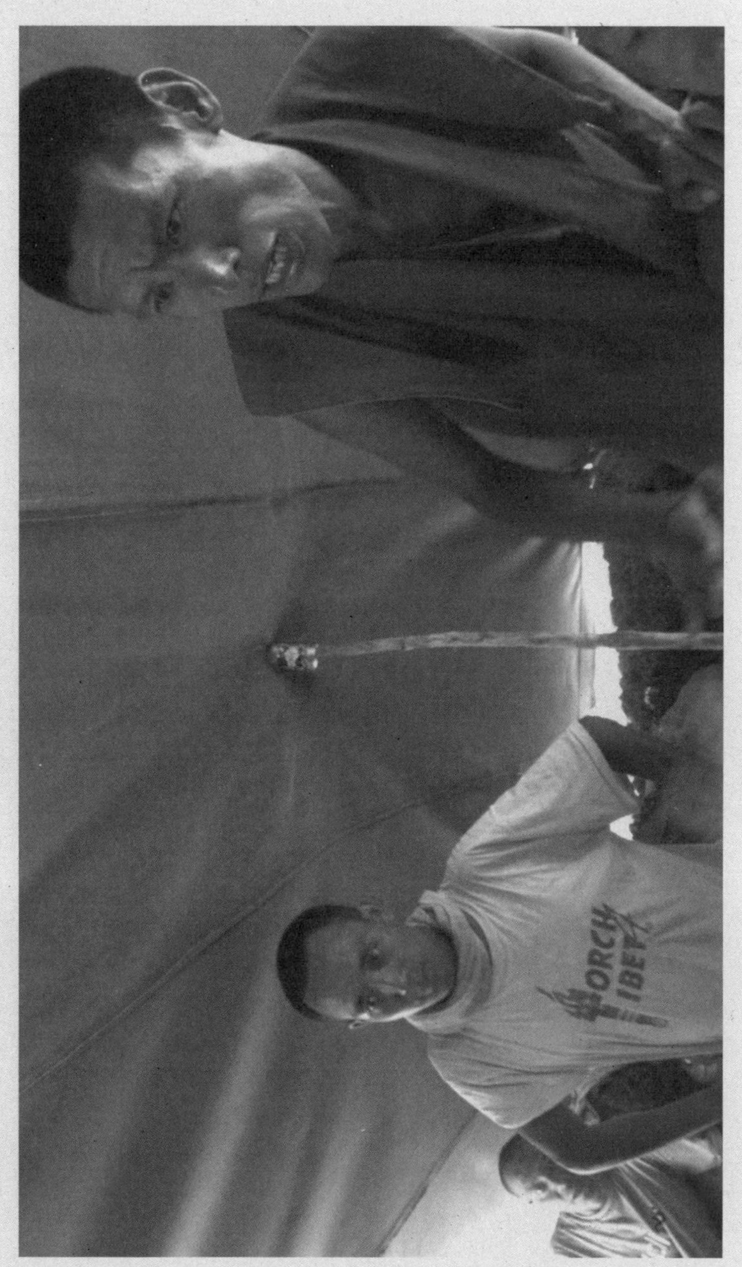

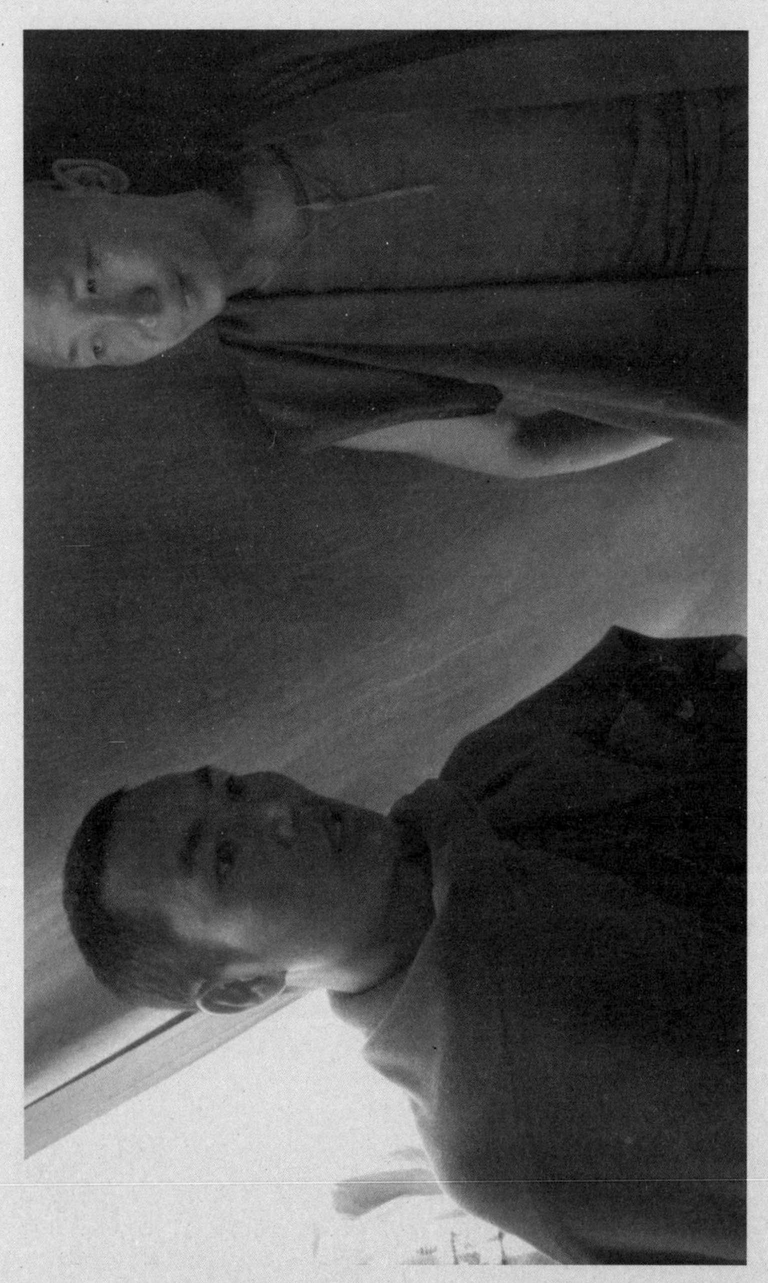

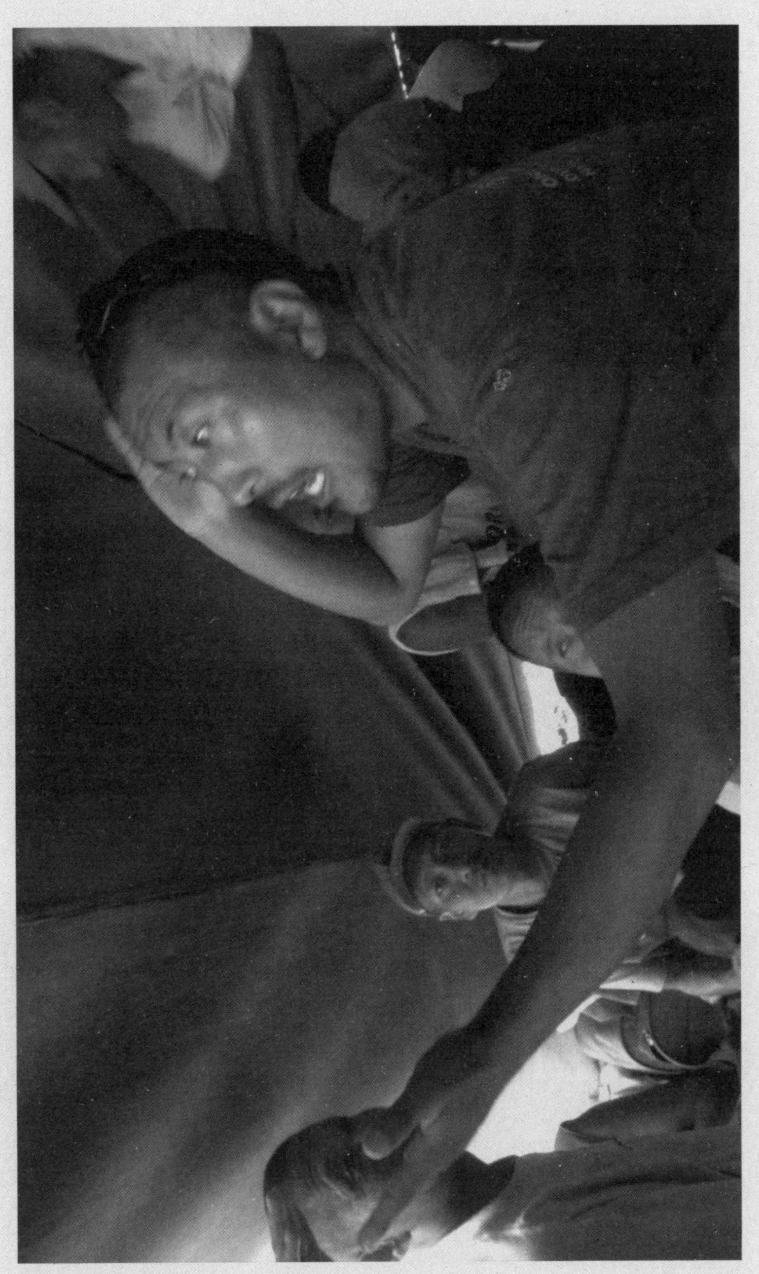

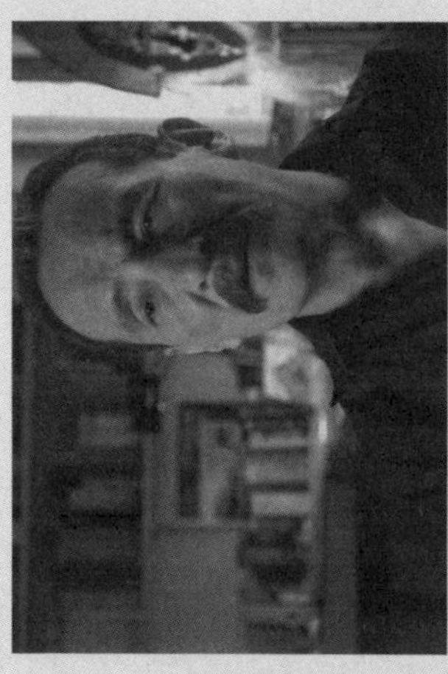

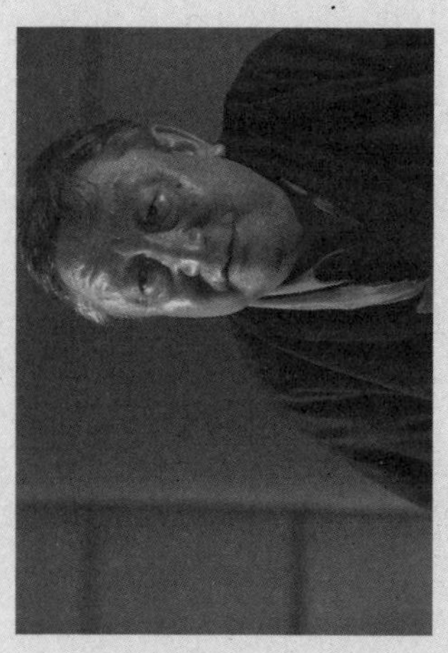

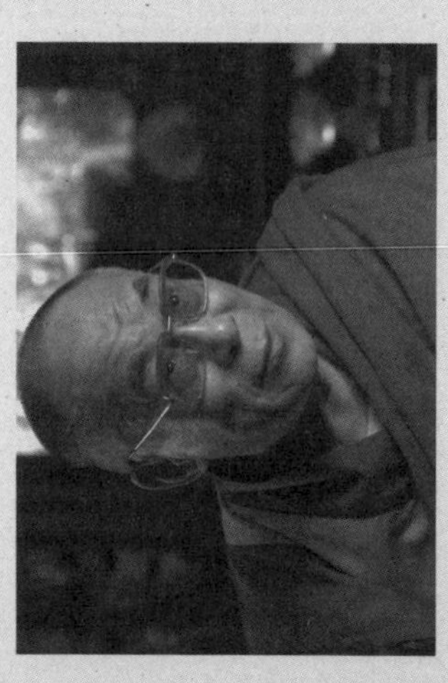

THE DALAI LAMA From a talk to the Chinese media in Seattle, April 12, 2008 (in English):

Then in the political field, about the concern for the future of Tibet, I always emphasize, we must act according to the new reality. The new reality is such that separation or independence, these are not very fitting, according to the new reality. In the new reality, everybody comes together.

So that is our basic thinking. Not separation. We must remain within the People's Republic of China. In the meantime we should have full guarantee of preservation of Tibet's own culture, Buddhism, and on top of that, the Tibetan environment is something very delicate. Therefore we need special care about the Tibetan environment. So that's my … or our … sort of thinking. We developed this "Middle Way" approach in 1974. This is a realistic approach and in the best interest of Tibetans and also a mutually agreeable solution … so from our side, since '74, we already made up our mind not to argue about independence but simply to try to gain meaningful autonomy.

Yes, certainly among the Tibetan community, outside Tibet and also inside Tibet, there are clear indications that more and more people now feel frustration. But still I usually tell these people who really criticize us… I ask them, okay, you want independ-

LODI GYARI, the Dalai Lama's special representative and chief negotiator with China (in English):

There is a widespread belief among the Tibetans, no doubt, and also among our friends, not only limited [to] the Tibetan friends, but international observers, that this whole exercise by the Chinese government in engaging the envoys of His Holiness is nothing but a tactical move to gain time. And even though it is my job not to believe in that school of thought because since my job is to definitely engage the Chinese seriously, but as an individual, as a human being, I told them this time, I said I am also sort of being compelled to lean to that school of thought, and it is for these reasons that we have this nagging sort of concern.

I really believe that resolving the issue is important not only for us, but I believe, for example, that His Holiness the Dalai Lama, this simple Buddhist monk, Tenzin Gyatso, can bring a fundamental change in the very character of that nation. Not just, you know, bring a kind of freedom to the Tibetans, bring unity between the Chinese and the Tibetans, and help bring stability to China and Tibet, but to bring about a fundamental change in the very character of that most important nation—the People's Republic of China. So when I see the changes, when I see some of the thinking of the leaders, that is where in fact I feel more optimism.

JAMYANG NORBU, writer, activist (in English):

No, absolutely not … it is not an emotional response. As I told you earlier, the whole idea is about first principles in philosophy … what is it that which defines your issue … and the Tibetan issue is completely defined by the fact that it was a separate country with a separate culture and separate … political existence from China and the problems that have emanated from Chinese occupation essentially come from that. So when you deny that and call it emotional, then you know … what you have left… These are the problems that the Dalai Lama faces … is that he does not understand the need of individuals for a land, for a country. He is operating in terms of spiritual reasons. For us, we are in many ways creatures of evolution. Normal Tibetans need territory … we are territorial … and in that sense … when you don't have that … people's … let's say, their self-respect … their dignity … it all sort of fades away.

I think the way the Dalai Lama looks at it … it's completely wrong … he is looking at it from a spiritual, rational way. Why don't we all live together? Why do we need nations? Why don't we all live as a family … this is what the Dalai Lama talks about all the time … but of course in reality … that is not taking into account dictators, the Saddam Husseins, the Burmese generals, Kim Jong Il.

ence, then how to achieve independence? No answer. Our "Middle Way" approach, we have some clear vision, yes …

* Talk to Tibetan community, Paris (in Tibetan):
In order for democracy to function, it is not appropriate that a lama leads the people. It should be based on elections. Secondly, the struggle is for a race. It's not a struggle of one generation, or of a few selected leaders, nor is it to benefit a small minority group. Therefore, the people must lead and work and not depend on one or two persons. Normally, on the lips of Tibetans, it's always, His Holiness knows best, His Holiness will do it. If you say such things, it is a mistake. It is also dangerous … to depend on one person. The Chinese also say that the Tibet problem is nothing, that it is dependent on one person, and that if this person passes away, then the issue of Tibet will also disintegrate. This is what they say, but this is not the truth, absolutely not. Therefore, we must be able to fight and struggle, generation after generation … we have to prepare ourselves for this. It is very important.

* Talk at Lerab Ling Buddhist Centre, South of France (in English):
So that's why, as I mentioned earlier, Tibet is now passing through a very, very difficult period and particularly, since 10th March, I described the Tibet problem as … I mentioned … the Tibetan nation, one ancient nation, with an ancient cultural heritage, is now passing through something like a death sentence. Very difficult. Now Guru remains helpless… . Guru full of … feeling of helplessness. The Tibetan people, they are putting a lot of expectation, a lot of hope on me. I am in a free country. Of course, I myself, everything is okay, but that moral responsibility in this case … helpless. Very sad.

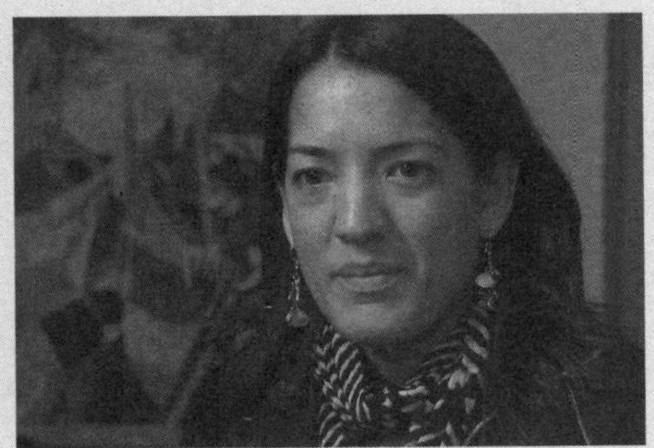

SAMDHONG RINPOCHE, Prime Minister,
Tibetan government-in-exile (in English):
That is why we need compassion. If there is fire and you need to extinguish the fire, you shall have to use something the opposite nature of fire. You need to put water or something that is of the opposite nature of fire. If there's fire, you put more fuel or more fire on it, it is not going to be extinguished. There's violence and there's hatred, there is domination, there is a misuse of power. We have to oppose them. How to oppose them? By using the opposite nature of those things. If there is hatred, it can be eliminated only by love. If there is anger, it can be eliminated only by kindness. If you react to hatred with hatred, then there will be only conflict and violence. There cannot be any resolution. So this is the law of nature. So we know that causality, the law of causality … the law of causality always says that if you need to eliminate something, you shall have to cultivate the opposite nature, so we are cultivating the opposite nature. The Tibetan people talk about compassion, but they are not really seriously cultivating compassion. If the Tibetan people eliminate their hate and anger against the Chinese rulers and have really matured compassion for them, I don't think that Tibet can be ruled for a single minute more by those powers. It is our weakness that

We cannot live as families … we have to live in entities where we can protect ourselves and where we feel we belong to each other and we share certain values and roles, and we do nothing of the kind with China.

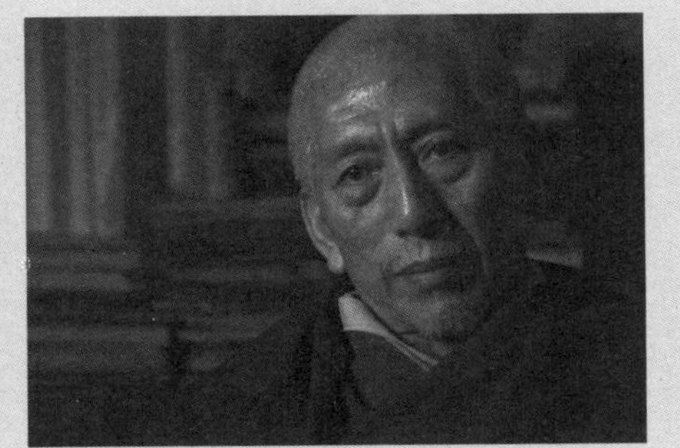

LHADON TETHONG, president,
Students for a Free Tibet (in English):
For our side to give up on the idea of Tibetan independence … completely … it's just … I think it's not … We do a great disservice to the Tibetans in Tibet and the future generations of Tibetans if we believe it's not possible. I think a lot of people see His Holiness' Middle Way … Middle Path … as a stepping-stone to independence, and I think the Chinese see that too. I mean, they're not dumb. They know that if the gun is removed from the back of Tibetans' heads, if Tibetans really have … inside Tibet … the right to speak freely and to govern themselves even just a little bit, well, they will see … we will see Tibetans say what they really want, which is China out, which is Tibet for Tibetans, which is Tibetans to be the masters of their own destiny, and so I think the Chinese leadership knows that.
I think we need to really take a long, hard look at our movement

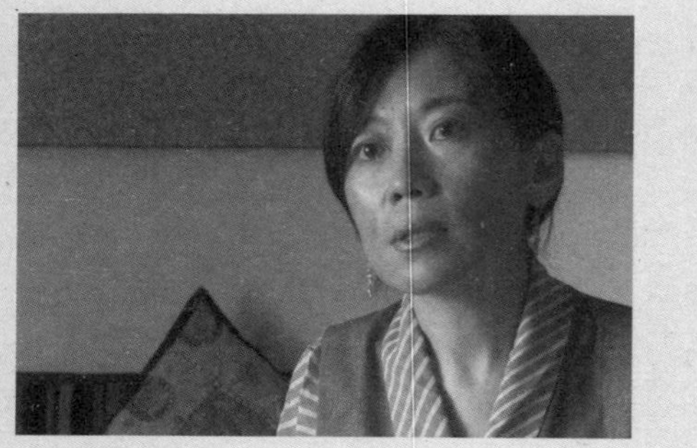

WOESER, dissident poet and writer (in Tibetan and Chinese):
I myself have lived in Tibet as well as inland China for so many years. Now I am in Beijing. I feel that the issue of Tibet can only be solved when the problem with China is solved. China's problem is mainly with the Communist Party, one-party system, a totalitarian regime. This kind of totalitarian regime has controlled not only Tibet but also all of China. Whether it is Tibetans, Hui, Mongolians, or many others, everyone is under the control of this regime. So under such circumstances, any kind of ethnic group, for example, the Tibetans … we cannot solve our problem alone. This is unrealistic or even impossible. A solution to Tibet's problem depends much on a solution to the problems of China. When there is an end to the one-party autocracy and when China is headed on the path of genuine democracy, there will be a chance for Tibet. Tibet will enjoy the chance for a new life, a chance to be her own master. But on the contrary, if such a system keeps on going in China, there will be no hope left for Tibet.
After dealing with the Chinese for many years, the "Middle Way" approach proposed by the Dalai Lama has not brought any constructive results, and many people do question this thinking and say that there should be a change in the method of the struggle.

we are not able to make the maturity of our compassion, our nonviolence. So we shall have to build up our powers in order to meet with the challenge of misrule.
The Tibet issue remained alive, not only alive but also a burning issue in the international scenario because of this Middle Path Approach. People should understand it. Emotionally, everybody likes the word independence, but emotion does not take us anywhere. They have to tell us how to do it. How to achieve it. If the Middle Path Approach does not achieve anything, for the seeking of *independence,* are they going to achieve it tomorrow or within six rounds of talks? Absolutely not. Everybody knows it is not going to be possible. Feasibility and possibility are the most important in politics. Particularly in the twenty-first century, everybody talks about pragmatism … pragmatism in politics, and everybody talks about this. Emotion has no place in the … reality and the politics of pragmatism.

and say, have we really truly employed nonviolent … strategies and campaigns in the best way? In the most effective way? Have we really, truly looked at and studied our enemy and figured out their weaknesses and devised strategies and trained ourselves to work and to exploit those weaknesses? I don't think we have. And I think if you just think time is running out, it just gives people this sense of just … loss, and like it's a hopeless cause and it's not, and so yeah, we try not to say that. We try not to … to use that analogy… ˙If there are Tibetans left in Tibet, however bad the situation is, we'll fight. We'll work for them, even if you told me today that we were going to lose the battle for independence, which I don't think we are, but even if you told me that now, then we'll fight, we'll continue to fight, we'll fight for every bit that we can get. That's what we owe people inside.

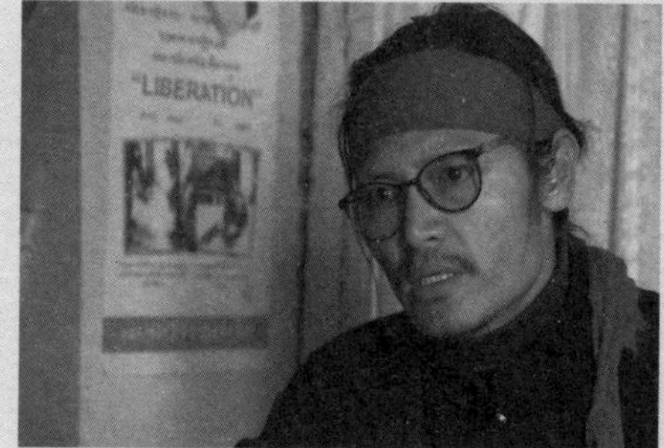

TENZIN TSUNDUE, poet, activist (in Tibetan):
I truly respect and have my deepest reverence for him, since His Holiness is a manifestation of the Buddha of Compassion, and has wide and deep insight and compassion. Nevertheless, we are humans and we cannot think exactly the way he does. So it

I think it's worth considering, however, when it comes to independence, whether this kind of demand is achievable. And taking
into consideration the actual situation in Tibet, it really seems
very difficult, and unachievable. But of course it is understand-
able that many Tibetans do have this kind of desire, considering
the current situation as well as historical facts. When these two
factors are placed side by side, it is natural that people have this
kind of demand, and this is unquestionable. But when such a
demand (for independence) is really put into practice, it seems
very difficult to achieve any result, given the fact that there is
great disparity in strength between Tibet and China. So I think we
should be well prepared. However, I myself totally support and
follow the proposition of the "Middle Way" approach. But at the
same time I do think everybody should be well prepared in case
a sudden opportunity arises … not an opportunity created by
Tibetans, but rather one prompted by a change from an external
factor. For example, in the 1940s, when there were lots of opportunities, Tibetans were just not able to grab them, and as a result,
this is what the situation is today. Therefore, taking a lesson from
history, we should work hard and be able to take advantage of
any opportunity that arises. However, talking about independence
alone, I don't think this is realistic.

These excerpts are drawn from the many interviews and
press conferences that we filmed. They give an idea of the
debate between the "Middle Way" approach for genuine
autonomy and independence as the goal of the Tibetan
movement.

is nothing but natural for us to have anger and to bear grudges
against the Chinese, against the government that is responsible
for all of the repression in Tibet. Moreover, although I agree that
his idea is highly regarded and respected, but great ideas and
intentions don't necessarily lead to good results . . .
For instance, achieving genuine autonomy through the "Middle
Way" approach does not depend merely upon our initiative. Like
we say, only two hands can make a clap. So without the coopera-
tion of the Chinese government, mere goodwill on the part of His
Holiness and the Tibetans won't bring about a positive solution.
The lack of political will on the Chinese side is like us waiting with
open arms for the mercy of the Chinese government.
The argument that Tibetans make against the Chinese government is about the rights of the fifty-six minority nationalities,
including Tibetans, in the constitution of the People's Republic of
China, which entitles all the regions inhabited by minority groups
to enjoy the same fundamental rights. Although this is a genuine
concern and a just demand, the Chinese reject it. Especially since
the areas of Kham and Amdo have been divided and incorporated
into five other provinces, it makes it all the more difficult for the
Chinese government to accept such a demand. This is because
they fear that giving special consideration to the Tibetans
would lead to similar kinds of demands from the other minority
nationalities. Besides, they also fear that such special consideration might also lead to the demand for an independent Tibet in
the future. Hence, keeping all of this in mind, I believe seeking
genuine autonomy cannot go further than being an idealistic
approach. Therefore, many people like me believe that it is better
to seek complete independence, because for this to happen, we
don't have to wait for China's approval.

INTERVIEW WITH TSERING SHAKYA

Ritu Sarin and Tenzing Sonam: Tsering, in your opinion, what were the reasons that impelled the recent demonstrations in Tibet, and how significant are they in terms of recent Tibetan history?

Tsering Shakya: Let's talk about the significance: it's really phenomenal, the size and the spread of the demonstration. You look at the map of Tibet in the whole of China. It constitutes something like 25 percent of the Chinese landmass, and the entire region erupted and was in revolt simultaneously. So in terms of the actual significance of the protests, this was unprecedented. Even in the 1950s the Tibetan revolt was a progression: it started in '54, '56, and built up a momentum in 1959, so it was a sort of gradual escalation. But what you saw between March 10 and 14 was the whole region simultaneously erupting, and then Tibetan students in Beijing and other parts of China were also joining in the protests, so it's almost as though the entire Tibetan people were involved in this.

This is particularly significant in that the Chinese have never witnessed such a wide geographical spread of such demonstrations, and the intensity, the involvement, of the ordinary Tibetan farmers, of monks, and also of students. The other significance is that the protesters were almost all under the age of fifty. That means they were all born and raised under communist rule. So they are not concerned about the feudal Tibet of the past. They are really what the party calls "the children raised under the bosom of the Communist Party." So they are turning against or rejecting their upbringing and asserting their Tibetan identity. The cause of the demonstrations in Tibet is … you can't say there's a single factor… I mean, there's a convergence of many factors. The immediate reason is almost now a sort of chicken-and-egg situation. What happened is that weeks before the demonstrations started, the Chinese National People's Congress [NPC] meeting was being held in Beijing. And during that meeting and prior to the meeting, there was an extensive media campaign in China about potential and possible threats from Tibetan and other nationalist sort of terrorist attacks in China. And even in Beijing it was announced that Tibetans shouldn't be allowed near the People's Congress, the parliament. There were notices put out to the taxi drivers that any Tibetans carrying large packages should be reported to the Chinese police, so there was an intensification of security all over the Tibetan area and in China, and huge media … sort of … publicity given by the Chinese government to the potential threat. Now that led to the intensification of security measures in all the Tibetan areas. The Chinese perceived that the National People's Congress meeting would become a potential focus of protests. At the time, I was thinking that the media campaign was launched to divert the public attention away from the NPC meeting that was happening. Now the intensification of the security measures both in Tibetan areas and in the Autonomous Region led to sporadic confrontations between the Chinese police and the Tibetans, especially the monks. The monasteries were cordoned off, surrounded by police, and so there was some sporadic fighting that happened. So from the Chinese point of view, they will say that the intensification of the security

measures was necessary because they had prior knowledge of the protests.
The Tibetans assert that the intensification of security became oppressive and
therefore led to the protests. So you have a sort of a chicken-and-egg situation
here. You cannot say which was the real cause of the protests. I can understand
that for the Tibetans the intensification of security measures became intoler-
able, and that led to anger and confrontation with Chinese security authorities.

**And how significant is the fact that these demonstrations spread to
areas of Kham and Amdo that are not part of the TAR (Tibet Autonomous
Region)?**

Well, if you look at the 1980s demonstrations, '87 to '89, the demonstrations
were mainly focused in Lhasa, in the Autonomous Region. Relatively, the areas
in Kham and Amdo did not participate in the demonstrations. So what we see
today is the demonstrations spreading to all the surrounding Tibetan-speaking areas. So in that way there is almost a collective Tibetan identity and a
collective Tibetan voice being heard. And so this is partly due to the success
the Chinese had in introducing technology, mobile communication. And what
you had in the eighties … the people in Amdo or Kham, far-flung areas …
actually didn't really know what was happening in Lhasa because the media
was controlled. But today they had a sort of independent source. Their relatives
from Lhasa were phoning saying what was happening in Lhasa. And this mobile
phone technology and the widespread use of text messaging and phones actually made for ease of communication.

**Is this sense of Tibetan identity among all these provinces something that
is recent, or is that something that was always there in the past, and if
it's recent, what was the cause behind it?**

Before 1950, whether it's in Kham area or Amdo or the Autonomous Region,
the Tibetans had the perception that they were living in a homogeneous and
exclusively Tibetan area. And that had existed for centuries, despite the different dynastic Chinese authorities in the region. So there has been a very strong
sense of that until today. And what you find today is the mass influx of Chinese
traders, temporary migrants, so there's this whole shift in the population that's
happening on the Tibetan plateau. So for the first time Tibetans are in much
closer contact with the Chinese population than they have ever been in history.
So being with the Chinese actually intensified their own sense of being Tibetan.

**In these demonstrations the people were reported to be shouting for the
long life and return of the Dalai Lama and also for Tibet's independence.
How do you explain this, particularly in the context of the fact that the
Dalai Lama has long rejected Tibetan independence?**

The demonstrations cannot be explained purely as a fight for independence or
for the return … it's a voice of so much resentment or legitimate grievances
Tibetan people have against the present Chinese policy and rule. So the shouting for the long life of the Dalai Lama or the call for independence is, to some
extent, a convenient political slogan. But nevertheless they see the present system in Tibet under Chinese rule as not working, and they do want an alternative,
but this alternative appears in many different guises, such as greater autonomy,
support for Dalai Lama's Middle Way, and outright independence. So it's not a

very coherent and unified voice. Actually there's much divergence of views in what they say.

What window of opportunity did these events create for Tibet—for the Tibet movement—and how have the Dalai Lama and the exile government responded to this crisis?

What is clear and significant about these protests is that Tibetans are unhappy under the present regime, and it is also a rejection of the current Chinese policy of development and the process that is a sort of Chinese paradigm for Tibet. It is a total rejection of this government's policy.

Secondly, in terms of opportunities for the Tibetans, actually for many years the Chinese have claimed that Tibetans are happy under the Chinese regime and they have made enormous progress. But clearly the demonstrations are indications that Tibetans are not satisfied. It doesn't matter how many participated in the protests, it is a sizable voice and an articulation of people who are willing to risk their lives and go to prison.

In terms of opportunity for the Tibetan diaspora politics, we see the Dalai Lama and his authority being enhanced by the protests in Tibet. But at the same time, in terms of actual policies adopted immediately and during the demonstrations, it's as if the exile government didn't know how to deal with that. At one level they are very mindful and very cautious not to be seen by the Chinese to be actually inciting demonstrations or being the main perpetrators of demonstrations. Therefore you would see very few statements from the Dalai Lama endorsing the demonstrations or in direct support of the demonstrations. In fact, he has avoided making any comment on the nature or course of the demonstrations or his own views on it. And there's a sense that he still hopes the Chinese government can see him as a reasonable person with whom they can negotiate. Now whether this policy of the Dalai Lama is quite realistic or naive is a matter of debate. Some will say that he should have grasped this opportunity and taken moral leadership and confronted the Chinese head on. Whereas others would have seen his position as very shrewd and trying to show to the Chinese that he is the only alternative solution to the Tibet problem.

What is the situation now in Tibet, and what do you think the Chinese government's strategy in regard to Tibet will be?

At present, you know, China is adopting the policy of knee-jerk reaction. In that sense, they are confronted with major protests, and their first immediate task is to develop a very repressive measure to keep the demonstrations from spreading further or developing into further protests. This is very important for China in the sense that the Olympics are coming, and the world's media attention is on China. The timing of the demonstrations is very significant for China; they see this not as a spontaneous or unplanned, uncoordinated event. Because of the way it happened, they see that the Tibetans had deliberately chosen that date to highlight the Tibetan issue during the Olympic year. So the present measures in Tibet are to curtail the demonstrations and arrest people, and the Chinese have announced that thousands of people have been detained and arrested.

The second tactic that the Chinese are trying to develop is to sort of portray China as the victim, not the Tibetans. China is seen as being harassed and victimized not only by the Tibetans but also by the whole of the Western world. In that they have managed very successfully to mobilize Chinese public opinion onto their side. For China, ultimately, it's really not so important what the West thinks or what our side thinks; what really matters is what the public in China thinks. So that sort of strategy has worked quite well for China.

So now, the fact that China has put itself forward as the victim of Tibetan violence, what do you think the long-term effect of this view—of the average Chinese person's view of Tibet—is going to be?

If you look at the petition submitted by the Chinese intellectuals, one of the first paragraphs mentions the one-sided propaganda as having a detrimental effect on China's ethnic relationships. And I think in the long term that will be one of the most damaging effects that it will have. Now in the Chinese populace's mind the Tibetans are ungrateful natives who will resort to violence. Remember that the demonstrations in Lhasa were continuously shown on Chinese television as being … sort of … Tibetans perpetrating anti-Chinese … an anti-Chinese people's struggle, and that the innocent Chinese civilians were the victims of this demonstration. So there will be for a long time this racial tension, ethnic tension. It's something that the government has built up. It's very hard to dispel. Another issue is the enhancement of Chinese nationalism that has been generated in China in the present period.

The Chinese have also been repeating the claim that Tibet was a slave society that they helped to liberate and that the Dalai Lama wants to return to this feudal past. Even though it sounds outrageous, many educated Chinese, even in the West, believe this. Is there any truth to this claim, and how can China expect to get away with such accusations?

The question of the condition of Tibet before the Chinese arrival in 1950s … the Chinese use that as a propaganda tool. To some extent you can see that the argument is an argument adopted by old colonial powers: the land and the people they conquer are uncivilized, and their mission is to civilize and develop the region. So in some ways this conforms to old colonial powers' perception of their own rule. Old colonial powers see themselves as beneficent, and benevolent rulers, so in that sense, the Chinese are adopting the classic sort of colonial ideas of civilizing the natives. Secondly, the question of the historical condition of Tibet really has little significance for the Tibetan people. As I said, the people who participated in the demonstrations are under fifty years old. So they have grown up under the present Chinese regime, and they compare the experience in their lives not with historical Tibet but with what they have endured in their own time. Even if the social condition in Tibet was worse than now, nevertheless, that sort of social condition, of bonded laborers, the sort of states that existed in Tibet, it existed in China also; its existence still continues in many developing countries. The social condition was neither worse nor better than in most Chinese villages before 1950s or '49. So it's really totally irrelevant; it's just one of the justifications the Chinese still use.

You've been in touch with educated Tibetans in Tibet and China. What is their view of what has happened, and what are their hopes and aspirations?

Since 1990 there has been quite intense debate among the Tibetan intellectuals, particularly among secularized intellectuals, and to some extent they adopt many of the modernist views adopted by Chinese intellectuals; particularly they take inspiration from great Chinese writers like Lu Hsun (Lu Xun) and the May Fourth Movement in China, to see the importance of revitalizing and creating new cultural conditions in Tibet. So many Tibetan intellectuals don't see the question of independence as the ultimate question, but essentially the question is about how to change Tibetan society, how to modernize Tibetan society, and how to deal with the present situation in an engaged way.

For the Tibetan intellectuals, in a way, it's quite complicated; at one level they support the demonstrations as expressions of Tibetan resentment and grievances against the present Chinese regime, so they are supportive. At the same time they see the sort of violent confrontation as hopeless, suicidal, and they recognize that Tibet has to engage in a much more creative form of protest; I mean in a creative engagement with the modern world. At one level they are emotionally sympathetic to what's happened, but at the same time they see this as detrimental to the long-term cause of Tibet in the sense that the Chinese will adopt more draconian measures against Tibet, and that certain aspects of liberalization and liberal policies that have been happening will be taken back, and it's … sort of … it's a step backward to what's going to happen now. And so they are caught between these views.

The Dalai Lama has stated that during these recent demonstrations he felt the same sense of helplessness that he did in Tibet in the Lhasa uprising of March 1959. What was his dilemma then, and is there a parallel with the situation today?

It's problematic for the Dalai Lama since his duty as the leader of the Tibetan people … he should be in the forefront of the protests, he should be leading the protests. It's like Nelson Mandela. When you look at any resistance movement or colonial protest movement, the leader is with the people, but in the case of the Dalai Lama, he is also the leader of the Buddhist community, and his primary identification is as a Buddhist monk. He believes in pacifism and nonviolence, and so there's a conflict in his duty as a leader of the Tibetan people and his own role as an international figure or symbol of peace and pacifism. So in that sense, if he were to lead the protests and endorse the protests, he would be damaging his own credentials as a Buddhist monk and an international symbol of peace, but if he adheres to this idea of pacifism and nonviolence, actually it leaves the Tibetan people without leadership.

This interview is an excerpt from film interviews
conducted by Ritu Sarin and Tenzing Sonam
© White Crane Films

INTERVIEW WITH ROBERT BARNETT

Ritu Sarin and Tenzing Sonam: In your view, what is the Tibetan struggle all about?

Robert Barnett: It's problematic to call it a struggle because I suppose that prejudges what the problem is and the nature of the way it's developed. I think it's becoming clearer nowadays that it's a division between two ways of seeing things—a primarily Tibetan way and what we can call roughly a primarily Chinese way of looking at the situation. As history has moved on, we now can't confidently say this is a simple struggle of an oppressed people for freedom. It certainly looked like that earlier on. Maybe it was, but as the world has changed, as the situation has become more complex and as China has become more powerful and, in a slight way, more articulate, it's started to become a conflict between two demands of how an issue should be seen.

One of the strangest and most troubling things about the Chinese approach to the Tibet issue has been that, apart from the government and the party and then almost only in written form, no Chinese people have dared to speak about the Tibet issue. It's almost unheard of for Chinese intellectuals, Chinese scholars to appear in their own name speaking to the public in the West about the Tibet issue.

For the first time this has begun to change. This is one of the results, good or bad, of the March events in Lhasa and Tibet in 2008. A Chinese movement has emerged of Chinese intellectuals who were going to speak about Tibet. The important thing about this dispute, this demand to have the right to speak, is that the Tibetans have almost no voice in it. The thing that has not been noticed by anyone is that, in the great movement of Chinese nationalist outrage of 2008 against what they call media bias in the West, there are no Tibetan voices. The Chinese are speaking on behalf of an imaginary Tibetan who they insist wants to be protected from an imaginary Western predator. And this is a problem: the Westerners reply to them, the Westerners attack the Chinese or support them. Again the Tibetan voice is left out of this. There's an exile Tibetan voice of a sort. A voice that's mainly expressed through protests and street actions and symbolic passion, suffering, sacrifice, determination, but that's not really entering into the actual high-level debate. In the corridors of power it is unclear who has the right to speak for Tibetans, and nobody is saying, where are the Tibetans? Where are the actual Tibetan voices in this?

You've worked closely with Tibetans in Tibet. What are their aspirations and how do they differ from the aspirations of the exiled Tibetans?

Well, this is an important question for people like me. We've dedicated most of our working time to trying to take the focus of the Tibet issue back to inside Tibet, where 97 percent of Tibetans are. For people like me, for the researcher community, that's the big movement of the last twenty years. The big shift in Tibet politics is the recognition, the sort of unstated recognition, that it is the Tibetans inside Tibet who are actually the heart of the issue; that's where the majority is. And this has not been matched very much by political thinking and political strategy. And there's a huge problem of communication, it seems, between exiles, Tibetans outside Tibet, and Tibetans inside Tibet.

Inside Tibet the experience of working there is that the kind of people that someone like me comes into contact with are people who don't have an ideological notion of politics; they don't even have a passionate notion of politics, generally speaking. For them, it's very, very deeply felt but something that has to be worked out for the best possible solution, in a largely pragmatic way. I see it as a kind of contract. It's about what they can get out of the Communist Party's offer to Tibet. And they are looking at a deep memory of the Communist Party and not at some ancient dynasty that's existed for centuries and that has some divine right like British kings or Chinese emperors. It is a very recent phenomenon that resides in power in China and inside Tibet because of a contractual deal Tibet made when Mao came to power sixty years ago, which was: we will give you these benefits—maybe equality, prosperity, international standing—if you let us have absolute power. This is the fundamental issue for Tibetans.

They were promised these things. They understand politics and state as being a contract where these rights have to be given. Within the intellectuals and the middle class in China, perhaps also for the peasants and for the nomads and so on, it's about demanding that the Chinese community should fulfill the contractual promises that it made fifty-six years ago, and that it in a way keeps on making. That means that Tibetan people will accept a reasonable offer from China, if my theory is right. They might very well all want independence. We can't really know for sure—of course some people we certainly know—but most people will say I want a practical solution, I want the deal that we were promised by the Communist Party at its best times.

This means that we have to reinterpret what we mean when we talk about nationalism in Tibet. We imagine, generally speaking, that there's only one kind of nationalism, that rather ugly, passionate, atavistic kind of drive that has done a lot of damage in the world in the past. That is what we see in a lot of Tibet politics, but inside Tibet that nationalism is quite rare. There's another kind of nationalism, which is much more subtle. It's a pride in a community and an immense pride in history and a sense of difference, and it's not necessarily about creating a separate state as far as we can tell. Of course many people wish to have a separate state, but they may not be demanding to have it. They may settle for a better deal if they feel that the Communist Party is keeping to its contract, the equality, and the notion of listening to the voice of local people. So this is the kind of nationalism that we don't know about in the West, a kind of contract-based nationalism. We are a nationality, we have rights, and you have obligations, and we are going to demand that you give them. This is something that really hasn't been discussed very deeply. It's very important because that kind of nationalism can produce solutions. The deep, passionate nationalism that we are used to, the kind that's been developed in the so-called free world, is a nationalism that really doesn't tolerate compromise. So in this sense there's more hope within Tibet than outside.

This year we saw widespread unrest all across Tibet, including greater Tibet. Did this come as a surprise to you, and what were the factors that sparked it?

The thing about the events of 2008 is that although we never knew if they would happen or when they would happen, the only strange thing about them is that they didn't happen earlier because the policies of China are so deeply provocative. The intensity of the demeaning nature of policy decisions made by the Chinese leadership is incalculable. I am speaking actually about the detailed things that really affect ordinary people's lives. People adjust to the general quality of living in an extremely authoritarian state; they don't exactly quarrel about that. What they quarrel about is when that authoritarian state does something that is specifically targeted at them and that has no possible rational explanation. So they don't find it strange that there are, say, restrictions on travel. That's normal in authoritarian states; we have it too. They may not even find it strange; they might understand it that, say, monks can't join a monastery till they're supposedly eighteen years old. It is not that unusual—we have similar rules—but there are certain things that the Chinese have introduced in the last ten, fifteen years in Tibet and have very much stepped up in the last three years that have no possible explanation and that not only don't happen anywhere else in China except Xinjiang but are actually illegal in China.

And the most obvious one of these is the ban on any form of religious practice for government officials, government employees, and their families in the Tibet Autonomous Region and the ban on any form of religious practice for students in the Tibet Autonomous Region. This is illegal in China: you go to prison in China, supposedly, if you stop someone from practicing a perfectly legal form of religion. There's no explanation for it.

So this kind of thing is not written down; you never read about it in the Western press; the exiles have missed it; they are too busy saying that all religion is being suppressed. Clearly that's not the case. Countryside people can have very extensive religious practices. The few people who are allowed to be monks and nuns, they're allowed quite a range of practice up to a point. But this complete ban on the students and the government sector, which may be half the educated population in the Tibet Autonomous Region, this is really an extraordinary decision for China to make.

Similarly the decision to ban the Dalai Lama, his pictures, worship of him, this really is one of the most provocative things that the modern government can choose to do. Remember, we are talking about a modern government that actually has been conscientious about avoiding racial discrimination in its legislation. Avoiding directly provocative measures—that's how the modern China has tried to display itself to its citizens.

So gradually we saw a splitting of Tibet from China, just the opposite of what China claims. It has huge investments, economic integration, while it separates Tibet and Tibetan areas from Chinese mainland, inland areas in terms of policies. If you practice religion, who can you worship? On the scale that these were done in Tibet, and to some extent in Xinjiang, this is a really serious provocation, and it's not surprising that people would eventually push back against this. There's another element that I think is important for people to remember. It's not surprising, but we tend to forget it. One of the issues for Tibetans that I think is endemic and that has been hugely accentuated is that they are not allowed to discuss sensitive policies. It's not just the question of whether China puts a railway line through the middle of Tibet or whether it's going to bring in Chinese people or bring in just tourists and goods. It's a question of whether Tibetan people are allowed to say, we don't like this, we are worried about this, this should be done, migration should be regulated, the benefit should be for locals. They were not allowed to discuss this. This is completely forbidden for discussion, for criticism. Now this is terribly important. We comfortably imagine that this is how authoritarian states work, but it isn't. China in the 1980s, in the early 1980s, allowed criticism of all kinds of economic policies. It didn't allow political questions like, Can Tibet be independent? You could never touch that. But economic issues like that, they were fair game until quite late in the 1990s, and then they were taken off the page.

The bringing in of Chinese migrants to Tibet, temporary or otherwise, no discussion was allowed after 1992. The whole issue of what in Chinese political language is called special characteristics—this idea that local areas can have different development policies from Beijing—banned basically. No discussion of that. Banned after 1992, 1993 because the state decided that this could be used to hide some secret nationalist agenda. What actually you and I would call moderates, Tibetans who are in the Communist party, these people were stopped from speaking, let alone ordinary Tibetans in society.

So this constant experience that it's a Chinese person who tells you what's good for you, it's a Chinese person who decides the policy, it's a Chinese person who regulates your life and who tells you that you are happy—I think eventually this has to collapse. It's a nonsustainable form of political control.

In 2006 the state also began very aggressive policies that were something like old-style social engineering, moving a quarter of a million farmers and villagers into new roadside housing that they had to pay half of the money for, reset-tling a hundred thousand nomads in settlements where there is no livelihood or prospects. So China has quietly moved to new phases of policy in Tibet in the last two to three years or so. It's not surprising that people after decades of this, remembering how the early parts of the 1980s were a much more open period, it's not surprising that people move back to the streets. The problem is, we don't know what this will achieve.

So do you think it has achieved anything?
Well, at first I thought it had certainly achieved one thing, which was it spoke very loudly to the Dalai Lama's contention that there is a single Tibetan territory if you like, an area that was never ruled by Lhasa historically but that is peopled by Tibetans and has common interests. So the fact that these protests in 2008 spread all across the Tibetan plateau, way beyond the little area that China calls Tibet, is very significant and must be deeply worrying for the Chinese, and even more worrying for the party analysts is the fact that this spread across the class categories: the peasants, the nomads very prominently involved, students, and some middle-class people also involved. This is very, very new and significant politically.

But the strange thing about this is that it hasn't played out politically like the 1980s unrest, when there were Westerners there who brought out extremely detailed accounts. There was press support from the Western media that was very effective and tried to be active this time as well, but they were quickly shut out of Tibet, and the Western movement on the Tibet issue has faltered. There was a brief period in March–April when the international community was more or less unified in its criticism of China for the handling of the Tibet issue. And that brief moment was lost, disintegrated: the Chinese were able to divide the French from the Germans, the other groups from other countries, and that fragmented again, and China was then able to take the initiative. Then the earthquake happened in Sichuan, and understandably there was a great return of sympathy for China. The great nationalist movement emerged, and the Chinese intellectuals of a certain kind were able to mouth a strong attack on Western support for Tibet. This has decimated the political impact of the 2008 events. They—the nationalist movement, the Chinese intellectuals—have been able to support the state in characterizing this movement as largely ethnic violence. This is done really by manipulation of televisual evidence, the visual material that China released of one protest that was very ugly in Lhasa when Chinese civilians were attacked brutally. But the other hundred or so protests of the following week and the following month, we have seen very little of those. They didn't involve attacks on civilians. So this has changed the image of Tibetans and the Tibetan political perception; it now looks like Tibetans are capable of violence, which people didn't really realize before, although it had always happened but there'd been no visual evidence of it on our screens. It now is easier for people to say this is just an ethnic problem, a developmental difficulty that really has to be dealt with internally.

This interview is an excerpt from film interviews
conducted by Ritu Sarin and Tenzing Sonam
© White Crane Films

WE
HAVE TO BE
VERY

CAREFUL THESE DAYS BECAUSE…

MEMORY FILES

The following thoughts are taken from a conversation conducted in September 2008 between Tashi Tsering, director and co-founder of the Amnye Machen Institute (AMI), the Tibetan Center for Advanced Studies in Dharamsala, India, and Aradhana Seth.

Most Tibetan books, even when published in Tibetan by exile governmental and non-governmental organizations or academic institutions, focus on religious works. Before 1959, many writings by lay individuals and religious women, whose works were historically neglected, were still undiscovered. The AMI was the first institute concerned with lay literature, culture and ethics, and in that stance, we believe, provided a role model for the future.

After 1959 we were worried that the rest of the world would know nothing about Tibetan history and culture. Because of its history, geography, and identity, we streamlined our efforts to try to inform and educate the world about Tibetan history and philosophy. At that time all our energy, funds, time, and knowledge were spent in translating into English and other European languages the writings on Tibetan philosophy and medicine that were first translated from Sanskrit eight-hundred years ago.

Honestly, this effort was not rewarding, as nothing really has "come back." No foreign publications were translated into Tibetan—apart from the Holy Bible, which was done by missionaries—a sign that we still live in intellectual isolation that has replaced the previous geo-political one.

After forty years operating in this field, we believe it is important for Tibetans to think like the rest of the so-called "developed world": if we want to work shoulder-to-shoulder with the West, we have to understand Western philosophy, science, and history.

But at the same time, we need to document our history and identity through collections of old photographs, such as those of dignitaries and places like monasteries that, after 1959, were destroyed. The whole landscape of Tibet has changed, and many of these photos, taken by British diplomats and trade agents between 1900 and 1947, witness places and events that younger Tibetans are not able to recognize.

We operate programs in several categories. On the one hand, we have created and are continuously enlarging various resource archives. The Rigdzoe (Cultural Treasury) program is a long-term project that aims to preserve, catalogue, and archive the wealth of available assets related to Tibetan culture. These encompass the collection from AMI's Film Reference Library; a collection of rare books and documents, some dating from the seventeenth century; a library of books and journals in Tibetan, English, Chinese, and other languages; the institute's own publications (in Tibetan and English); the institute's collection of maps and atlases; and its audio collection of interviews, oral histories, lectures, music, recitations, etc., on compact disc, tape, and gramophone records.

The Visual Archive is a catalogued and widely accessible archive of visual materials comprising photographic collections such as the Tsarong Collection, which is probably the largest collection of photographs existent in Tibet and was taken by two Tibetan photographers, a father and son, from about the 1920s to

the late '50s. The Kasur Lhamo Tsering focuses on documents from the Tibetan
resistance movement. The Shelton Collection consists of photographs of the
American missionary Albert Shelton of his mission in Batang, Eastern Tibet.
For instance, we have gathered photographs of three generations, or three
successive incarnations of Rinpoches, and of ruling families, tribal chieftains,
and princely states. Once in possession of this material, we have tried to
identify and research its background in order to build some mnemonic and
visual information that speaks for itself. Ordinary photographs of young girls,
aristocrats, business-
men's wives, and group
portraits present the
transformations within
Tibetan society, which
are hardly found in the
writings of the period
(in the '30s and '40s,
for instance, people
rarely wrote about the
marginal activities of
their lives, such as what
kind of powder they
used, what they smoked
or what brand of lipstick
they used).

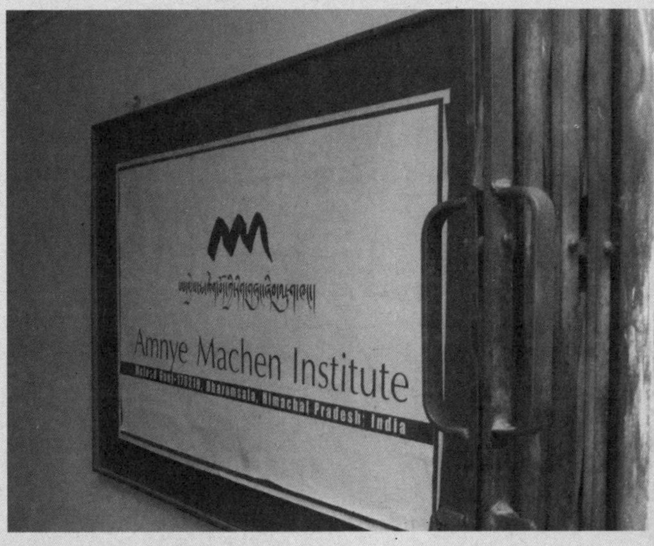

Shuttered doorway, Dharamshala, India

But our foremost
endeavor is a series of programs in the areas of Tibet studies, China studies,
and publishing. These range from literature and folklore, the arts, and Tibetan
history to cartography, urban and architectural studies, and women's studies.
This last subject alone consists of three branches: there is the women's studies
journal; collected writings by Tibetan women writers which, by now, covers
twenty-five to thirty volumes; and a series of biographies of Tibetan women
which covers fifteen to twenty volumes.

Before 1959 Tibet was not worried about its own identity. In the years during
and following the Cultural Revolution, the few photographs we still have depict
people who appear to live simple lives and act humbly. They didn't want to
give the impression of being, for instance, confident aristocrats, as at the time
China was experiencing serious class struggles. But from the late '80s to today,
Tibetans have once again begun styling themselves in order to display their
identity and traditions, by means of hairstyles, dresses, and various ornaments
(swords, knives) that emphasize how their culture, as ethnic minority, is unique
and different from Chinese culture.

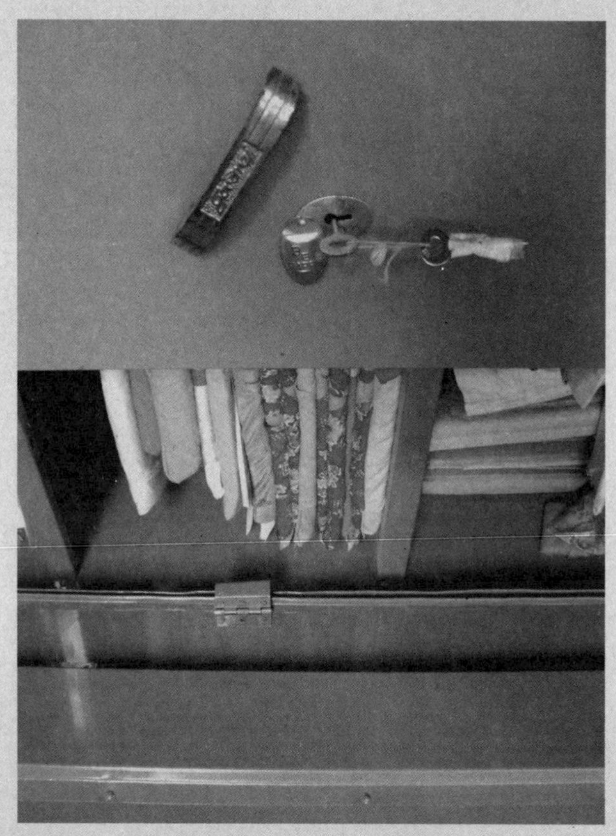

ARADHANA SETH
REAL MEMORY, 2008

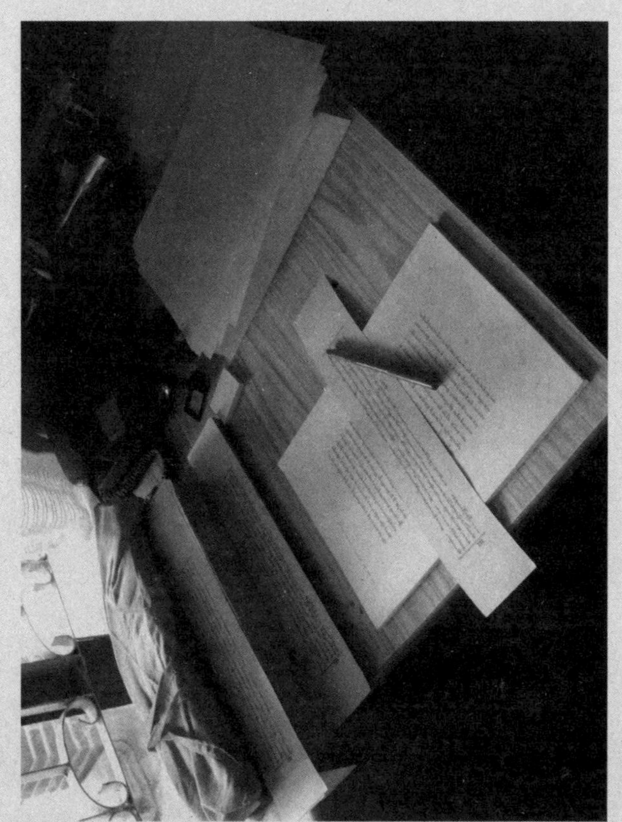

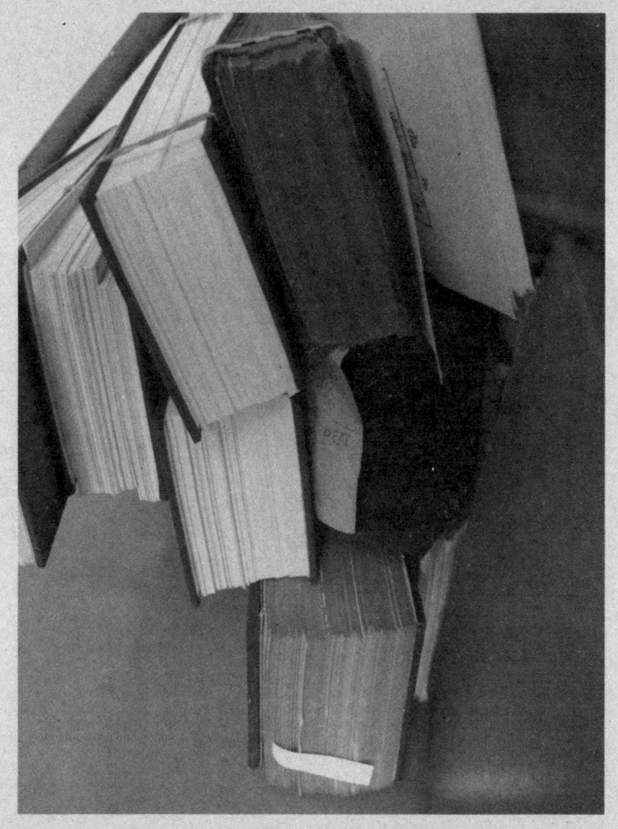

A LANGUAGE TO COME

How then to speak and document what had passed because so little remains on which to hold? And how to attest to the veracity of an attestation and what precisely is it that it attests to? As Maurice Blanchot wrote: "Enlaced, separated: witnesses without attestation, coming towards us, also coming towards each other, at the detour of time that they were called upon to make turn."[1] The question becomes what is the relationship between testimony and a record of what has come to pass, between the document and the archive.

Writing on the archive, Paul Ricoeur has suggested that it is "constituted by the set of documents that result from the activity of an institution or of a physical or moral person" designating not only an "organized body of records" but also an "authorized repository."[2] More than that Ricoeur views the archive as synonymous with the trace and the document.[3] The document or record, he writes, is "contained in the initial definition of archives … the notion of a trace implicitly contained in the notion of a deposit."[4] The document serves as evidence of a course of events and thus if "history is a true narrative, documents constitute its ultimate means of proof. They nourish its claim to be based on facts."[5] The document functions therefore as a trace left by the past. Collected and organized this body of material becomes the theoretical premise and material basis for the construction of the archive and the writing of history. From this perspective, therefore,

TRACES ARE NOT SIMPLY RESIDUAL REMAINS, SIGNS AND CLUES, BUT THE MATERIAL EVIDENCE, THE STUFF OF HISTORY, THE ARCHIVE.

Pointing to the link of passing and pastness whereby what passes by leaves a trace of what has past, Ricoeur remarks on the apparent paradox. The thing has passed or the passage is no longer, while the trace exists and remains.

And yet to admit to this paradox is to recognize the discontinuity and heterogeneity of the trace to its originating referent, to the event. The appearance of the trace then would be a past that has never been present, a past which no memory, no thing could resurrect, capture, represent as present. It is rather bound to the future, always coming after, opening onto a horizon that exceeds its referent. But nor does the trace have a phenomenal presence or plenitude. The materiality that the trace assumes is then witness to the fracture of its own condition. But if the trace itself is heterogeneous, what then of the archive and what properly belongs to the archive and its authority as authorized evidence of an event? Does not the archive require for its well-being a repression of this distance, a distance recognized within the failure of the testimonial to attest to anything but its own survival and hence a distance from that which has disappeared? Yet, the archive cannot admit the testimonial for this reason. It will appeal to the notion, as Ricoeur does, that the trace is bound to its originating referent, the unique moment of truth that occurs prior to the separation of origin and representation.

Correspondingly, the concept of the document, as Allan Sekula has suggested in writing on his photographic archive, "entails a notion of legal or official truth, as well as a notion of proximity to and verification of an original event."[6] Photography reflects the truth of that which it represents either by viewing a linear progression from past to present or by virtue of the fact that the camera as a mechanical form of reproduction provides a "source of factual knowledge" and "objective evidence."[7] The document it produces therefore becomes the source and foundation of the archive and the archive itself authorized the veracity of the document through its incorporation. Photography and the archive function interdependently in so far both entail transferring the world to image. Tied to the referent, the photographic trace secures it livelihood and becomes critical to the practice and authority of the modern archive.

— CHARLES MEREWETHER

Excerpt from: Charles Merewether (2002), "A Language to Come: Japanese Photography After the Event".

1. Blanchot, Maurice (1992), "The Step Not Beyond", trans. by Lynette Nelson, Albany: State University of New York Press, p. 76.
2. Paul Ricoeur citing "Encyclopedia Universalis" and "Encyclopedia Britonnica". See Ricoeur, Paul (1988), "Time and Narrative", vol. 3, trans. by Kathleen Blarney and David Pellauer, University of Chicago Press, p. 116.
3. Ibid., p. 119.
4. Ibid., p. 117.
5. Ibid., p. 117.
6. Sekula, Allan (1983), "Photography between Labour and Capital", in "Mining Photographs and Other Picture: A Selection from the Negative Archives of Shedden Studio Glace Bay, Cape Brecon 1948-1968", photographs by Leslie Shedden, Benjamin H.D. Buchloh and Robert Wilkie (eds.), The Press of Nova Scotia College of Art and Design and the University of Cape Breton Press, p. 199.

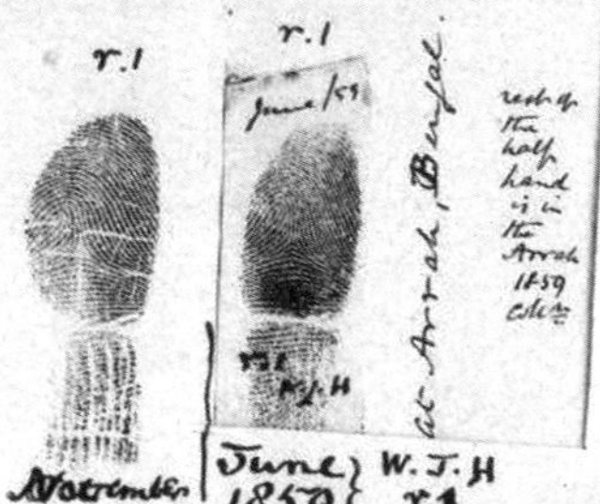

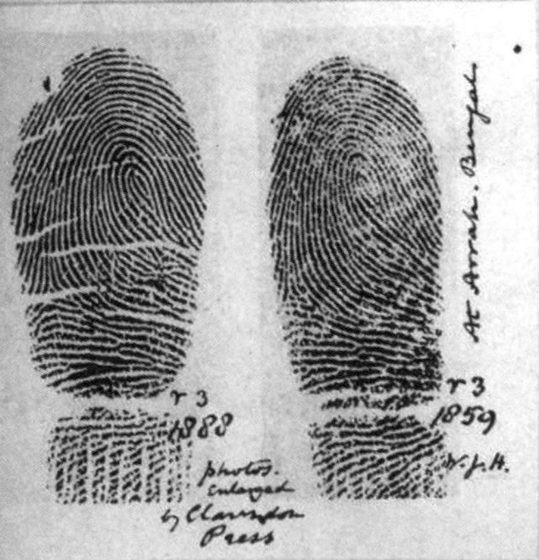

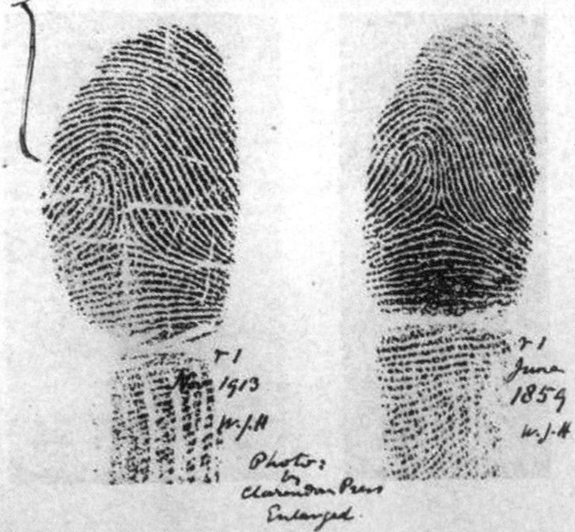

Beginnings of Finger-printing
An early experiment in finger printing
29 years interval
An early experiment in finger-printing
54 years' interval
The longest known proof of persistence

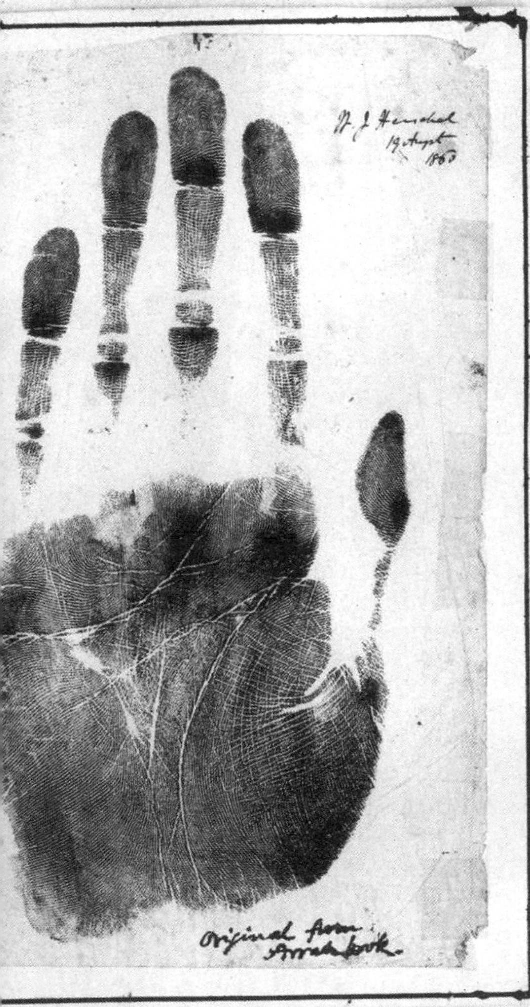
N. J. Herschel
19 August
1860
original from
arrack book.

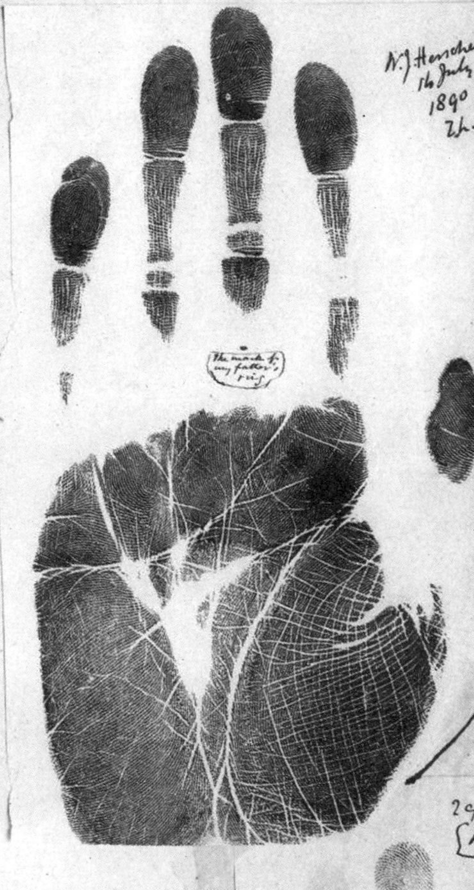
N. J. Herschel
16 July
1890
Zh.
the marks to
my father's
print

WORKS IN THE EXHIBITION

AMAR KANWAR
The Torn First Pages, 2004–08
19-channel film installation
Varying durations, color and b/w, sound
Dimensions variable
The Torn First Pages film installation and
book project are co-commissioned by
Thyssen-Bornemisza Art Contemporary, Vienna,
and Public Press, New Delhi

DETAILS
Part I
Six projections
The Face: 4 min 35 sec
Thet Win Aung (a): 4 min 35 sec
Thet Win Aung (b): 4 min 35 sec
Ma Win Maw Oo: 4 min 35 sec
The Bodhi Tree: 7 min 4 sec
Somewhere in May: 38 min

Part II
Seven projections: 24 min 53 sec

Part III
Six projections: 23 min 26 sec

TECHNICAL CREDITS
Part I
Camera: Dilip Varma, Amar Kanwar
Editing: Anupama Chandra
Sound: Maria Bustnes
Assistance: Sandhya Kumar

Part II
Camera: Dilip Varma
Editing: Sameera Jain
Sound: Marc Hebert

Part III
Editing: Ajay Saini
Installation designed with Sherna Dastur

ACKNOWLEDGEMENTS:
Aung Din, Aye Chan Naing, Khin Maung Win, Thida Thin
Myat Tha, Soe Win Nya, Nelson Ku, Myat Htay Kyi, Htet
Aung Kyaw, Khin Hnin Htet, Aye Aye Mon, Nang Kham
Kaew, Htun Htun, Dr. Zaw Win Aung, Nay Mya Mya Swe,
Soe Myint, Sein Myint, Zaw Lwin Htun, Chit Kyi, Nyein
Chan, Kyaw Thet, Christiane Erharter, Gargi Sen, Eyrun
Thune, Jan Bull, Per Bjarne Boym, Ritu Sarin, Tenzing
Sonam, Garima Bajpai, Dilip Simeon, Steve Lehman,
Susanne Ghez, Ute Meta Bauer

Office for Contemporary Art, Norway; Democratic
Voice of Burma, Norway; Democratic Voice of Burma,
India; Mizzima News, New Delhi; Nordland Art
FilmSchoolkunst , Lofoten

HEMAN CHONG
Deleted Scenes, 2008
5 collages on paper
Each 105 x 75 cm
Commissioned by Thyssen-Bornemisza
Art Contemporary
Courtesy of the artist and Vitamin Creative Space,
Guangzhou / Beijing

GONKAR GYATSO
My Identity, 2003
4 photographs
Each 61,5 x 78 x 3,4 cm
Courtesy of Fabio Rossi, London

MARINE HUGONNIER
An Artwork Which Is Not An Artwork, 2008
Handbound book-box containing pages increasing
in numbers, changing elements
Commissioned by Thyssen-Bornemisza
Art Contemporary
Courtesy of the artist and Max Wigram Gallery, London

NIKOLAUS HIRSCH & MICHEL MÜLLER IN COLLABORATION WITH THE CYBERMOHALLA ENSEMBLE
Cybermohalla Hub, 2008
Multimedia installation
300 x 600 x 500 cm
In collaboration with Sarai/CSDS (Delhi), Ankur –
Society for Alternatives in Education, Manifesta 7,
AbK Stuttgart (Matthias Acksel, Krasimir Anastasov,
Alexander Gaus, Steffen Sendelbach, Sylvia Stoll, Letizia
Valsecchi), Engelsmann Peters Ingenieure, Daniel Dolder
and the Cybermohalla Ensemble
Courtesy of the artists

AMNYE MACHEN INSTITUTE (AMI)

Books, magazines, maps
Courtesy of AMI, Dharamsala

ARADHANA SETH

Real Memory, 2008
Single-channel video on monitor
67 min, color, sound (engl.OV)
Commissioned by Thyssen-Bornemisza Art
Contemporary

Memory File 1
Amnye Machen Institute
Tibetian Center for Advanced Studies,
Dharamsala, India
Tashi Tsering, director AMI
24 min 17 sec

Memory File 2
Tibetan Manuscript Library
Library of Tibetan Works & Archives,
Dharamsala, India
Lhasang Shastri, librarian AMI
5 min 53 sec

Memory File 3
Bookworm
The Complete Bookshop, Dharamsala, India
Lhasang Tsering
Poet and essayist, owner of *Bookworm* and
co-founder of the Amnye Machen Institute
8 min 7 sec

Memory File 4
Dharamsala, India
Tenzin Tsundue, writer and activist
28 min 33 sec
Camera: Aradhana Seth; Editing: Sameera Jain;
Sound: Aradhana Seth; Sound Post: Asheesh Pandya

(CONTESTED) EVIDENCES

p. 1

Ma Win Maw Oo, a high school student, is carried
by two medical students after being shot dead
by Burmese soldiers during the 1988 student
protests. Capturing worldwide attention as a news
photograph for a day, her picture drops from public
memory shortly thereafter. See also: Amar Kanwar,
The Torn First Pages, 2004-08.

pp. 20/21

The "Four People's Desires" and "Four Objectives"
formulated by the Burmese military regime,
which by law must be included as the first page
in any book or printed matter published in Burma.
State Peace Council and Development Council,
Government of Myanmar.

pp. 54/55

E-mail source: "A british agency shot this photo on
20. 03. It shows "monks", who acted violently at
this day in Lhasa.
We do hope, this pic will cross all borders and all the
world will see the photo.
The chinese soldiers will change their clothings ...
the rest of the story is well known .....
- Groovemeister Binglebrain -"

pp. 84/85

Translation: "Announcement – Every resident of Larong
monastery, Sertha County, is ordered to clean up the
wood from the destroyed residence and other property
before July 20, 2001. Thereafter, the local government
would remove them. Sertha County Government, July
8, 2001."
Private collection

pp. 122/123

Visualization based on:
Map of Lhasa City, published by Amnye Machen
Institute, Dharamsala, 1995

pp. 172/173

Part of Sheet One of a "Collection of selected finger-
prints 1858–1877 and later".
Although Sir William James Herschel developed the
technique of fingerprinting, he only ever used it as an
administrative tool. He did not realise that it could be
used to catch criminals—it was Francis Galton and
Edward Henry, building on the foundations that Herschel
had laid, that turned fingerprinting into a tool for fighting
crime.

ARTISTS' BIOGRAPHIES

AMAR KANWAR

was born in 1964 in New Delhi, where he lives and works. He has established a distinctive voice through several films that emerge from his exploration of the politics of power, violence, sexuality, and justice. The films are characterized by a unique, poetic approach to the political. He had solo exhibitions at the Haus der Kunst, Munich (2008); Whitechapel Art Gallery, London, and the Apeejay Media Gallery, New Delhi (2007); at the National Museum, Oslo (2006), and The Renaissance Society in Chicago (2004), among other venues. He has participated in numerous group exhibitions, including Documenta 11 (2002) and 12 (2007) in Kassel, Germany, the Sydney Biennial (2006), *Image War: Contesting Images Of Political Conflict* at the Whitney Museum, New York, and *Territories*, Kunst-Werke Berlin KW Institute of Contemporary Art (2004).

HEMAN CHONG

was born in 1977 in Malaysia and raised in Singapore. He is currently based in Berlin and Singapore. Chong received his M.A in Communication Art & Design from The Royal College of Art, London, in 2002. His art practice involves an investigation into the philosophies, reasons, and methods of individuals and communities actively imagining the future. Charged with a conceptual drive, this research is then adapted into objects, images, installations, situations, and texts. Chong's work has been shown in solo exhibitions at Hermes Third Floor (Singapore), Vitamin Creative Space (Guangzhou), Art In General (New York), Project Arts Centre (Dublin), Ellen de Bruijne Projects (Amsterdam), The Substation (Singapore), Künstlerhaus Bethanien (Berlin), and Sparwasser HQ (Berlin). He has also contributed to several group exhibitions and biennials. In 2003 Chong represented Singapore at the 50th Venice Biennale.

GONKAR GYATSO

was born in 1961 in Lhasa. He graduated from the Fine Art Department of the Central Institute of Nationalities, Beijing, and from the Chelsea Art & Design College, London. He is the founder of The Sweet Tea House, a contemporary Tibetan art gallery in East London. He received a Leverhulme Fellowship in 2003 and has been artist in residence at the Pitt Rivers Museum in Oxford. His work has been exhibited internationally, in galleries and museums such as The Chinese National Art Gallery (Beijing), The Glasgow Gallery of Modern Art (Scotland), the Courtauld Institute of Art (London), the Weleld Museum Rotterdam (Netherlands), and the Colorado University Art Museum and Collections (USA). Works by Gyatso are now held in collections of the Newark Museum (USA), the Pitt Rivers Museum (UK), and numerous private collections. Gyatso lives in London and is a visiting teacher at the London Institute.

NIKOLAUS HIRSCH & MICHEL MÜLLER

The work of Frankfurt-based architects Nikolaus Hirsch and Michel Müller focuses on experimental institutional projects such as the Bockenheimer Depot Theater in Frankfurt (with William Forsythe), the European Kunsthalle in Cologne, Unitednationsnationsplaza in Berlin (with Anton Vidokle), and, currently, the Cybermohalla Hub in Delhi and a studio structure at The Land in Thailand. Their installations include the music pavilion *Soundchambers* at Museu Serralves in Porto, *Intervention* for *Kraft der Negation* (Cologne/Berlin), Autobahn-Tower (with Thomas Bayrle, MMK Frankfurt), and *Node House* (with the Raqs Media Collective, Frankfurt / Kunstmuseum Bern). They are currently devising an extruded structure for the *Indian Highway* exhibition at the Serpentine Gallery in London.

Nikolaus Hirsch, born in 1964 in Karlsruhe, Germany, is a professor at Städelschule in Frankfurt and has previously held academic positions at the Architectural Association in London, the University of Pennsylvania in Philadelphia, and the Institute for Applied Theater Studies at Gießen University. He has curated *ErsatzStadt: Representations of the Urban* at Volksbühne Berlin and is a member of the Curating Architecture program at Goldsmiths College in London.

Michel Müller, born in 1961 in Ludwigshafen, Germany, is a professor at the Academy of Fine Arts in Stuttgart and was previously a researcher and teacher at the Technical University in Darmstadt, where he earned his dissertation on planning methods for flexible architecture.

MARINE HUGONNIER

was born in Paris in 1969 and currently lives and works in London. She holds a Master of Anthropology from the Nanterre University, Paris. Hugonnier's films, photographs, and works on paper have been exhibited internationally, including in solo exhibitions at the Stedelijk Museum voor Actuele Kunst, Gent (2006), the Fondazione Sandretto Re Rebaudengo, Turin (2006),

the Musée d'art moderne et contemporain, Geneva
(2007), the Philadelphia Museum of Art (2006), and the
Kunsthalle Bern (2007).

CYBERMOHALLA ENSEMBLE

is a network of young researcher-practitioners in
various working-class neighbourhoods in New Delhi.
The group's members work out of self-administered
media labs and studios in their own neighbourhoods
alongside practitioners from Sarai-CSDS and Ankur:
Society for Alternatives in Education. In the last eight
years, close to 450 young people have constituted the
Cybermohalla network. Instigating a diverse range
of small-scale interventions, the Ensemble creates,
gathers, shares, and transforms materials, as well
as builds conceptual resources and vocabularies by
which to think the contemporary urban environment.
Cybermohalla Ensemble has produced a body of
works—books, broadsheets, installations, radio
programmes, blogs, etc—that circulate in different
locations. (www.sarai.net/practices/cybermohalla)

Contributing practitioners: Jaanu Nagar, Lakhmi Chand
Kohli, Rakesh Khairalia, Shamsher Ali, Suraj Rai,
Yashoda Singh, Love Anand, Azra Tabassum, Babli
Rai, and Tripan Kumar are part of the Cybermohalla
Ensemble.

KHIN KHIN SU

is the first Burmese transsexual artist. She was born
in 1978 in Central Africa. Moving with her externally
displaced Burmese parents, Khin Khin Su has lived on
five continents. At the age of eleven, Khin Khin Su found
sex, and at thirteen she decided that she wanted to be
an artist. Su became transsexualized in the early 2000s.
Currently Khin Khin Su lives and works in Australia.
She holds no degree from Harvard University, Yale
University, or Oxford University, and has never worked
for the UNHCR.

RAQS MEDIA COLLECTIVE

Jeebesh Bagchi (*1965 New Delhi), Monica Narula
(*1969 New Delhi) and Shuddhabrata Sengupta
(*1968 New Delhi)
Raqs is a word in Persian, Arabic, and Urdu that
describes the state that whirling dervishes enter into
when they whirl. It is also a word used for dance.
At the same time, Raqs could be an acronym,
standing for Rarely Asked Questions. Formed in 1991,
the members of Raqs Media Collective have been
variously described as artists, media practitioners,
curators, researchers, editors, and catalysts of cultural
processes. Their work has been exhibited widely
in major international spaces and events, including
at Documenta 11 in 2002, the Walker Art Center in
2003, the Venice Biennial in 2005, and in the Museum
van Hedendaagse Kunst Antwerpen in 2008. Raqs'
work locates them squarely at the intersections of
contemporary art, historical enquiry, philosophical
speculation, research, and theory, and it often takes
the form of installations, online and offline media
objects, performances, and encounters. They live and
work in Delhi, where they are based at Sarai, Centre
for the Study of Developing Societies, an initiative
they co-founded in 2000. They are members of the
editorial collective of the Sarai Reader series, and have
curated *The Rest of Now* and co-curated *Scenarios* for
Manifesta 7 (2008), Bolzano, Italy.

PAK SHEUNG CHUEN

was born in 1977 in Fujian, China. He emigrated to
Hong Kong when he was seven years old. He currently
lives and works in Hong Kong and Beijing. Pak is a
conceptual and performance artist who is well known
as a regular visual art columnist in the Hong Kong
newspaper Ming Pao. He has published two books:
"Odd One In: Hong Kong Diary" and "See Walk What
on 1 July". He was awarded an Overseas Exchange
Prize (Chinese Performance Art) from Macao Museum
of Art in 2005. He received the Lee Hysan Foundation
Fellowship in 2006 from the Asian Cultural Council,
which supported him while he worked in New York. His
solo exhibition *Page 22* is permanently installed in New
York's 58th Street Branch Library. He participated in
the Yokohama Triennial (2008), the Guangzhou Triennial
(2008), the Busan Biennale (2006), and in the exhibition
China Power Station II at the Astrup Fearnley Museet for
Moderne Kunst, Oslo (2007). Pak is a core member of
2nd Floor 5 Sons Studio.

RITU SARIN AND TENZING SONAM

White Crane Films was formed in 1990 in London by
Ritu Sarin, who was born in New Delhi in 1959. She
finished her schooling in London and completed her
undergraduate studies at Delhi University. She holds a
Master of Fine Arts in Film and Video from the California
College of the Arts in Oakland. Tenzing Sonam was born

in 1959 in Darjeeling, India, to Tibetan refugee parents. After graduating from Delhi University, he worked for a year in the Tibetan Government-in-exile in Dharamsala. He then specialized in documentary filmmaking at the Graduate School of Journalism, University of California, Berkeley. In 1987, they moved to London to help the Meridian Trust, a Buddhist film and video archive, develop its archives. As part of their efforts, they documented on video a number of historic trips made by the Dalai Lama, including the one he took to attend the Nobel Peace Prize ceremony in Norway. In 1990, they made *The Reincarnation of Khensur Rinpoche*. Their subsequent films, some of which were commissioned by the BBC, include *The Trials of Telo Rinpoche, A Stranger in My Native Land* and *The Shadow Circus: The CIA in Tibet*. Their most recent work is a video installation, *Some Questions on the Nature of Your Existence,* which was commissioned by Thyssen-Bornemisza Art Contemporary. In 1996, they moved to Dharamsala in India to be closer to the exile Tibetan community about whom they planned to make a feature film. That project, *Dreaming Lhasa,* was shot in the winter of 2003 with a predominantly non-professional cast and completed in January 2005. It was executive produced by Jeremy Thomas and Richard Gere. Tibet, in all its dimensions, has been the focus of Sarin and Sonam's work. Through their films, they have attempted to document, question, and reflect upon the issues of exile, identity, culture, and politics that confront the Tibetan people.

ARADHANA SETH

is a filmmaker, designer, art director, and photographer. She has made over fifteen films, some of which were commissioned by the BBC and Channel 4 (UK); among her credits are *DAM/AGE* (made with Arundhati Roy), *The Magnificent Ruin, Hanging by a Thread, What Is our Choice?,* and *Art for Cry.* Feature-length films on which she has worked include *Earth, Stiff Upper Lips, The Guru, The Bourne Supremacy,* and *The Darjeeling Limited.* Seth has designed cafés and stores, co-edited a book of photography with the artists Graciela Iturbide, Raghu Rai, and Sabastiao Salgado, and researched the India section of the book "Nonfiction Film: A Critical History," by Richard M. Barsam. As an artist, she has participated in the exhibition *Click! Contemporary Photography from India* at the Vadehra Art Gallery, New Dehli (2008), and her photographs have been published in major national and international catalogues. Seth lives and works between India, Europe, and the United States.

QIU ZHIJIE

is a calligrapher, painter, stone carver, and computer and-video artist. His works have been presented worldwide by a series of publications and museum exhibitions, including *Inside Out: New Chinese Art*, San Francisco Asian Art Museum, and Asia Society Gallery, New York, *Transience: Chinese Experimental Art at the End of 20th Century*, and *Fresh Cream*. He was born in 1965 into a scholar's family in Fujian Province, China. He studied calligraphy under his learned grandfather. His teenage years coincided with China's opening to the West, and its resultant cultural ferment. In 1988, he enrolled in the printmaking department of the Zhejiang Academy of Fine Arts in Hangzhou. He was given faculty support to travel abroad in 1989, but the travel restrictions imposed after the June Fourth Movement shuttered his ambitions. Qiu stayed in China and began collaborating with fellow artists Wu Shanzhuan and Zhang Peili. Together they engaged in anti-establishment activities designed to eradicate "the personal" from their artwork. By putting traditional Chinese art in a conceptual context and raising questions about the essence of the traditions he has inherited and studied, Qiu has made himself into one of the most thought provoking artists active in China today.

AUTHORS' BIOGRAPHIES

JEEBESH BAGCHI

Born in 1965 in New Delhi, Jeebesh Bagchi works as an artist as a member of Raqs Media Collective and as a practitioner for Sarai-CSDS and Ankur: Society for Alternatives in Education in Delhi.

DIANA BALDON

Diana Baldon is an Italian curator and writer currently based in Vienna. She is one of the curators of the 2nd Athens Biennale, opening in June 2009. She received a Master's degree in Creative Curating at Goldsmiths College, University of London, in 2002. Since then, she has realised exhibitions around Europe, including, among others, *Left Pop* at the 2007 Moscow Biennale, *Marietjca Potrc/Kyong Park* at London's Cubitt Gallery, *After Effect* at Centre d'Art Neuchâtel. Between 2007–08 she was Curator In Residence at the Academy of Fine Arts Vienna, where she devised the Demonstrationsraum exhibition programme and taught the seminar Curatorial Studies within the Department of Art Theory and Cultural Studies. She regularly contributes to international art magazines, including Artforum International. Her critical writing has appeared in artists' catalogues as well as in the critical readers "Men in Black—Handbook of Curatorial Practice" (2004, Revolver Books) and "LAND, ART: A Cultural Ecology Handbook" (2006, Royal Society of Arts).

ROBERT BARNETT

is currently adjunct professor of Contemporary Tibetan Studies and Director of the Modern Tibetan Studies Program at Columbia University, New York. He ran an annual summer program for foreign students at Tibet University in Lhasa from 2000 to 2005, and teaches courses on Tibetan film, television, biography, and other subjects. Barnett has edited or written a number of books on modern Tibet, including "Cutting Off the Serpent's Head: Tightening Control in Tibet 1994–1995" (Human Rights Watch Asia), "Resistance and Reform in Tibet", "Lhasa: Streets with Memories," and "Tibetan Modernities: Notes from the Field on Social and Cultural Change," co-edited with Ronald Schwartz. Recent articles include "Women and Political Participation in Tibet," in Janet Havnevik and J. Gyatso (eds.), "Women in Tibet: Past and Present" (Columbia University Press, 2006).

MONIQUE BEHR

Monique Behr is a curator and exhibition organizer in Frankfurt am Main. Her most recent curatorial project at the Jüdisches Museum was the exhibition *Christian Boltanski, Rainer Ganahl, Michaela Melián.* At the Museum für Kommunikation, she is in charge of exhibition planning and realization. Her last exhibition there was *Cataloonia! Ein Land zeichnet sich in die Zukunft*, presented during the 2007 Book Fair in collaboration with the Guest of Honor, Catalonia. In 2006, she first invented Raqs Media Collective to present their project *KD Vyas Correspondence Vol 1.* in an exhibition. In 2008, she began teaching exhibition conception at the Johann Wolfgang von Goethe Universität, Frankfurt am Main. She has published on her research focus, the work of Peter Roehr, in a variety of media.

GABRIELLE CRAM

Born in 1979 in Falkirk, Great Britain. Gabrielle Cram lives and works in Vienna, Austria. She studied semiotics and film theory with a focus on postcolonial questions, popular culture as well as sex-gender related issues at Vienna University, graduating in 2001. In 2005, she graduated from the Academy of Fine Arts in Vienna, where she studied conceptual art practice. As curator, artist and theoretician she explores modes of display and representation and seeks to combine artistic and cultural practice with theoretic approaches.

T. J. DEMOS

is a critic and a lecturer in the Department of Art History, University College London. The author of "The Exiles of Marcel Duchamp" (MIT Press, 2007), his essays on modern and contemporary art have appeared in international journals such as *Artforum, Grey Room, October,* and *Texte zur Kunst.* He is currently working on a new book, provisionally titled "Migrations: Contemporary Art and Globalization." Demos is also curator and director of *Zones of Conflict: Rethinking Contemporary Art During Global Crisis* (November 2008–February 2009), comprising both an international group exhibition at Pratt Manhattan Gallery in New York, and a series of research workshops in London (in partnership with Iniva, Tate Modern, Tate Britain, and UCL's Centre for the Study of Contemporary Art).

FRANCESCA VON HABSBURG

Born in Switzerland in 1958, Francesca von Habsburg is founder and chairman of Thyssen-Bornemisza Art Contemporary. Her studies lead her from Switzerland to London, where she studied art at St. Martin's School of Art and History of Modern Art at the ICA, as well as to New York and Los Angeles. In 1989, von Habsburg became chief curator of special exhibitions of the Thyssen-Bornemisza collection at the Villa Favorita in Lugano. In 1991, she founded ARCH Foundation, which is dedicated to the preservation and restoration of cultural heritage and in 2002 Thyssen-Bornemisza Art Contemporary in Vienna, Austria.

SYBILLE KRÄMER

was born in Trier in 1951. She studied philosophy, history, and political sciences in Hamburg and Marburg. In 1989, she was appointed professor of theoretical philosophy at the Institute of Philosophy at Freie Universität, Berlin. Krämer is leader of a project group within the interdisciplinary research project *Kulturen des Performativen*. Between 2005 and 2008, she was a permanent fellow at the Wissenschaftskolleg zu Berlin. She is an expert on the panel of the European Research Council, and directed a number of projects in the philosophy of language and media theory that received support funding from the German Research Foundation. Selected publications: "Schrift. Kulturtechnik zwischen Auge, Hand und Maschine" (ed. with Grube/Kogge, 2005); "Stimme" (ed. with Doris Kolesch, 2006); "Spur. Spurenlesen als Orientierungstechnik und Wissenskunst" (ed. with Grube/Kogge, 2007); "Medium, Bote, Übertragung. Kleine Metaphysik der Medialität" (2008).

CHARLES MEREWETHER

is an art historian and writer on contemporary and postwar art who has taught at universities in the United States, South America, Europe, and Australia. He is deputy director of the Cultural District, Saasiyat Island, in Abu Dhabi. In 2007 he was the Arts and Culture Consultant for the Emirates Foundation in the United Arab Emirates, and between 2004 and 2006 he was the Artistic Director and Curator of the Bienniale of Sydney. Born in Scotland and educated in Australia, he received his bachelor's degree in Literature and his doctorate in Art History at the University of Sydney. In 1991 he was named inaugural curator of the Museo de Arte Contemporáneo de Monterrey (Mexico) and between 1994 and 2004 was the collections curator at the Getty Center in Los Angeles. His recent publications include "The Archive" (MIT Press, 2006) and "Ai Weiwei: Under Reconstruction" (University of New South Wales Press, 2008).

KEIKO SEI

is a writer and curator who advocates for independent media. After running an organization for independent video and video art in Japan, she moved to Eastern Europe in 1988 to research the media scene of the communist bloc. Since 2002 she has been based in Bangkok, where she continues her research on independent media. She has initiated and worked for various projects such as *The Media Are With Us!: The Role of Television in the Romanian Revolution* in Budapest (1990), *The Age of Nikola Tesla* in Osnabruck (1991), *EX-ORIENTE-LUX – Romanian Video Week in Bucharest* (1993), *Orbis Fictus – New Media in Contemporary Arts* (1995) and *POLITIK-UM/new Engamement* (2002), both in Prague, and the documenta 12 magazine (2006–2007). She has taught and given lectures on media art and independent media at numerous institutions, among which is HFG-Karlsruhe, where she currently teaches. She writes for publications worldwide, including *springerin* (Austria).

TSERING WANGDU SHAKYA

Born in Lhasa, Tsering Wangdu Shakya fled to India with his family. He graduated from London University's School of Oriental and African Studies (SOAS), and received his Ph.D. in Tibetan Studies in June 2004. Shakya currently holds the Canadian Research Chair in Religion and Contemporary Society at the Institute for Asian Research, University of British Columbia, Vancouver. As an independent consultant and widely respected analyst, Shakya is regularly invited to advise Western governments on Tibet/China policy. Shakya's published works include "Fire Under the Snow: The Testimony of a Tibetan Prisoner" (Harvill Press, 1997), which is now regarded as a standard text on the history of modern Tibet, as well as the first anthology of modern Tibetan short stories and poems, "Song of the Snow Lion: New Writings from Tibet" (University of Hawaii, 2000). Tsering's feature articles have been published in numerous international journals and magazines, including *Time* and *New Left Review*.

DANIELA ZYMAN
Born in 1964 in Vienna, Austria, Daniela Zyman
is currently curator of Thyssen-Bornemisza Art
Contemporary. As chief curator at the MAK
– Austrian Museum of Applied Arts / Contempo-
rary Art in Vienna between 1995 and 2001, she
was a founding member of the MAK Center for
Art and Architecture at the Schindler House in Los
Angeles, which she has directed for several years.
Zyman has earned her MA in art history at the
University of Vienna and her MFA at New York's
Columbia University.

ACKNOWLEDGEMENTS

Text references

pp. 78-79: "First Information Report" by Raqs Media Collective was originally published in German translation as part of "Umfrage: Dokumente sprechen nicht: Stimmen zu alten und aktuellen Dokumentarismen in der Kunst", *Texte zur Kunst,* no. 51 (September 2003), pp. 93-95. Reprinted with kind permission by *Texte zur Kunst.*

pp. 80-83: Sybille Krämer "On the 'Grammar of Witnessing'", excerpt from: Krämer, Sybille (2008), "Medium, Bote, Übertragung. Kleine Metaphysik der Medialität", Frankfurt am Main: Suhrkamp. Reprinted with kind permission by the author. Translation by Gerrit Jackson.

pp. 100-101, 108: Excerpts from: Cybermohalla Ensemble (2007), "Trickster City", texts by Azra Tabassum, Jaanu Nagar, Lakhmi Chand Kohli, Rakesh Khairalia, Yashoda Singh, Kiran Verma, Suraj Rai, Neelofar, Kulwinder Kaur, Shamsher Ali, Babli Rai, Ankur Kumar, Dilip Kumar, Love Anand, Nasreen, Rabiya Quraishy, Sunita Nishad, Saifuddin, Arish Qureshi, Tripan Kumar. Translated from Hindi to English by Shveta Sarda. [Orig.: Bahurupiya Shehr, Rajkamal Publication, Delhi 2007]

pp. 102-107: Reprint of: Paper Weights/Waits. A Reflection by Cybermohalla Ensemble (unpublished compilation of texts by Cybermohalla practitioners, http://www.sarai.net/practices/cybermohalla/minor-practices/collecting-documents/cm_paper_waits.pdf) Reprinted with kind permission by Cybermohalla Ensemble.

pp. 154-163: Excerpts from film interviews conducted by Ritu Sarin and Tenzing Sonam. Copyright White Crane Films.

pp. 170-171: Excerpt from: Charles Merewether (2006), "A Language to Come: Japanese Photography After the Event", in Charles Merewether (ed.), "The Archive", Cambridge: MIT Press.

Photo credits

Ill. p. 1 © Steve Lehman, Ill. pp. 22-27 © Amar Kanwar, Ill. pp. 28-29 © Marino Solokhov, Ill. p. 40, 42-43, 112-113, 164-165 © Khin Khin Su, Ill. pp. 57-59, 61-63 © Raqs Media Collective, Assistant: Amitabh Kumar, Ill. pp. 65-69, 71-72 © Marine Hugonnier and Max Wigram Gallery, London, Ill. p. 70 © Michael Strasser/T-B A21, Ill. pp. 76-77 © Heman Chong, Ill. pp 86-89, 91, 94-95 © Nikolaus Hirsch & Michel Müller, Ill. pp. 99, 102-107, 108-109 © Cybermohalla Ensemble, Ill. pp. 116-121 © Pak Sheung Chuen, Ill. pp. 112-123 © Amnye Machen Institute, Dharamsala, Ill. pp. 133-139 © Qiu Zhijie and Long March Project, Beijing, Ill. pp. 141-143 © Gonkar Gyatso and Rossi & Rossi Ltd., London, Ill. pp. 147-152 © Ritu Sarin and Tenzing Sonam/White Crane Films, Ill. pp. 167-169 © Aradhana Seth.

A QUESTION OF EVIDENCE

Thyssen-Bornemisza Art Contemporary
Chairman: Francesca von Habsburg
Curatorial team: Daniela Zyman, Diana Baldon
Associate Curator: Aradhana Seth
Curatorial Assistant: Gudrun Ankele
Tibet21: Tsewang Gyatso
Exhibition Architect: Philipp Krummel
Collection Management: Barbara Horvath
T-B A21 team: Eva Ebersberger, Alexandra Hennig,
Verena Platzgummer, Markus Schlüter, David Weidinger
Archival Research: Markus Schlüter
Administration and Finances: Samaela Bilic-Eric,
Elisabeth Mareschal, Barbara Simma
Press and PR: Christina Werner / w.hoch.2wei
Project communication: Kristina Pia Hofer

Our most special thanks go to all the artists and practitioners who have engaged with the topic
of this exhibition and agreed to participate in this wide-ranging project. We very much appreciate the generous support from the authors and writers who have contributed texts, statements,
and interviews for the publication. This project would have not been possible without the support,
collaboration and advice from many many advisers, supporters and friends in all the stages of its
realization, especially the world of Tibetan and Burmese activism.
In particular, the T-B A21 team and the curators would like to thank the following individuals:
Barbara Buchbauer, Zoe Butt, Chris Dercon, Daniel Dolder, Cosmin Costinas, Ferdinand Feldgrill,
Alexandra Grausam, Tina Köhler, Nicola Lees, Kathleen Madden, Sarat Maharaj, Melanie Nief,
Hans Ulrich Obrist, Maren Richter, Fabio Rossi, Keiko Sei, Steffen Sendelbach, Brian Sholis, Marino
Solokhov, Zhang Wei, Tashi Tsering, Tseten Zochbauer, the Friends of Tibet in India, and all mem-
bers of T-B A21´s hard-working technical team.

This exhibition is generously supported by: Wiener Städtische

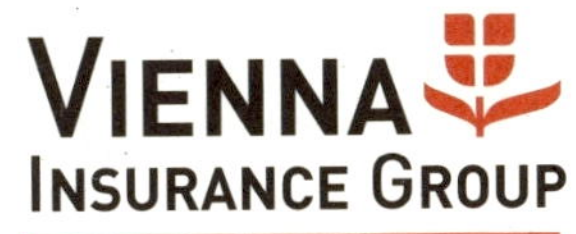

The listed Vienna Insurance Group is one of the leading insurance groups in CEE headquartered in Vienna. Outside of its home base in Austria, Vienna Insurance Group is active, through subsidiaries and insurance holdings, in Albania, Bulgaria, Germany, Estonia, Georgia, Croatia, Latvia, Liechtenstein, Lithuania, Macedonia, Poland, Romania, Russia, Serbia, Slovakia, the Czech Republic, Turkey, Hungary, Ukraine and Belarus. There are also branches in Italy and Slovenia. On the Austrian market, the group positions itself with Wiener Städtische Versicherung, Donau Versicherung and Sparkassen Versicherung.

Cultural Engagement

As the leading Austrian insurance company, the Vienna Insurance Group clearly perceives its social responsibilities and has been a reliable sponsoring partner of cultural projects for many years. Numerous museums and galleries have insured their collections with Vienna Insurance Group. The main objective in doing this is to promote the international exchange of arts and culture.

Architecture in the Ringturm

Since 1998 the Vienna Insurance Group frequently presents architecture exhibitions – ranging from the works of Austrian architects to international and award-winning projects – at its head-quarters, the Ringturm in Vienna. By this way the architecture of the countries, in which the Vienna Insurance Group operates, is made accessible to a wide public.

WIENER STÄDTISCHE Versicherung AG
Vienna Insurance Group
Schottenring 30A-1010 Wien
Tel.: +43 (0) 050 350 – 20000
Fax: +43 (0) 050 350 – 20000
E-Mail: mail-us@staedtische.co.at
http://www.viennainsurancegroup.com

IMPRINT

This catalog was published on the occasion of the exhibition *A Question of Evidence*,
November 19, 2008 to April 5, 2009 at Thyssen-Bornemisza Art Contemporary,
Himmelpfortgasse 13, 1010 Vienna, Austria

Editor: Thyssen-Bornemisza Art Contemporary, Vienna
Concept / edited by: Daniela Zyman / T-B A21 & Diana Baldon
Editorial assistance: Gudrun Ankele
Translators: Eric Abrahamsen, Lee Ambrozy, Gerrit Jackson
Proofreading: Karen Jacobson, Gerrit Jackson, April Lamm
Graphic Design: Christian Schienerl, assistance: Eva Hebenstreit / SCHiENERL / ppfmd, Vienna
Project administration: ARCH Communications GmbH
Printed by: REMAprint, Vienna
This publication is printed on 100% recycled paper (Cyclus Recycling Offset)

Published by
Verlag der Buchhandlung Walther König, Köln
Ehrenstr. 4, 50672 Köln
Tel. +49 (0) 221 / 20 59 6-53
Fax +49 (0) 221 / 20 59 6-60
Email: verlag@buchhandlung-walther-koenig.de

Die Deutsche Bibliothek – CIP-Einheitsaufnahme
Ein Titelsatz für diese Publikation ist bei
Der Deutschen Bibliothek erhältlich

Printed in Austria

Vertrieb / Distribution:

Schweiz / Switzerland
Buch 2000
c/o AVA Verlagsauslieferungen AG
Centralweg 16
CH-8910 Affoltern a.A.
Tel. +41 (0) 44 762 42 00
Fax +41 (0) 44 762 42 10
a.koll@ava.ch

Außerhalb Europas / Outside Europe
D.A.P. / Distributed Art Publishers, Inc.
155 6th Avenue, 2nd Floor
New York, NY 10013
Tel: +1 212-627-1999
Fax: +1 212-627-9484
eleshowitz@dapinc.com

UK & Eire
Cornerhouse Publications
70 Oxford Street
GB-Manchester M1 5NH
Tel. +44 (0) 161 200 15 03
Fax +44 (0) 161 200 15 04
publications@cornerhouse.org

ISBN 978-3-86560-569-6

WITH CONTRIBUTIONS BY
FRANCESCA VON HABSBURG / DIANA BALDON /
AMAR KANWAR / GABRIELLE CRAM / AUNG
MYINT HTET / T. J. DEMOS / RAQS MEDIA
COLLECTIVE / MARINE HUGONNIER / SYBILLE
KRÄMER / MONIQUE BEHR / JEEBESH BAGCHI
/ CYBERMOHALLA ENSEMBLE / CHARLES
MEREWETHER / TENZING SONAM / ARADHANA
SETH / DANIELA ZYMAN

EDITED BY
DANIELA ZYMAN & DIANA BALDON